Listening with a Feminist Ear

# Listening with a Feminist Ear

*Soundwork in Bombay Cinema*

Pavitra Sundar

University of Michigan Press
Ann Arbor

For questions or permissions, please contact um.press.perms@umich.edu

Published in the United States of America by the
University of Michigan Press
Manufactured in the United States of America
Printed on acid-free paper
First published July 2023

A CIP catalog record for this book is available from the British Library.

*Library of Congress Cataloging-in-Publication data has been applied for.*

ISBN 978-0-472-13248-5 (hardcover : alk. paper)
ISBN 978-0-472-03937-1 (paper : alk. paper)
ISBN 978-0-472-90366-5 (open access ebook)

DOI: https://doi.org/10.3998/mpub.11713921

Library of Congress Control Number: 2023935021

This book is made possible, in part, through a generous subvention from Hamilton College.

Some material in this book was previously published and is included here by permission. A part of chapter 1 appeared as "Gender, Bawdiness, and Bodily Voices: Bombay Cinema's Audiovisual Contract and the 'Ethnic' Woman," in *Locating the Voice in Film: Critical Approaches and Global Practices*, edited by Tom Whittaker and Sarah Wright (Oxford University Press, 2016). An early version of some sections of chapter 2 appeared as "Romance, Piety, and Fun: The Transformation of the Qawwali and Islamicate Culture in Hindi Cinema," in *South Asian Popular Culture* 15, no. 2 (2017), https://www.tandfonline.com/doi/full/10.1080/14746689.2017 .1407550

The University of Michigan Press's open access publishing program is made possible thanks to additional funding from the University of Michigan Office of the Provost and the generous support of contributing libraries.

Cover image: Singing Microphone and a Photograph, 2013, 32 x 9 x 25 in | 81 x 23 x 63.5 cm. By Shilpa Gupta. Courtesy of Shilpa Gupta.

*To patti*

# CONTENTS

## Listening

## Speaking

## Coda

Digital materials related to this title can be found on the Fulcrum platform via
the following citable URL: https://doi.org/10.3998/mpub.11713921

# ILLUSTRATIONS

# VIDEOS

Video 1.1. "Choli Ke Peeche," *Khalnayak* (dir. Subhash Ghai, 1993): https://doi.org/10.3998/mpub.11713921.comp.1

Video 2.1. "Parda Hai Parda," *Amar Akbar Anthony* (dir. Manmohan Desai, 1977): https://doi.org/10.3998/mpub.11713921.comp.2

Video 2.2. Nusrat Fateh Ali Khan's "Afreen Afreen," *Sangam* (1996): https://doi.org/10.3998/mpub.11713921.comp.3

Video 2.3. Rahat Fateh Ali Khan and Momina Mustehsan's "Afreen Afreen," *Coke Studio*, season 9 (2016): https://doi.org/10.3998/mpub.11713921.comp.4

Video 2.4. "Khwaja Mere Khwaja," *Jodhaa Akbar* (dir. Ashutosh Gowariker, 2008): https://doi.org/10.3998/mpub.11713921.comp.5

Video 2.5. "Kun Faya Kun," *Rockstar* (dir. Imtiaz Ali, 2011): https://doi.org/10.3998/mpub.11713921.comp.6

Video 2.6. "Q Funk," *Oorja* (1995): https://doi.org/10.3998/mpub.11713921.comp.7

Video 2.7. "Kajra Re," *Bunty Aur Babli* (dir. Shaad Ali, 2005): https://doi.org/10.3998/mpub.11713921.comp.8

Video 2.8. All India Bakchod's "Creep Qawwali" (2015): https://doi.org/10.3998/mpub.11713921.comp.9

Video 3.1. "Goli Maar Bheje Mein," *Satya* (dir. Ram Gopal Varma, 1998): https://doi.org/10.3998/mpub.11713921.comp.10

## ACKNOWLEDGMENTS

There are many genealogies to trace as I think about how *Listening with a Feminist Ear* came to be. One of them begins with my Carnatic music teacher T. S. Anantharaman, who predicted when I was fifteen that I would write about music. I guffawed at his comments then, but here I am, decades later, with a book on listening. This is not quite what he expected me to write, but the love of music he inspired has shaped both my intellectual trajectory and my listening habits. Long before vocal lessons, came dance. It was my Bharatanatyam teacher, the late Komalavalli Krishnamani, who sparked my imagination through bodily movement and performance. In retrospect, I understand *paatu* sir and dance *patti* as imparting early lessons in research. Under their tutelage, I came alive to the pleasures of laboring over a single note, a single gesture, a single set of ideas.

I am grateful to my undergraduate teachers Hugh Egan, Claire Gleitman, Carla Golden, Jonathan Gil Harris, and Nancy Rader for carrying me through my student years at Ithaca College and beyond. Their lessons in cultural critique, theory, and gender politics paved my path to the interdisciplinary program in Women's Studies and English at the University of Michigan. While this book is entirely different from my doctoral dissertation, that project oriented me in crucial ways and taught me to read across disciplines and fields. From the bottom of my heart, I thank my chair Nadine Hubbs and committee members Simon Gikandi, Christi Merrill, Sumathi Ramaswamy, Derek Vaillant, and Jennifer Wenzel, all staunch supporters from the start. Well after I had left Ann Arbor, Sumathi and Christi continued to open doors for me and encourage me to step out more boldly. Among others who extended a kind hand was Elizabeth Wingrove, whose fierce thinking and teaching continue to inspire me. That I return to insights first gleaned in my work with these graduate mentors speaks to their foundational influence.

A Mellon postdoctoral fellowship took me to Dartmouth College, where I was ensconced in a wonderful community of scholars affiliated with the

Department of Film and Media Studies, the Women's and Gender Studies Program, and the Leslie Center for the Humanities. I thank Mary Desjardins for her immense indulgence as I began growing, ever so gradually, into a cinema and media studies scholar. I remember Doug Haynes, Amy Lawrence, Adrian Randolph, and Mark Williams fondly as well, for their guidance and good cheer. In those early years, I was a regular lurker at the feminist preconference at Madison and part of the first cohort of the American Institute of Indian Studies' dissertation-to-book workshop. I am thankful for the funding earmarked for graduate students (Michigan), adjuncts (Oberlin), postdocs (Dartmouth), and untenured faculty (Kettering) that enabled me to hook into these formative institutional structures. My colleagues in the Department of Liberal Studies at Kettering University were impressive in the way they persisted in their teaching and research in the face of significant constraints. Our humanities reading group was a breath of fresh air, and I will be ever grateful for friendships forged over dinners with Dave Golz, Christine Levecq, David Marshall, Laura Mebert, Laura Miller-Purrenhage, Greg Schneider-Bateman, and Denise Stodola. With David and Greg, I enjoyed the kind of wonderful bond that can only emerge as one hurtles down the highway over seventy miles an hour, several days a week, come rain or shine (or Michigan snow).

I consider myself fortunate to have landed next at Hamilton College, in the Department of Literature and Creative Writing. My colleagues' rethinking of the historical contours of English as a discipline and as a department allows me to do my work every day. I have the privilege of teaching courses in literary and cultural studies, cinema studies, and sound studies to fabulously engaged students. They keep me on my toes and teach me about my own work. The actual writing of this book would not have been possible without the substantial material support of the Dean of Faculty's office. A generous start-up package allowed for regular conference travel, professional development opportunities, and subvention monies for the open-access publication of this book. Departmental and Dean's office funds also supported the hire of two stellar undergraduate research assistants: Yassine Dahlek, who helped populate my Zotero library, and Clara Walling, whose eagle-eyed editing and whip-smart comments eased me through the final stages of revision. Most of all, it was institutional backing for a manuscript workshop and a summer fellowship at the National Humanities Center that put me on the path to completing this book.

I am infinitely grateful to Michele Hilmes and Sangita Gopal, the primary readers at my manuscript workshop. I could not have asked for better interlocutors than the two of them—their vote of confidence and incisive advice helped me see the potential of my project more clearly. I am still amazed by Michele's incredible support for a junior scholar with whom she had no previous connection. Sangita, for her part, joined via Skype (at dawn!) after an April snowstorm stymied her travel plans. Michele's and Sangita's deep engagement with my work despite the circumstances meant the world to me. Tom Wilson, Onno Oerlemans, and Margaret Gentry were instrumental in securing funding for the workshop, and I thank them for their faith in me. Over the course of several lunch conversations with Tom and Benj Widiss during our leave year, and with helpful advice from Kyoko Omori, Margie Thickstun, Lisa Trivedi, and Steve Yao, I dreamed up a set of events unlike any that Hamilton had previously hosted. My deep thanks to all my afore-mentioned colleagues and others who read my work and participated in the day's activities, including Abhishek Amar, Marissa Ambio, Jennifer Ambrose, Beth Bohstedt, Celeste Day Moore, Mariam Durrani, Tina May Hall, Jessie Jia, Jeff McArn, Faiza Moatasim, Vincent Odamtten, John O'Neill, Andrew Rippeon, and Arjun Shankar. Myriad others helped with the logistics, including Gill King and Carolyn Mascaro—no mean feat, since the workshop was scheduled at the busiest time of the spring semester.

My month-long residency at the National Humanities Center was blissful. With no interruptions and all the support in the world, I worked out some theoretical knots and drafted another essay. Tania Munz, Lynn Miller, and the rest of the administrators and staff at the Center left no stone unturned in making the space as conducive to writing and research as possible. The conviviality of that summer's cohort was second to none: thanks especially to Masha Belenky, Esther Fernández, Iván Ramos, and Jennifer Nolan for many a fun lunchtime and cocktail conversation.

Similar pockets of intellectual and social solidarity at Hamilton kept my research moving along. The sound studies seminar I organized with Celeste, thanks to an interdisciplinary collaborations grant from the Hamilton Humanities Center, was key to me finding my footing at the College during my first year. Jennifer Stoever's visit and talk were a fitting culmination to a semester's worth of exciting sonic explorations with Jeff, Kyoko, Amy James, Rob Knight, Scott MacDonald, Janet Oppedisano, the late Sam Pellman, Ian Rothenberg, and Chris Willemsen. Regular work sessions with the Junior Faculty Writing Club and, more recently, with my friends Quincy Newell and Kristen Burson have kept me sane and on track with my writing. Big thanks are also due to the RAVE group—Kristen, Rhea Datta, Courtney Gibbons, Elaine Harrigan, Anna Huff, Wes Kramer, Alex List, Max Majireck, Megan Smith, and Darrell Strash—for creating a gentle space of research support across disciplines and ranks. The Feminist Killjoys, the Decolonial group, Contingent Hamilton, and the AAUP crew (shout-out to Susan Jarosi and Jeanne Willcoxon, in particular) also helped ground me during some difficult times.

Over the course of writing this book, I have connected with several overlapping communities of scholars of cinema, music, and sound. Among the colleagues I am happy to cross paths with regularly are: Isabel Huacuja Alonso, Uma Bhrugubandha, Iftikhar Dadi, Manishita Dass, Swarnavel Eswaran Pillai, Teja Ganti, Lotte Hoek, Anuja Jain, Shikha Jhingan, Sangeet Kumar, Madhumita Lahiri, Neepa Majumdar, Darshana Sreedhar Mini, Deepti Misri, Navaneetha Mokkil, Madhuja Mukherjee, Anupama Prabhala, Ratheesh Radhakrishnan, Kristen Rudisill, Natalie Sarrazin, Meheli Sen, Gohar Siddiqui, and Samhita Sunya. Thank you for transforming conferences from dreaded occasions for professional grandstanding to much-awaited moments of camaraderie and inspiration. Madison and Utrecht, in particular, will forever be tied in my mind to you and others who were part of those lively conversations. Friends in music circles, particularly Shalini Ayyagari, Jayson Beaster-Jones, Nilanjana Bhattacharjya, John Caldwell, Nina Sun Eidsheim, Kaley Mason, Anna Morcom, Kathy Meizel, Sarah Morelli, and Zoe Sherinian, keep me from feeling like an interloper among musicians and (ethno) musicologists. Several colleagues provided feedback on prior iterations of my arguments, including Rajinder Dudrah, Ajay Gehlawat, Janell Hobson, Constantine Nakassis, S. Shankar, Aarti Wani, Tom Whittaker, and the excellent anonymous reviewers of my manuscript. With others, I read books that stayed with me long after our Friday afternoon chats: I'm thinking here of the queer theory reading group with Ben Aslinger, Megan Ankerson, and Sarah Murray. I have also benefited from the generosity and advice of Jigna Desai, Sara Dickey, Caryl Flinn, Frances Hasso, Priya Jaikumar, Purnima Mankekar, Sujata Moorti, Anu Needham, and Jyotika Virdi.

Closer to home, I found a lively community through the Central New York Humanities Corridor and New York Six Liberal Arts Consortium's cinema and media groups. Corridor funding afforded Anaar Desai-Stephens and me more occasions to meet and exchange writing, and my work is all the better for it. It also opened up a fruitful connection to the George Eastman Museum and its South Asia archive, and brought me into the company of Tula Goenka, Harleen Singh, Nimanthi Rajasingham, among other wonderful colleagues. The virtual gatherings that Lisa Patti organized with Rebecca Burditt, Ani Maitra, and Samantha Sheppard were enormously helpful in the early days of the pandemic. Patty Zimmerman's talent for convening interesting occasions for deep dives into film and media never ceases to amaze. I thank her, Leah Shafer, and Rachel Shaff for widening the reach of my work through the Finger Lakes Environmental Film Festival and Conversations Across Screen Cultures.

It took me a while to acknowledge that writing a book is not simply an intellectual feat; it demands emotional and institutional labor as well. Regular check-ins with Tina L. Peterson and Kristina Vassil keep me steady—hard to believe we've been meeting for over five years now. Gina Velasco and Jessica Andruss have cheered me on each time I worked my way back to my scholarship after a break. I have also benefited tremendously from Michelle Boyd's writing advice: thank you for helping me settle into my work. My relationship with the University of Michigan Press began with Mary Francis. Her interest in my project and keen feedback on my proposal had me hooked from the start. The credit for bringing this book to fruition, though, belongs to Sara Jo Cohen. I am grateful to her for not only taking over editorial supervision of the project midway through the review process, but shepherding it through the grueling pandemic years. Her patience and thoughtfulness, not to mention her diligence in answering all my questions about open-access publishing and Indian editions, assured me that I had found the right person and editorial team for this project. For the gorgeous image that graces the cover, I thank Shilpa Gupta. I know her art will continue to inspire me for years to come.

Had it not been for my weekly writing group in Ann Arbor, with Greg, Megan Ankerson, Hui Hui (Tung-Hui) Hu, and Aswin Punathambekar, I would not have dared imagine a book project. Aswin, in particular, has my profound thanks for his encouragement and advice every step of the way. Likewise, I am indebted to Laura Brueck and Praseeda Gopinath, whose friendship over the years has fed my thinking and buoyed my spirits. Even as I worked on this book, I engaged in several cowriting ventures, each of which expanded my intellectual horizons immeasurably and introduced me to colleagues with interests and questions adjacent to mine. Heartfelt thanks to Aswin, Praseeda, Debashree Mukherjee, and my friends in the Accent Research Collaborative, Pooja Rangan, Akshya Saxena, and Ragini Tharoor Srinivasan. Time and again, I have retuned my thinking after listening to, and reading, Vebhuti Duggal, Usha Iyer, Monika Mehta, Matt Rahaim, and Amanda Weidman. Thank you to each and every one of you for sharing your writing, and for always engaging closely with mine. You inspire me not just with your dazzling intellect, but also with your grace and kindness.

The Happy Hour group was my rock through the most isolating phases of the pandemic. To the late John Bartle, Jason Cieply, Lydia Hamessley, Mireille Koukjian, Nancy Sorkin Rabinowitz, Peter Rabinowitz, Franzi Schweiger, Frank Sciacca, and Wei Zhan: I am infinitely grateful for your friendship and wisdom. Our daily virtual gatherings seem like a dream now. John's sudden passing was a horrible blow, as was the equally sudden loss of Sam Pellman a few years earlier. I will always cherish the twinkle in Sam's eyes, as I will John's big smile. I am privileged and amazed to also call Margo Okazawa-Rey a close friend. Maureen McDonnell and Laura Halperin have been with me through thick and thin, anchoring me with their laughter as much as their strength. Clare Counihan and I have conspired to hang out over good food and drink in lots of different locales. That she is an editor extraordinaire is also a gift to me—had it not been for her, chapter 3 would have remained a sloppy draft. My dear pals Toy (Sharmadip) Basu, Varuni Bhatia, Sameena Dalwai, and Nihal Satpute were a salve during a recent trip to India, just as my lifelong friends Devi Pottath, Ed Sketch, and Claire Whittemore were on a similarly hectic jaunt across the United Kingdom.

Most of all, thank you to Aimee Germain. Words fail as I try to express all the ways in which you sustain me. Thank you for your love and constancy, for the many adventures and laughs, and, of course, for hiking the face of the mountain with me. I adore Edith for reminding me that I, too, am a creature of habit, and for doubling down on the importance of treats. To the rest of my kith and kin: whether you know it or not, you are all behind this book of mine. Thank you for gently asking me how it was going and then graciously not asking me about it. I dedicate this book to my grandmother, whose desire to learn is matched by none.

# Introduction

*Listening with a Feminist Ear*

My love of cinema as a child was sonic. When I think back to my growing years in Bombay, I do not remember going to the movies much. I remember listening to the radio and fussing over my collection of cassette tapes. I remember watching the film-song shows *Chhayageet* and *Chitrahaar* on television. I remember evenings spent on a neighbor's stoop playing *antakshari* with friends. This popular pastime, which became a successful television game show in the 1990s, involves players taking turns singing Hindi film songs; each song must begin with the letter (*akshar*) on which the previous player's turn ended. Thus, while *antakshari* is typically thought of as a test of musical memory and fandom, it is in fact a *sonic* game, driven by the consonants that begin and end the opening refrain of film songs. To put it in the terms of chapter 3 of this book, *antakshari* (lit. last letter) conceives of both music and language as sound. Such aural and oral engagements with cinema are by no means a thing of the past. Think, for instance, of the bombastic citing of film dialogues in daily life, often laughed away as dialogue-*baazi*.[1] Think of the ringtones and caller tunes people use to personalize their sonic identity on mobile phones; most of these musical refrains are culled from popular film soundtracks.[2] Think also of #Kolaveri, the wildly popular Twitter hashtag that cited a viral film song in order to critique the Indian political establishment.[3] Each of these examples illustrates what is well known about Indian film songs: they have a life of their own and circulate independently from the films for which they were initially composed. What is true of film songs is also true of other sonic fragments from films. They pervade everyday life and remind us that the pleasures and politics of cinema in India are aural, not simply visual.

Many before me have lamented the hegemony of the image in contemporary scholarship.[4] The problem is not so much that we live in a world rife with visual media and metaphors, but that we continue to disregard other ways of organizing and experiencing the world. We tend to dismiss other sensory data, including the sonic, in our research. Most pertinent to this book is the fact that despite decades of film sound and music criticism, the fallacy that cinema is a visual medium, rather than an audiovisual one, persists. The inattention to the aural is surprising in the South Asian context, given the importance of music in many of the subcontinent's film traditions. Song-dance sequences have long been considered a distinguishing mark of mainstream films, and a crucial moneymaking device. Over the last four decades, scholars of Indian cinema have challenged Hollywood- and Eurocentric frameworks in film studies, probing questions of genre, theatricality, and verisimilitude. But much of this work rehearses the visual predilection of the discipline, paying little heed to any sounds apart from dialogues and, occasionally, song lyrics. Music is relegated to the realms of pleasure and economics; film sound is reduced to words; and films continue to be "watched," not heard.

*Listening with a Feminist Ear* bridges the gap between the quotidian aurality of my (and other fans') cinematic engagements and the visual focus of film studies as a discipline. I home in on the aural domain of mainstream Bombay cinema to unpack its political ramifications and possibilities, identifying singing, listening, and speaking as key sites of cultural politics.[5] In the first two chapters, I think through the sound of Indian womanhood and the Islamicate in Hindi films from the mid-twentieth century through the present. Noting the dramatic morphing of these constructs since the advent of economic liberalization in the early 1990s, I argue that underlying the dynamic terrain of gender, sexuality, and ethnic and communal (religious) identity in mainstream Hindi cinema are fundamental changes to aurality and visibility in Indian public culture. In the following chapter, I listen for how the materiality of language can stretch the boundaries of city and nation, and reframe the relationship between cinematic speech, song, and sound design. Keeping in play the many different sonic elements that films use, as well as the interaural fields in which those sounds register, helps us chart new paths through the history of cinema. It generates counterhegemonic understandings of identity and belonging so sorely needed in our times.

If my interventions are audible now, it is due to the concert of voices surrounding my project that have also been touting the significance of the aural for the past several years. Analysis of Hindi films was resolutely focused on visual narratives until the publication of two books: Sangita Gopal and Sujata

Moorti's edited volume *Global Bollywood* (2008), which tracked the many itineraries of Hindi song-dance sequences, and Gregory D. Booth's ethnography of Bombay film musicians, *Behind the Curtain* (2008).[6] The conceptual and methodological challenges posed in these key studies—one situated primarily in cinema and media studies, the other in ethnomusicology—echoed those posed by Alison E. Arnold in "Hindi Filmī Gīt" (1991) and Peter Manuel in *Cassette Culture* (1993), as they pivoted away from ethnomusicology's traditional foci of classical and folk music.[7] This important scholarly corpus has grown substantially in recent years, clarifying the production and circulation networks undergirding Indian film and music industries, and specifying the musical features associated with various genres, music directors (composers), and time periods. Posing an implicit challenge to the ocularcentrism of Indian cinema studies, this body of work is a companion to my own attempt to initiate scholarly conversations about aurality in the Indian context.[8] I build also from the work of those feminist scholars who incorporate the aural into their analyses and treat the film song as more than just a musical plot device.[9] Last but not least, I write in the company of other South Asianists who have recently turned their attention to the noisy soundscapes and diverse sound cultures of the subcontinent.[10] In *Listening with a Feminist Ear*, I use the generative possibilities of this nascent sonic turn to listen more deeply, and a bit differently, to Hindi cinema.

Even as I pursue questions of interest to scholars of film music, I follow Neepa Majumdar in asking how we might theorize sound in Bombay cinema "beyond the song sequence."[11] What is to be gained in "thinking sound," as Alexander G. Weheliye puts it, not just thinking *of* sound in this cinema?[12] One approach might be to think beyond "song"—that is, to attend not just to musical elements like melody, rhythm, and instrumentation, but also to other aural, visual, and performative elements that constitute the "sound" of a song. What might we learn from listening to vocal timbre and accent, for example? How might a singer's or music director's broader oeuvre and the "re-animation" of songs in extracinematic contexts shape the meanings attached to a particular song?[13] How might we conceive of the sound-image relationship in terms other than "song picturization"? Another approach might be to think beyond the musical "sequence"—that is, to expand aural analysis beyond song-dance numbers, which are typically understood as "interruptions" to the narrative.[14] This work demands listening to so-called background music (orchestral score), dialogues, voice-overs, ambient noise,

and sound effects.[15] What happens to song when we conceptualize it in relation to such apparently nonmusical elements in the rest of the diegesis? What
is the relationship between music and speech? How do we conceive of the
sound of words or that of silence?

In this book, I propose a third approach, one that encompasses the aforementioned but generates more expansive theoretical questions about singing, listening, and speaking in cinema. The capacious conception of the aural
I embrace in this book ("soundwork") and the interpretive practice it enables
(what I dub "listening with a feminist ear") shift the intellectual terrain of
Indian cinema studies. I ask very different questions of Bombay cinema and
the Hindi film song than previous studies have. How might our understanding of individual films, and of cultural history more generally, shift if we centered listening in our methodological and epistemological frameworks? What
would Hindi cinema sound like if we kept in mind different—nonmusical,
nonfilmic, even non-Hindi—histories and contexts? What if aural and oral
figures drove our analyses? What can we glean from recasting familiar concepts in sonic terms? How might such critical listening inflect our understanding of Hindi cinema and Indian public culture at large? Jonathan Sterne
writes that "to think sonically is to think conjuncturally about sound and culture."[16] This is the project I pursue in *Listening with a Feminist Ear*.

The three chapters of this book demonstrate a few different ways of put-
ting into practice the ambitious theoretical and methodological reach of my
project. Together they offer a way of attending to Hindi cinema that amplifies
the aural without diminishing the importance of the textual, the visual, or
anything else. My task, at its most fundamental, is to reorient (Indian) cinema studies toward the aural, to infuse it with a sonic sensibility. More mod-
estly, I aim to convince my fellow scholars and fans to *listen* as carefully as
we watch. I seek to undermine the assumption that sound simply augments
visual narratives. The emergence of sound studies as a distinct field of inquiry—in particular, the burgeoning of feminist media studies and South Asian
studies scholarship on sound—is crucial to my effort to coax cinema studies
to listen. Historian Mark M. Smith proposes that we understand sound studies "as a desirable 'habit' of historical inquiry. . . . By 'habit' [he means] methodological, epistemological, and even ontological embeddedness—a way of
examining the past that becomes second nature so that evidence is read, consciously and even subconsciously, for tidbits of the acoustic, smatterings of
the auditory, gestures of silence, noise, listening, and sound."[17] I agree, and
I want to extend such a "habit" beyond historical research. What would it

take to bring one's "habit" of sound studies to other modes of analysis? I seek with this book to make listening with a feminist ear a habit for all subsequent scholarship on Indian cinema.

## Listening as Habit and Hermeneutic

Like my fellow scholars of the aural, I take not just music but all sound to be "a social formation that is constituted by struggle and struggled over; one that is both overdetermined semantically and yet manifold in its semiotic possibilities."[18] Recognizing that soundwork is a discursive realm of both constraint and possibility, we must become "sound students." The term is Jonathan Sterne's tongue-in-cheek adaptation of a dismissive epithet ("cultural students") from the US culture wars of the 1990s. He writes: "sound students produce and transform knowledge about sound and in the process reflexively attend to the (cultural, political, environmental, aesthetic . . .) stakes of that knowledge production."[19] That is to say, if we acknowledge sound to be a site of culture and politics, we must listen—and we must listen as carefully, thoughtfully, and reflexively as we do all else. Along with Nina Sun Eidsheim, Charles Hirschkind, Roshanak Kheshti, Kate Lacey, Lisbeth Lipari, Jennifer Lynn Stoever, and others, I conceive of listening as a critical and ethical endeavor.[20] Listening is not a passive exercise but an engaged and interpretive one. It is a "directed, learned activity," a way of engaging with aural material that is cultivated over time. Thus, listening requires the physiological faculty of hearing, but is not reducible to it.[21] The disciplining of auditory perception, or what Sterne calls "audile technique," is a wholly social and cultural experience.[22] It is steeped in the specificities of time and place, context and genre.

While scholars of cinema (Indian and otherwise) have been slow to pick up on the importance of soundwork and the cultural politics of listening, key Indian nationalists and music reformers of the early to mid-twentieth century were well aware of what was at stake in listening. Most famously and apropos to the history of Bombay film soundwork, B. V. Keskar sought in his position as Minister of Information and Broadcasting (1952–62) to reform the nation's listening practices. His ban on Hindi film songs and simultaneous encouragement of classical music on All India Radio was designed "to forge a soundscape for the new nation by educating, and more importantly by disciplining, citizen-listeners."[23] While radio listeners roundly rejected Keskar's plan to police what "good" music and listening entails, his emphasis on listening as a *cultivated* practice, something that is learned and not self-evident or fixed, and his assertion of its relevance to national identity are notable. Further, certain listening formations and auditory practices that are commonplace in India today owe their shape to discursive, institutional, and industrial developments of prior decades. I demonstrate this claim in the first two chapters of this book by tracing conventions of vocalizing, watching, and listening in Hindi cinema that have become so familiar over time that they go unremarked in both scholarly and popular discourse. Histories of soundwork can fix our "ways of listening" as they do our verbal, vocal, and musical practices.[24] In this book, I propose listening with a feminist ear as an unlearning of some of those aural and interpretive tendencies.

Listening with a Feminist Ear names a hermeneutic—a mode of listening, if you will—that both clarifies and undoes normative conceptions of embodiment and belonging that take shape in sound. To listen with a feminist ear is to attend to aural and oral manifestations of social hierarchies. It is to heed the intersections of gender, sexuality, nation, and other vectors of identity, and to note how the aural forms of these constructs exclude as much as they include. It is to listen in situated and reflexive ways, attentive not just to geographic and historical context but to what Pierre Bourdieu calls "habitus," for those socially conditioned dispositions shape how we listen.[25] It is to ponder how we consume individual texts or performances, as well as how we conceptualize listening itself. In the case of Bombay cinema, it means probing not just what we hear, but how we have come to hear femininity or regional belonging, or even the Hindi of Hindi cinema. How, in other words, have particular sounds and particular ways of interpreting what we hear (on screen) become institutionalized and normalized? How have various currents in public culture disciplined our listening habits, and how might we listen otherwise? In short, to listen with a feminist ear is to tune in to questions of power.

As the final question in the list above indicates, Listening with a Feminist Ear also proceeds from the belief that we *can* listen against the grain, in defiance of disciplinary and textual structures. In *Living a Feminist Life* (2017) and again in *Complaint!* (2021), Sara Ahmed invokes the figure of the "feminist ear" to discuss "how you hear what is not being heard."[26] The metaphor names her "research method as well as an institutional tactic," a way of registering the silences, refusals, and complaints that trouble the official narratives of the institutions in question.[27] Histories of music, radio, and listening on the Indian subcontinent include many instances of audiences sidestepping the diktats and desires of cultural and political authorities. To listen with a feminist ear is to be keyed in to those alternative listening formations and practices. It is to amplify voices and sounds that are otherwise devalued, denigrated, or dismissed. It is also, crucially, to sound out alternative temporal, spatial, and relational possibilities. I indulge such counterintuitive sonic imaginaries in my analyses of the accented soundwork of *Satya* (1998) and the whiskey-and-music scenes of *Aligarh* (2015). The point is not simply to offer an oppositional reading of these delicate but dark films; rather, it is to sit with what becomes possible and tangible when one centers sound. What happens when we listen to Hindi cinema with a feminist ear?

Readers will recognize in my theorization of listening the twin impulses—critical and utopian—that drive many a feminist exploration of music and sound. My early encounters with (new) musicology taught me that gender, sexuality, and race are aural constructs as much as they are visual ones.[28] I began to sense that social categories are reified not just in sound, but in the way we make sense of sounds. The critical move was thus also a utopian one, for perhaps new ways of interpreting music could reconfigure hegemonic aural imaginaries. My recent ruminations on the topic have focused on listening as a site of peril and promise. For example, Jennifer Lynn Stoever traces the racialization of the sonic regime ("the listening ear") in the United States while also gesturing to the promise of agency inherent in listening: "listening is a dynamic historical and cultural practice, an embodied critical sense shaping how and what we think, *and* an ethical act shaped by our thoughts, beliefs, experiences, and ideologies, one both subject to discipline and offering agency."[29] Roshanak Kheshti is even more hopeful about the radical potential of listening. She describes her project of "playing by ear" as being, in part, about identifying and enacting "an ethical listening practice that opens up a set of possibilities that continue to be emergent, a practice of listening through which the listener relates differently to pleasure."[30]

I, too, write from a desire to disrupt the listening relations that structure contemporary life. If listening is a matter of schooling, of embracing historically and socially specific conventions, then we might be able to teach ourselves to listen differently. Condensing the critical and the utopian in a single phrase, *Listening with a Feminist Ear* reminds us that inhabiting social structures and seeking to transform those structures are intimately related endeavors. In my conceptualization, listening does not represent anything radical in and of itself—not necessarily, anyway. As I demonstrate in chapter 1, "haptic listening" (Irina Leimbacher) or "reduced listening" (Michel Chion), which prioritizes the textures of sound (or voices), can reify ethnocentric, racist, and sexist assumptions about the body and difference that constitute the listening ear. The same dangers lurk in the xenophobic interpretation of certain speaking voices as "other," as I argue in chapter 3 of this book and in my other writing on accent. Certain modes of "listening out" (Kate Lacey) that I discuss in chapter 2 can reinforce gendered and communal divides; others can be profoundly solitary and irrelational in nature. In short, listening is not the panacea it is sometimes thought to be. This is why we must consciously and pointedly listen with a feminist ear.

Wary of the many universal claims about listening in the literature, I do not prescribe a singular methodological or theoretical approach to cinema or sound in this book. *Listening with a Feminist Ear* is but an invitation to inhabit a critical and principled orientation to, and in, sound. We must listen to the power dynamics and the social, political, and industrial histories that have shaped our ways of listening. We must listen for how we have been taught to listen—taught to recognize certain sounds as liberatory and others as oppressive, some voices as sexual and others as pious, some forms of speech as proper and others as uncouth. Nina Sun Eidsheim might call this "listening to listening."[31] In listening thus, we learn to listen anew. We learn to notice voices and sounds that typically go unnoticed or underappreciated. We learn to turn up the volume on those "othered" sonic forms and tell other stories about them. To attend to silences and muted sounds, to follow aural associations to "other times, other places," is akin to Michael Denning's project of "decolonizing the ear."[32] It is to continue the struggle over meaning, power, and pleasure in sound. It is to conjure new ways of being and thinking and feeling through sound. In listening in new and different ways, in listening awry to that which is familiar as well as to "unheard melodies," we reconstitute both sound and the many entities (individual and collective) articulated in sound.[33] This, then, is the radical potential of listening with a feminist ear.

## Soundwork

The conceptual move I attempt in this book, from music to the aural broadly conceived, requires not just an ethical listening practice but an expansive one. Michele Hilmes's term "soundwork" is helpful, for it can encompass the many different elements audible in films. Hilmes uses the term for "media forms that are primarily aural, employing the three basic elements of sonic expression—music, speech, and noise—to create a lively economy of sound-based commodities and institutions, ranging from radio to recorded sound to, at the more visual limit, the soundtracks that accompany visual media."[34] Hilmes notes elsewhere that speech is the dominant element of the new digital soundwork to which she refers; in other words, cinema is not the medium her critical term is meant to describe.[35] And yet, thinking of my object of study as soundwork shifts the intellectual terrain just enough to help me listen better—more deeply, more widely, more critically. It helps me theorize the aural in Bombay cinema in more nuanced ways.

A comparison to Emily Thompson's use of "soundscape" may be in order. Building on R. Murray Schafer's and Alain Corbin's use of the term, Thompson deploys "soundscape" to mean not just an "auditory or aural landscape . . . [but] a way of perceiving that environment; it is both a world and a culture constructed to make sense of that world."[36] Likewise, I use "soundwork" to name not just what I listen to in Hindi cinema, but also how various cultural currents allow those sounds to resonate as markers of gender, sexuality, ethnicity, and nation. Whereas "soundscape" brings to the fore the relationship between sound and notions of place—a matter I dwell on in chapter 3 of this book—Hilmes's term enfolds a gesture to "work" that I appreciate very much. I leave it to other scholars and practitioners to elaborate the labor involved in crafting cinematic sound. In this book, I take on the complementary task of explicating the inordinate cultural work that screen sounds perform.

To study cinematic soundwork is to listen to a whole host of material that films offer the ear, including speech, sound effects, music, ambient noise, and other elements of sound design. Listening across different categories of sound is all the more important today because Hindi cinema has changed in striking ways in the last two decades. Contemporary filmmakers' innovations in genre and style have led to the emergence of the "songless" film, where song-dance sequences "retrea[t] into the soundtrack."[37] Yet, even as the erstwhile musical sequence has "disappeared," the film-music industry has enjoyed phenomenal growth. While these twin developments may appear contradictory at first blush, what they suggest is that contemporary film songs are quite different than those of the past, both in form and in function. Music directors today conceptualize sound and music differently than their predecessors did, and their compositions bear traces of this shift in thinking. Lines between song-dance sequences and the rest of the diegesis, between those sequences and "background" music, and between sound and music are far less clear.[38] The industry has begun paying more attention to other aspects of aural production besides music composition and playback singing; the roles of the sound engineer and sound designer, for example, are recognized more now than ever before. The sound of speech in Hindi cinema has also changed dramatically, with filmmakers opting for language that is more colloquial, more vernacular, and, thus, more hybrid and regionally specific. It is imperative that we shift our conceptual categories to grasp these and other changes afoot in the sound of Bombay cinema. To be clear, I am not suggesting that the interdisciplinary paradigm of this book is only applicable to the study of "new Bollywood" of the early twenty-first century.[39] After all, I devote two of my three chapters to tracing shifts in soundwork from the 1950s through the present. What I am proposing is that contemporary experiments in song, film sound, and speech emerge alongside, and demand, different listening practices. This should cue different ways of thinking about sound in our scholarship as well.

The term "soundwork" is valuable in the study of Hindi cinema because it keeps my aural analysis from being limited to song—even as I study song. It does not rehearse the distinction between the musical and the nonmusical. The term is also a useful alternative to "soundtrack," which, in the Indian context, refers primarily to song-dance sequences and occasionally to the so-called background score. Soundwork steers us away from visual metaphors such as "background" that sustain the fallacy that films are primarily visual media. At the same time, it teaches us to *not* discount the image in thinking about sound. Consider such concepts as voice-overs, sound bridges, playback singing, and song picturization. These terms all name different articulations of sound and image. The first two are well established in cinema studies' vocabulary. They represent a visual approach to analyzing sound, in that they describe audible material in terms of what is visible on screen. By contrast, the latter two concepts are widely used in studies of Indian cinema, but are not considered integral to the discipline as whole. They prioritize sound over image, for they describe the practice of composing and recording sonic material and *then* "picturizing" it. While playback and song picturization are certainly accurate descriptors of important industry practices, it is important to pause over the theoretical implications of those concepts. In framing my analysis in terms of soundwork, I seek to correct cinema studies' overemphasis on the image to the detriment of sound. At the same time, I resist the temptation to simply flip the hierarchy and claim that the aural is more important than the visual. To study soundwork is to watch and listen at once, mindful that the relationship between sound and image in cinema is protean and context specific. Put differently, soundwork names an interdisciplinary approach to the aural that takes as its starting point Hilmes's observation that "sound [is now] a screen medium."[40] Other feminist scholars also point to imbrication of the aural and the visual in constructing gender, sexuality, and race, in such apparently disparate arenas as nineteenth-century Italian opera performances, YouTube clips of *Britain's Got Talent*, and post–World War II radio broadcasts in the United States.[41] Accordingly, I take soundwork as a call to think creatively about, and with, the conjunction of sound and image in Bombay cinema.

## Interaurality

Studying soundwork requires that we listen as fans—voraciously and with little heed to conceptual borders that academic disciplines draw around diverse sounds. Fans of film and film music tend to have extensive repertoires. They—*we*—listen to and revel in more than just film music. Songs are never consumed in isolation; they are always understood in relation to other sounds, in a film, across films, and across public culture generally. It is imperative, then, that we harness our cinephilia and audiophilia to our scholarly projects. As idiosyncratic as our preferences and knowledge as fans may be, fandom teaches us to chart connections across different aural spheres, not limiting ourselves to film or to a singular linguistic domain. In addition to multiplying and diversifying what we listen to in films, we must listen beyond cinema (and certainly beyond *Hindi* cinema).

Conceptualizing film soundwork as part of histories of sound, music, dance, and performance, I take research into popular music, radio, and television, as well as public culture more broadly, to be fundamental to film studies. This book thus represents an eschewal of disciplinary divisions that separate sound studies from musical analysis, and sound from other aspects of performance in cinema. In making my case, I build on the insights of performance and media studies scholars who note that in India, as elsewhere in the world, artistic genres and media forms are not as distinct in practice as they seem to be in scholarship.[42] It goes without saying that Bollywood is a culture industry characterized by "convergence" and intermedial connections of all sorts.[43] What I emphasize is that ways of thinking about sound in putatively extracinematic domains—for example, expectations of what particular sounds mean, how particular bodies ought to sound, or how sounds are related to images— have structured conventions of listening to and viewing Hindi cinema over the years. Listening to soundwork with a feminist ear thus demands a firm commitment to interdisciplinarity, to the crossing of all borders that need to be crossed and that *are crossed by* sound. My interventions work in tandem with those of Usha Iyer, who calls for rethinking Hindi dance sequences by foregrounding choreography and performance style.[44] They are also aligned with those of Vebhuti Duggal, who has consistently theorized film song and listening beyond diegeses. Likewise, Isabel Huacuja Alonso's and Laura Kunreuther's histories of radio on the subcontinent, and Amanda Weidman's extended body of work on the politics of voice in South India, have pushed me to conceptualize my project with wanton disregard for the boundaries of cinema and cinema studies.[45] The challenge is to understand films as being rooted in interocular and intertextual fields as well as what we might call "interaural" ones.[46] Conceived as a way of naming new digital media forms, soundwork carries within itself a gesture to other aural (and visual) media besides film. In *Listening with a Feminist Ear*, I argue for a still broader notion of interaurality, one that includes not just popular media forms but also the way singing, listening, and speaking are understood and experienced in public culture at large. All in all, I demonstrate the need to expand what constitutes the aural not just in cinema but in the *study* of cinema.

## Politics of Nation

Soundwork's roots in radio studies cue a rich body of feminist scholarship critiquing aural figurations of gender, race, and nation. Contestations over "the nation's voice" were as audible in the early days of radio in the United States (consider, for example, the role of minstrelsy in the development of the medium) as they are in Spanish-language radio today.[47] Likewise, in Britain, France, and Germany, broadcasting developed in the context of war and empire; discourses of gender and modernity that sustain nationalist and imperial enterprises are thus crucial in the scholarship on radio in these locales.[48] Emerging research on broadcast media and public sound cultures in other parts of the world, from Argentina to Nepal to Nigeria, also highlights similar struggles over gender and citizenship.[49] This feminist corpus in sound and media studies helps contextualize the centrality of nation in *Listening with a Feminist Ear*. While mine is not a historiographic project in the way the aforementioned work is, it is motivated by a similar set of theoretical concerns.

Such an insistence on the continued importance of nation as an analytic might seem counterintuitive in these global times, when research on Indian cinema has taken both a transnational and a regional turn.[50] Scholarship on South Indian film industries, in particular, has challenged the hegemony of Hindi cinema as well as the national-cinemas framework that undergirds much of the work in cinema studies, South Asian and otherwise. Ratheesh Radhakrishnan, S. V. Srinivas, Ravi Vasudevan, and Aarti Wani have discussed "region" as a potential framework, while Ranjani Mazumdar used the city as a frame in *Bombay Cinema: An Archive of the City* (2007) well over a decade ago.[51] *Listening with a Feminist Ear* hears these important calls to unsettle nation as a category of analysis, even as it insists on the need to unpack the aural politics of nation and/in Bombay cinema. To study the politics of nation is not to deny that Hindi films have long been oriented beyond the borders of the nation-state: they are consumed the world over and grapple with the tensions between the "home and the world," between India and the West. Nor is it to ignore the crucial challenges posed by other "cinemas of India" or by region as a framework for the study of Bombay cinema.[52] However, given the paucity of research on Hindi film soundwork, I submit that discerning how nation is signified and resignified in the aural domain remains a critical task. Following Jyotika Virdi, I "deploy 'national' critically, [as] a heuristic device enabling understanding of how cinema articulates its local milieu, while simultaneously interrogating its hegemony."[53] I demonstrate that listening to Hindi film soundwork does not merely make room for otherwise marginalized bodies and texts. It challenges the temporal, spatial, and performative contours of "nation" and "national cinema."

What little work there is on the sound of nation in Hindi cinema has mainly focused on the voice of Lata Mangeshkar.[54] The very sound of Mangeshkar's voice—deemed "pure," virtuous, and long suffering—came to stand for ideal Indian womanhood in the postcolonial period, so much so that as late as the 1990s hers was the voice against which all Hindi film singers were judged. Notwithstanding my own investment in, and writing on, the subject, I believe it is time that cinema studies interrupts the legendary playback singer's hegemony over the field. In *Listening with a Feminist Ear*, I extend the theorization of voice and nation in two directions. First, I bring our understanding of vocality into the present, by juxtaposing the grand dame's voice with those of playback singers who have arrived on the scene more recently. Adding other voices to the story, I revise extant understandings of the relationship between voice and body, sound and image. Second, I elaborate how cinematic speech is also inflected with connotations of local, regional, and national belonging. In tuning my ear to speaking voices, I model how we might move beyond the song sequence and playback singing, while also blurring the lines between sound, speech, and song. Throughout, I demonstrate that the oral and aural politics of nation are intertwined. That is, the politics of voicing is inextricable from that of listening. Thus, any study of cinematic soundwork must attend to not just the way voices are sounded out but also the way listening is conceptualized and experienced.

## Singing, Listening, Speaking

*Listening with a Feminist Ear* is oriented around questions of singing, listening, and speaking. I begin by tracing sonic representations of gender and community across seven decades of Hindi film history. Chapter 1, "From Singing to Musicking: Women's Voices, Bodies, and the Audiovisual Contract," is a study of playback singing, Indian cinema's decades-old convention of using professional singers' voices (and not the actors' voices) for musical sequences. I reframe playback in terms of Michel Chion's notion of the "audiovisual contract" to emphasize the complex relay between the aural and the visual that undergirds all cinematic representation.[55] Foregrounding the sound-image relationship clarifies the fact that audiences do not just *see* gender, sexuality, and nation on screen; they *hear* those constructs as well. Further, in anchoring the audiovisual contract in three distinct periods in the history of women's voices in Bombay cinema, I temper the universalist thrust of Chion's theoretical construct and extend the historiography of playback singing. I specify how the audiovisual contract worked during Lata Mangeshkar's vocal monopoly, from the 1950s through the 1990s, before laying out how ideas about voice and body integral to that contract—what I call the "somatic clause"—were undone over the next two decades. The transformation was gradual and uneven, but it marked a radical shift in conceptions of gender and voice. At the heart of my argument is a juxtaposition of Mangeshkar's hegemonic voice—high pitched, sweet, and contained—with the "ethnic" and pop voices that surfaced in the 1990s in the context of economic liberalization. Dramatic changes in the media landscape brought to the fore artists like Ila Arun, who challenged the aural ideal of Indian femininity and gave singers a more visible media presence. It would take until the early 2000s, however, for the moral connotations of the "old" audiovisual contract to dissipate. I conclude with a discussion of women's millennial soundwork to show that voice is no longer construed as the manifestation of an authentic inner self, but understood, in more postmodern vein, as a variable bodily technology.

Chapter 2, "Re-Sounding the Islamicate: The Qawwali and its Listening Publics," extends the previous chapter's concern with gender and soundwork by listening closely to the qawwali, a genre frequently used to evoke a Muslim milieu in Bombay cinema. Marshall G. S. Hodgson's widely accepted term "Islamicate . . . refer[s] not directly to the religion, Islam, itself, but to the social and cultural complex historically associated with Islam and the Muslims, both among Muslims themselves and even when found among non-Muslims."[56] This definition is apt, for the Islamicate genre of the qawwali signifies far more than a faith community in Hindi cinema. Sound and listening are of crucial importance in many strands of Islamicate thought and practice, and in Sufism in particular. I argue that Hindi cinema of the mid-twentieth century borrowed from this philosophical and musical tradition to craft a listening public that was synonymous with the nation. In this "classic" iteration, the cinematic qawwali emphasized the relationship between singers and listeners, interpellating not just an amorous couple on screen but a community with shared religious and cultural desires. Love, listening, and collectivity were articulated as one. The classic qawwali thus represented both the romance of secularism and the secularism of romance, ideals critical to India in its postindependence years. These twin ideals were severely tested over the decades, their diminishing importance registered in the gradual waning of the qawwali on screen. When it reappears in the postliberalization period, the cinematic qawwali (and the affiliated form of Sufipop) marks a different set of political aspirations and cultural emphases. I consider the "dargah" (shrine) qawwalis of the early 2000s to be part of the broader Sufi performing arts vogue, a liberal cultural response to the political ascendancy of the Hindu right.[57] I argue that in this second cinematic iteration, the genre animates the figure of the "good" Muslim man by drawing on entrenched notions of difference and impassioned religiosity. Through shifts in vocal and musical arrangement, performance style, mise-en-scène, cinematography, and other aural and visual features, the dargah qawwali calls up a markedly different listening public—one that is religious but not national. For its part, Sufipop turns inward in an apparent rejection of the relational and collective ethos that characterizes the qawwali. It also evinces a startling de-Islamicization, despite the fact that its distinguishing sonic feature—the plaintive male solo voice, bright and high—evokes the sound of two famous Muslim artists:

the qawwal and world-music legend Nusrat Fateh Ali Khan, and the leading music director of Hindi and Tamil cinema, A. R. Rahman. Finally, in its
"item number–esque" avatar, the qawwali moves from spirituality and male
homosociality back to its "classic" investment in heteronormative romance.
Crucially, however, it no longer accords much importance to listening. As
gender and romance are reconfigured, so too is the genre's conceptualization
of listening publics.

In training my ears on an Islamicate genre and arguing that the qawwali
was paradigmatic of how the nation was imagined in the Nehruvian era, I
"listen back" to hegemonic discourses about India that cast Islam as "other."[58]
Centering soundwork also undercuts the overemphasis on the visual in discussions of Islam, in India as much as in the West, where the veiled Muslim
woman figures as an object of pity and oppression. The qawwali hearkens
instead to a rich history of syncretism and Islamicate aesthetics on the subcontinent. That said, the generic shifts I identify in this chapter—the move
from romance to piety (and back) and from the stage to the *dargah* to the
dance floor—are more than about changing notions of the Islamicate. They
add nuance to a key term in sound studies: listening publics. In the history I
chart, we find examples of "listening out" that are as open, ethical, and welcoming of difference as Kate Lacey, Lisbeth Lipari, and other theorists of listening propose.[59] Equally, though, the cinematic qawwali and other Sufi forms
call up listening publics (and, at times, nonpublics) that are riven by narrow
conceptions of identity and belonging. Listening to the cinematic qawwali
with a feminist ear, thus, recalibrates our understanding of listening itself.

Note that while chapters 1 and 2 of this book center musical performance,
they are not about song-dance sequences per se. What they offer, rather, is
a study of cinematic conventions of voicing and listening. They reveal the
disciplining of our eyes and ears. If difference is constructed in the very act
of listening, what is at stake in being heard? What is at stake in being heard
*as different* and in being the one who is invited to listen? I demonstrate that
a sound-sensitive, feminist interpretive practice can name—and, in so doing,
undermine—the social boundaries Hindi cinema draws through soundwork.
I argue, further, that mutating sounds can themselves suggest new possibilities. To listen to the "ethnic" voice of a singer like Ila Arun is to understand
Indian womanhood in a wholly new way. To recognize the voice of Nusrat
Fateh Ali Khan or A. R. Rahman as *the* sound of the qawwali is to reimagine Muslim masculinity as pious and inclusive. To listen thus is to reject the
specter of the aggressive Muslim "other" conjured by Hindutva (Hindu right-

wing) forces and the United States' "war on terror." The first two chapters of *Listening with a Feminist Ear* thus approach implicitly a question I take up more explicitly in the next chapter and coda of this book: what is at stake in listening differently?

Chapter 3, "Speaking of the Xenophone: Language as Sound in *Satya*," extends the notion of cinematic soundwork by attending to the materiality of the spoken word in *Satya* (dir. Ram Gopal Varma, 1998). Building on Rey Chow's notion of the "xenophone," I argue that the sound of speech in this film works in tandem with song lyrics and sound design to call up the freighted history of language ideologies in India, a history that was remaking the city of Bombay in the mid-1990s. In my analysis, the *tapori*-turned-gangster gets cast as an aural figure whose hybrid, accented performance complicates our understanding of the city and its cinema. I demonstrate that listening to *taporis*' (vagabonds') accents and to the way dialogues are placed in relation to the rest of the soundwork in *Satya* opens up a different—more diverse and accommodating—conception of Bombay than the one claimed by nativist groups. The quintessential cinematic city becomes a space that questions the certitudes of linguistic nationalism, and thus a space from which to reimagine the aural politics of nation.

Bringing a feminist ear to the city the Hindi film industry has long called home, this chapter showcases the critical utopianism, cine- and audiophilia, and sonic sensibility that form the core of this book. In probing the nuanced pronunciations of belonging audible in this film, I also demonstrate that the aurality of language is as crucial in cinema as it is in other communicative and performative contexts. Pausing over blurred distinctions between sound and speech, I elaborate *Satya*'s argument against the policing of borders, and model analysis that captures both the historical and formal complexity of speech in cinema. Finally, I push cinema studies to look and listen beyond a single region and single language. What would the study of Hindi cinema be like if we were to start from a place of polyphony? How might we multiply the languages, places, and cinematic and performance traditions that anchor this cinema? I propose that conceiving of language as sound—and vice versa, sound as language—alerts us to the plurality in/of Bombay cinema that may be audible but is not always visible. Acknowledging the multiplicity of idioms and accents in films forces us out of the implicitly monolingual national-cinemas framework that has dominated the study of cinema. It decenters Bombay cinema and reveals both the city and its favorite industry as entities sustained by cross-regional, cross-national, and cross-media travels.

*Listening with a Feminist Ear* closes with a coda that pursues the uto-pian potential of soundwork in what is otherwise a deeply sad and poignant film. In "Listening, Loving, Longing," I contemplate how the soundwork of *Aligarh* (dir. Hansal Mehta, 2015) conjures configurations of desire and tem-porality that are not otherwise legible, or even possible, within the terms of the narrative. I tarry in scenes of listening and reading, noting how the film braids song, sound, and speech. In a world of sundered ties, the protagonist, Siras, finds connection and affirmation in what we might call "songless" song sequences—that is, in the film song reimagined as soundwork. Thus, while I begin this book by asserting the importance of nation to the study of cin-ematic sound (and vice versa), I conclude with the more radical notion that critical listening can produce alternative genealogies and futures.

As I hope is amply evident, *Listening with a Feminist Ear* draws its energies from four overlapping interdisciplinary formations: cinema and media studies, sound studies, South Asian studies, and women's and gender studies. It pushes the boundaries of Indian cinema studies, which has yet to see a monograph that places the aural (broadly construed) center stage and presents feminist analyses grounded in listening. With its focus on Bombay cinema, a case as instructive as it is powerful in reach, my work has important implications for cinema and media studies and sound studies as a whole. On the one hand, it tempers the universalism of these fields, which tend to base their claims in Euro-American contexts. On the other, it demonstrates that certain insights derived from the Indian case—regarding unquestioned assumptions about gendered constructs like "voice" and "body" or the monolingualism of the national cinemas frame-work, for example—travel beyond the subcontinent quite well. For its inter-rogation of gender, sexuality, and nation in soundwork, my book is indebted to the persistent questioning of these constructs in transnational feminist, women-of-color, queer, and postcolonial critique. It uses an important South Asian cultural site to extend feminist scholarship that theorizes how sound constitutes hierarchies of gender, race, and nation, and enact the possibility of undoing those normative structures through listening.

A word on what this book is not. While I draw on musical vocabulary and theory as needed, *Listening with a Feminist Ear* is ultimately not a work of musicological analysis or music theory. I do not offer here a comprehensive history of Hindi film music or film song sequences—both worthy projects. Nor is this book a study of all the ways in which sound has been, and is, used in Bombay cinema. That, too, would be a very welcome, if impossibly large, project. My task, rather, is to probe some of the ways in which the aural domain of Bombay cinema articulates and amplifies—and perhaps even transforms—social, cultural, and political currents. My task is also to interpret a few examples of cinematic soundwork so as to question commonplace assumptions about gender, nation, sound, and cinema.

# Singing

## CHAPTER 1

# From Singing to Musicking

## *Women's Voices, Bodies, and the Audiovisual Contract*

In "Female Singers' Adda," a 2017 interview for the digital platform *Film Companion*, veteran film journalist Anupama Chopra speaks with four contemporary singers of the Hindi playback world: Neha Bhasin, Jonita Gandhi, Neeti Mohan, and Aditi Singh Sharma.[1] Their conversation revolves around the singers' gendered experiences in an industry that prioritizes men and actors, and the vast changes in their line of work in the past decade. At one point, Chopra draws them out on the question of their "replaceability"—on the fact that Bombay cinema no longer boasts a singular playback star with a distinctive voice and an iconic reputation. Neeti Mohan's explanation is that contemporary audiences' greater exposure to music from around the globe means they are hungry for "fresh" sounds. Jonita Gandhi emphasizes the fact that we hear many more voices today, and that "a lot of singers who are getting their due now . . . are people who might not have been noticed a decade ago, because there was 'no room for them' at that time." She and Neha Bhasin argue that the competition pushes them to take matters into their own hands. They constantly "reinvent" themselves, fashion themselves as singer-songwriters, rather than "just" playback singers, and experiment with various formats and platforms to cultivate a fanbase that exceeds the bounds of cinema. Even as she agrees with these positions, Aditi Singh Sharma highlights the cutthroat nature of the playback industry: for every woman singer today, there are ten or more not so lucky as to have their versions of the song chosen for the film. Moreover, the sheer number of artists competing for stardom means that even those who make it big are not immediately recognizable—in part, because they do not, and cannot afford to, sound "the same" across songs. To recast these artists' experiences using the vocabulary of this chapter: Hindi cinema's audiovisual contract has changed such that in place of the aural stardom and voice recognizability of yesteryear, we find in wom-

en's millennial soundwork an emphasis on versatility, visibility, and musicking bodies. In what follows, I unearth the logic that undergirds this radical
transformation.

Remarkably, even as the interlocutors in "Female Singers' Adda" stress
that the business of singing today is very different than it was in "that era,"
not once do they utter the name of the late Lata Mangeshkar, the venerated
singer famous not just for her melodic voice, but for her grip on the Hindi
playback industry from the 1950s to the 1990s. They do not speak of how
the moral labor of representing women in the Bombay film song was split
between Mangeshkar and her sister Asha Bhosle, the latter singing for the
more risqué and modern characters. I appreciate this strategic silence on
Hindi cinema's "good-girl" and "bad-girl" voices. Narrating the history of
playback using that dichotomy does little to unsettle the saintly discourse
surrounding Mangeshkar. If anything, such a narrative extends her hegemony from Bombay cinema to the *study* of this cinema and its soundwork. It
does not clarify how other singers navigated—and continue to navigate—the
political and ideological terrain specific to their times.[2] To tell a different,
more nuanced story, we must sharpen our understanding of the relationship
between sound and image, and between body and voice, in Bombay cinema.
Doing so can dislodge commonplace assumptions about women's voices and
bodies that continue to shape not just industry practices and public discourse
in India, but cinema studies scholarship as a whole.

My attempt to listen to playback with a feminist ear begins with the following question: what conceptual framework enabled audiences to conceive
of voice as a disembodied entity? As counterintuitive as it seems, focusing on
the logic of the Mangeshkar era decenters the grand dame of Hindi cinema
from the historiography of playback singing. While the decades-long preference for her voice is remarkable, so too is the fact that a wholly different
set of conventions of voicing and listening became institutionalized in the
first decade of the twenty-first century. Therefore, I ask: How has the audible
sound of women's bodies changed in recent years? What explains the "aural
lag" in the history of film and popular music in India, the fact that aural representations of women did not change as quickly as visual representations did?
What ideas about voice, body, femininity, and technology are operative in the
industry today, and how do they differ from those of the mid- to late twentieth century? What does the materiality of voice in contemporary soundwork
tell us about the way we listen to cinema? What does it tell us about the way
we watch music?

I approach these questions via the concept of the "audiovisual contract."[3] This is the term film-sound theorist Michel Chion uses to describe the linking of sound and image in cinema. Audiences agree to treat the sounds played over the speakers as being of a piece with the images that flash across the screen in front of them. Discussing playback singing using the vocabulary of the audiovisual contract clarifies that this dubbing practice is not simply a quirk of the Indian film industry, but a convention that has been foundational to *all* cinema, at least since the arrival of the talkies. Far from being a marker of difference and distinctiveness, lip-synched songs are signs of Hindi cinema's *similarity* to other cinematic traditions whose audiences are also called on to effect a perceptual meld of sound and image. Lest this statement be taken as affirmation of the universalism of Chion's theoretical construct, I hasten to add that the power of the audiovisual contract lies in the specific ways in which it operates in each cinematic tradition. In identifying the six "clauses" of Bombay cinema's audiovisual contract and elucidating the imprint of other media, paratexts, and gendered public discourse on the sound-image relationship in cinema, I underscore the need to locate Chion in particular historical and cultural contexts.

Grounding Chion's term also helps me parse the notion of the body, a key concept in analyses of women in cinema and film-sound scholarship. Even the most astute theorists of gender, film, and sound discuss the body in exclusively visual terms, ignoring other ways of perceiving and experiencing corporeality. We speak of the voice-body relationship in cinema, forgetting that we do not just see bodies—we touch, smell, and *hear* them as well. Claudia Gorbman reminds us that voices emit all manner of bodily sounds: "The film voice is, of course, not merely a vehicle for words as text. Voices scream, cough, laugh, cry, sing, growl, and moan, and they carry distinctive accents, pitches, timbres, and rhythms."[4] She adds that although Roland Barthes's concept of the "grain of the voice" is cited often, few scholars attend closely to the sound of actors' speaking voices (I take up this very task in chapter 3).[5] Moreover, as Britta Sjogren observes, the "grain of the voice" is interpreted differently by different critics: some use it to refer to vocal tone, others to timbre, and still others to the way the voice exceeds the body or the way the body exceeds signification altogether.[6] Voice is the primary means through which bodies, regardless of their gender, are audible. But until recently, few have analyzed the materiality of the body in terms of the voice that emanates from it.[7] The conceptual slippage between body and image implies that voice is necessarily "disembodied," which in turn explains the near-exclusive focus on Lata Mangeshkar in both film studies and popular discourse on singing voices.

In a sharp departure from other studies of voice in cinema, I foreground the sound-image relationship. The audiovisual contract reminds us that the body is not just a visible entity but also an *aural* one. Along with film scholar Ian Garwood, I treat voice as having the potential to "bring its body to the fore."[8] While all voices originate in the body, some just do not let us forget their corporeal origins. These "bodily" voices prompt us to ask: When, and in what historical contexts, do we hear the body in voice, and what does that audible body mean? What work do such gendered, corporeal voices perform in relation to visual representations of women's bodies (and vice versa)? How do discourses that vilify the body deal with the affective and representational possibilities to which such bodily voices gesture?

Such questions do more than emphasize the materiality of voice; they also undercut simple celebrations of voice as a metaphor for political presence and agency. To "have a voice" and to "make one's voice heard" is to shape conversations in the democratic public sphere. The vociferous debate initiated in postcolonial and gender studies by Gayatri Chakravorty Spivak's essay "Can the Subaltern Speak?" implies that while such speaking may not be entirely possible, it is desirable.[9] This is in part because voice is the presumed locus of modern subjectivity and authenticity. Naturalized links between voice, speech, subjectivity, and political participation flatten what voice means, even as they valorize it. They reduce voice to the linguistic "content" of speech. As my discussion of language and accent in chapter 3 demonstrates, such inattention to the sound of bodies is more than a bête noire of mine. It has political ramifications, erasing as it does an important site for the construction and articulation of identity. That said, folding comments about the materiality of voice into a celebratory discourse about social, cultural, and political representation is not enough.[10] One must ask: is the mere sound of voices a good thing? As I demonstrate in my discussion of the "ethnic" singer Ila Arun, it is all too easy for particular sounds and voices to be interpreted in the terms set out by sexist, Orientalist, and other ideologically freighted discourses. So the question is not just whose voices we hear, but how—on what terms—particular voices enter the contested terrain of public culture. To what extent does the inclusion of diverse vocal timbres, accents, and styles of singing entail a democratization of public culture?

If having a voice is considered a good thing, so too is being visible. It is difficult to make political claims if one is not readable and identifiable as a legitimate, rights-holding entity. Consider the spatial metaphor of "coming out." To be "out" is to be seen in the public sphere, to be identifiable as "gay," and to demand rights and recognition on the basis of that visibility. But visibility can be a problem for gender and sexual queers, just as it is and has been for various other minority groups. Often, to be visible is to be targeted. What is all the more troubling about the hurrah-for-visibility discourse is that it assumes that identity is, and should be, readable on the surface of the body. This assumption not only misses the myriad embodied dimensions of experience and identity, it also neglects long histories of oppression that hinge on what bodies are thought to signify. For example, with its historical entrenchment in notions of sexuality, desire, and passion, the body has been a problem for discourses that idealize women as keepers of tradition, morality, national identity, and so forth. More precisely, the body has been a problem for *women*, for it is often associated with inappropriate, even "unfeminine," qualities like loudness, brashness, and assertiveness. To discuss the sound of women's bodies as I do in this chapter, then—to do so without demeaning either those sounds or those bodies—is to critique assumptions about gender, sexuality, and nation so widely held that they seem commonsensical.

All this to say that the project I undertake in this chapter is fourfold. First, I join other feminist scholars of sound and music in insisting that arguments about the social construction of gender account for the aural. The challenge is to the persistent ocularcentrism of film studies, but also to the hegemony of the image in other scholarly realms. I contend that identity gets read in the sound of bodies (in voices) as much as it does in those bodies' visible manifestations. The *interaction* between sound and sight is crucial in how particular bodies negotiate the world—in this case, the world of film and television. My analysis of the various "clauses" of the audiovisual contract clarifies how expectations about women's bodies—how women ought to look and sound, and what those visual and aural representations mean—have changed over time. What is at stake, then, is nothing less than the social construction of gender and sexuality in public culture.

Second, in centering the body in my analysis of women's playback singing, I am embracing what nationalist leaders and advocates of social and musical reform in late nineteenth- and early twentieth-century India vehemently critiqued. In their efforts to defend and "purify" Indian society, these activists sought to erase the physicality of women's bodies from the ambit of national culture. While I am by no means the first or only critic of this history, there is still a certain pleasure in thumbing my nose at centuries of masculinist discourse. Building from the work of scholars such as Neepa Majumdar, Gregory D. Booth, and Amanda Weidman, who have written insightfully about playback as a technological and industrial system, I offer a reframing of some of their insights using Michel Chion's vocabulary.[11] Thinking of playback history in terms of the audiovisual contract highlights just how constructed and historically contingent Mangeshkar's "pure" voice was. It reminds us that Mangeshkar's rise to fame was not a given, that playback in Bombay cinema could have sounded and looked different had we, the audience, agreed to a different contract. If her voice matched the look of the ideal Indian woman in film after film, it was because very specific ideas about sound, image, and performance were being mobilized as the postcolonial nation-state came into being. As I denaturalize gendered ideals about voice and body that sustained nationalist rhetoric in India for much of the twentieth century, I also challenge scholarly assumptions about those very constructs. I amplify contemporary singers' bodily voices to undercut the binary construction of voice and body that still drives much of the scholarship on singing and dubbing in cinema.

Third, I extend our understanding of aural stardom in Bombay cinema into the present moment. I argue that Mangeshkar's vocal monopoly did not fade until the audiovisual contract undergirding playback singing in India itself changed. In particular, what needed to change was what I call the "somatic clause," which turned on morally weighted ideas about voice and body. The extensive media and cultural changes inaugurated by economic liberalization in the early 1990s—changes that were writ large on television—led to a shift in dominant conceptions of the body, particularly women's bodies. Where once bodily display was frowned on, now it became the norm in popular cultural representations. As the sexualized body became more visible and more audible—as the sound of the body came to be heard more clearly and more often in women's playback singing—it ceased to be a sign of otherness and immorality. Instead, it came to represent modern, cosmopolitan Indian identity. Women's playback singing today boasts a diverse array of vocal timbres and styles, as evidenced by the artists featured on "Female Singers' Adda" as well as others like Shefali Alvares, Rekha Bhardwaj, Sunidhi Chauhan, Harshdeep Kaur, Alyssa Mendonsa, Shilpa Rao, and Nandini Srikar. This diversity is indicative of a move away from the notion of body-as-vice in cinema to one that recognizes women's bodies as musicking entities. Thus, the dismantling of Lata Mangeshkar's hegemony in Hindi cinema was much more than the eclipse of a star singer. It entailed a radical shift in thinking about gender and sexuality, particularly the way gendered and sexualized bodies performing in public articulate national identity in contemporary India.

Keeping sound and image in play at all times clarifies why the visual representation of women changed faster than the singing voices of those same characters. While "ethnic" characters could sing in bodily voices, Hindi cinema's leading women continued to sound Mangeshkar-esque well into the 1990s. I argue that this "aural lag" was crucial in maintaining the modesty of heroines who began to dress and dance as provocatively as the vamps of the past. The integral connection between sound and sight also bears on the transformation of the somatic clause in the 2000s. I demonstrate how changes in the visual representation of popular and film music have dislodged the long-held belief that voice represents the true essence of a character—and by extension, the notion that the aural is more important than the visual in Bombay cinema. *Seeing* women make music has reconfigured our understanding of their singing voices. Where once voice was disembodied, now it is treated as a bodily musical technology. Thus, while playback singing as a profession has changed dramatically in recent years, what persists is the relay between the aural and the visual. This is, moreover, a relay fundamental to the concept of soundwork I develop in this book.

Mooring Chion's abstractions in Indian historical and cultural contexts is the fourth critical intervention of this chapter. Such contextualization is important not because it reveals the particularity of Bombay cinema—its "difference" or departure from Eurocentric cinematic norms—but because it clarifies all that Chion takes for granted. For example, assumptions about the fundamentally disembodied nature of sound that are built into his terminology simply do not hold when we attend to the sound of Hindi cinema (or of other cinemas, for that matter). My analysis also suggests that different expectations attach to the cinematic image and sound depending on whether the characters in question are men or women. The relationship between sound and image is relentlessly gendered and sexualized. It follows, then, that we must consider these and other relevant identity constructs as constitutive to the audiovisual contract, whether in the Indian, the US, or the French case. In this chapter, I take on the urgent task of undoing of such "silences" about identity in cinema studies' theoretical vocabulary. As I contemplate changes in playback singing across seven decades, I demonstrate how Bombay cinema's engagement with other media forms—television, in particular—extends and transforms the audiovisual contract that is its very condition of possibility. In a sense, the power of the audiovisual contract is that it is a dynamic construct, responsive to the challenges of media and social history.

In the following two sections, I explicate and refine Chion's concept by identifying the rules—or "clauses"—that pertain to Bombay cinema's multifaceted audiovisual contract. Having specified how the six clauses sustained what singer Neha Bhasin and her colleagues cryptically refer to as "that era" and how they continue to foster pleasurable disjunctures of sound and image, I move to a discussion of the postliberalization period. Singing on television in the 1990s was an important avenue through which perceptions of the body—women's bodies, in particular—were recalibrated. Homing in on the rapidly shifting media landscape of this time helps explain the emergence of Ila Arun and her "ethnic" voice, which I argue both undermined and temporarily extended Mangeshkar's vocal monopoly. In the final two sections of this chapter, I discuss how changes set in motion in the postliberalization years enabled the sound of women's bodies in cinema to catch up (so to speak) with the shifts in the visual realm. Millennial soundwork is marked not by an aural lag, but by the heightened visibility of musicking bodies. Seeing women sing in a variety of contexts, genres, and platforms forces a revision not just of Hindi cinema's audiovisual contract, but of the demarcations of sound and image on which constructs such as "voice" and "body" rest.

## Conjoining Sound and Image

In framing the sound-image relationship in cinema as a "contract," Chion reminds us that it is "the opposite of a natural relationship arising from some sort of preexisting harmony among the perceptions."[12] The aural and the visual tracks work together, each influencing our perception of the other. This only happens because we (the audience) treat the two tracks as allied entities, as composing a single, if not always coherent, entity. While we may notice moments when sound and image seem mismatched, those moments only register as disjointed because of the expectations imposed by the contract, which has our tacit approval.[13] Such moments point to our complicity in the existing audiovisual contract even as they hold out the promise—and the *thrill*—of a new configuration of sound and image.

The audiovisual contract bridges temporal and spatial divides in the production process. This bridging requires a well-timed technological apparatus. The audience can only uphold its part of the contract when presented with aural and visual material simultaneously: "*Synchresis* (a word [Chion] forged by combining *synchronism* and *synthesis*) is the spontaneous and irresistible weld produced between a particular auditory phenomenon and visual phenomenon when they occur at the same time. The join results independently of any rational logic. . . . *Synchresis* is what makes dubbing, postsynchronization, and sound-effects mixing possible."[14] Chion's neologism "synchresis" encapsulates both the technology that synchronizes the two tracks and the psychological phenomenon that is a response to the synchronized sound and image. The importance of temporality in tying the aural and the visual is encoded in the very name of the system of film-song production operative in India: playback. Prerecorded songs are "played back" on set during the shooting of the song-dance sequence so that actors and dancers can time their movements to the song. The process thus involves both temporal and spatial separation (the prerecording of the music in a recording studio) and the partial erasure of that separation via lip-synching on set while the song-dance sequence is being filmed. Actors' precise mouthing of the lyrics heightens the impression that the voice we hear comes from the body moving its lips and limbs on screen.[15]

While Chion does not go this far himself, I would venture that the audiovisual contract was a function of the technology and the processes used to produce films from the start. In the "double system" that quickly became the norm in the talkie era, sound and image were recorded simultaneously, but on different strips of film (or on a disc). The two tracks were synchronized at a later stage in the production process or during exhibition. This technological separation of sound and image in the initial stages of production was not unlike the separation of the two "tracks" in the silent era: images shimmered on the screen while live narrators and musicians provided aural accompaniment from the side of the stage or in orchestra pits. The imperative that audiences mentally fuse sound and image has thus shaped the cinematic experience since the earliest days of the medium, not just in South Asia, but around the world. In an important sense, *all* sound in cinema is separated from its source. Technological mediation separates cinematic sound from its source, space, and moment of production. The beauty of the audiovisual contract is that it enacts a *disciplined forgetting* of this fact.

This "forgetting" entails a bevy of expectations arising from technological affordances, industry practices, and sociocultural conventions that have trained film audiences over decades to listen and watch in particular ways. In other words, playback is not simply a function of audiences' Pavlovian response to tight lip-synching. The perceptual "welding" may not be rational, but there is indeed a *logic* to it—a logic that is as historically and culturally specific as it is universal. It is because Indian audiences agreed to a *different* audiovisual contract than, say, Hollywood viewers have, that we took as both "natural" and desirable the pairing of a single voice with thousands of women's bodies on screen. While Chion pays little heed to the ways in which social, historical, and technological conventions shape the audiovisual contract, I argue that attending to such matters elucidates both the specificity and the complexity of the sound-image relationship as it operates in different cinemas.[16]

The disparate ways in which sound and image are paired in different cinematic traditions are apparent even at the level of terminology. Chion distinguishes between "dubbing" and "playback" based on whether the actor's movement or the unseen actor or singer's dubbed voice is recorded first.[17] I do not find such a distinction useful, and instead follow other scholars of the musical in using the term "playback" interchangeably with "song dubbing." My reluctance to draw a sharp distinction resides in the fact that in India, the term "dubbing artists" is used to refer to two sets of sound workers. The first group includes voice actors who dub dialogues. When an actor's linguistic skills are deemed inadequate or when shooting schedules demand it, a dubbing artist may be called in to serve as a voice double for the star. Alternatively (but also in that first group), dubbing professionals may render dialogues for films being released in languages other than the one in which they were initially shot.[18] The second group includes singers whose voices stand in for playback stars. A song may be picturized using that anonymous singer's recording; later in the editing process, this temporary version is generally replaced by the star singer's recording. Sometimes the dubbing artist's rendition is used in the final cut of the film, giving the aspiring singer a chance at stardom. In the past, dubbing artists spent inordinate amounts of time learning to match their own timbre, style, and technique to that of the star singer for whom they temporarily stood in.[19] In one sense, the practice of dubbing for a playback star has faded away, now that the Bombay film industry makes room for more vocal styles and timbres, and as routes into the playback industry have multiplied. In another sense, the practice persists in new form. As Aditi Singh Sharma notes in "Female Singers' Adda," it is quite common today to ask multiple singers to record "demo" versions of a film song. Thus, Indian playback artists often sing without knowing whether their voice will be used in the final cut of the film. Thinking through these and other intricacies of dubbing in Bombay cinema does more than demonstrate the specificity of this Indian case—it helps sharpen Chion's extraordinarily useful, if overly universal, construct.

In the next section, I delineate the contractual "clauses" that operate in the Indian context. My six clauses build on the key elements Chion discusses: audience participation, synchresis, and the role of technology in creating conjunctions and disjunctures. Tracking the ways in which these clauses have morphed over time—particularly the "somatic clause," which deals with women's bodies—demonstrates that the study of soundwork has important implications for our understanding of women in cinema.

## Playback Singing and the "Old" Audiovisual Contract

As in other parts of the world, the system of prerecording songs was instituted in India in response to various technological and logistical problems: loud cameras, fragile, nondirectional microphones, the fact that musicians had to be hidden within the set, and so on.[20] Although playback was introduced in 1935, it would take over a decade for the separation of acting and singing talent to become the norm in India.[21] From 1931, when the first talkies were released, to the late 1940s, when playback artists began gaining recognition, the illusion of the actor singing in his or her own voice was preserved, for either actors' own voices or those of uncredited "ghost" singers were used in film songs.[22] In the years leading up to, and immediately following, independence in 1947, a number of social and industrial changes allowed a handful of singers, especially Lata Mangeshkar, to dominate playback singing in Bombay cinema. Mangeshkar's talents and the exigencies of the historical moment helped solidify not just the institution of playback singing but also the audiovisual contract on which it rested.

The precise terms of this widely understood contract have changed over the years, as the Hindi film industry embraced new talent, new media forms and formats, and new markets.[23] But what is remarkable about the "old" audiovisual contract is its longevity: it operated from the 1940s well into the 1990s. The last decade of the twentieth century was a transitional period, when certain assumptions about women's bodies and about the relationship between sound and image were shifting, while others were proving more stubborn to change.[24] Women's musicking bodies would eventually come to be construed in altogether new ways, and now, twenty years on, soundwork in Bombay cinema is markedly different than it was in the Mangeshkar years. Even so, I describe all but one of the clauses of the audiovisual contract using the present tense. This is because most of the clauses still matter. The notable exception—the clause that distinguishes millennial soundwork in Bombay cinema—is what I call the "somatic clause." By only shifting tense in my discussion of this final clause of the audiovisual contract, I bring to the fore the persistent logic underlying playback singing.

## Clause 1: Song/Speech Disjuncture

Bombay cinema's audiovisual contract primes audiences to expect that a character will sound very different when she sings than when she speaks. Specifically, she will have a different voice in the song sequence than she does in other, nonmusical sequences. This foundational clause represents a sharp divergence from the many music-drama traditions to which Indian cinema is indebted, where there tends to be a lack of distinction between sung and spoken segments. The notion that a character may be a *multivoiced* figure—a composite entity drawing on the vocal talents of an actor, dubbing artist(s), and playback singer(s)—is also a departure from norms instituted by Hollywood's audiovisual contract. Indeed, Chion misses this distinction between song and speech in his account of the audiovisual contract because he takes for granted the hegemonic form of cinema in the West today, one that cares little for lip-synched musical sequences. Unlike the US context, where the mere revelation that an actor has not sung "her own" songs may be cause for consternation, Hindi film audiences expect a character's singing and speaking voice to be "mismatched." Here, I am riffing on Jennifer Fleeger's notion of "mismatched women," singers whose voices are thought to be at odds with the way they look.[25] In citing this concept in relation to a wholly aural disjuncture (rather than an aural/visual disjuncture, as I do in clause 2), I draw attention to the fact that audiences often have different expectations for verbal and musical performances.[26] The idea that the sound of speech should be aligned with that of song, or that a single actor should do all the speaking and singing their role demands, is not as self-evident a construct as it might seem to those only familiar with Euro-American cinema. In the 1940s, Bombay filmmakers tried to match the singer's voice to the voice and personality of the actor (whose voice was presumably used in the spoken segments). This practice of voice-casting quickly faded as playback voices came to be lauded for their own qualities, rather than for their ability to be a voice double of the actor.[27] The phenomenal stardom of Lata Mangeshkar over the next several decades meant that the *fact* of the mismatch—and the plainness of a character's speaking voice in relation to her singing voice—amplified the beauty and power of the latter. These and other disjunctures secured the protagonist's innate goodness (a point I elaborate in my discussion of the "somatic clause" later in this section) and Lata Mangeshkar's position as facile princeps of the playback world.

## Clause 2: Sound/Image Disjuncture

Bombay film audiences know and expect a disjuncture of sound and image in song sequences. Given the common practice of dubbing dialogues, Indian audiences are quite aware that a character's speaking voice may not be that of the actor on screen; it may belong to a dubbing artist.[28] Audiences also know that regardless of whether dialogues have been dubbed by someone other than the actor, song sequences are *defined* by such a disjuncture. A very specific pairing of bodies is required to mend this sound/image split, to turn the disjuncture into a spectacular conjunction of star bodies. Otherwise put, this audiovisual contract requires us to acknowledge that the body that seduces us in the song sequence is a composite star text: the voice belongs to one star and the image to another.

In his discussion of the politics of dubbing in *Carmen Jones* (dir. Otto Preminger, 1954), where white opera singers sang for some Black actors, Jeff Smith observes that the film "employs dubbing to create a kind of phantasmic body that registers visually as black but sounds 'white' in terms of the material qualities of its 'voice.'"[29] For close to five decades, Lata Mangeshkar's voice performed a similar function to that of the white singers in the "all-black" musical. The sound of her voice conveyed qualities that were not necessarily readable in the images of the heroines. Film after film paired Mangeshkar's pristine voice with the images of glamorous actors who lip-synched to her songs, from Nargis in *Mother India* (dir. Mehboob Khan, 1957) to Meena Kumari in *Pakeezah* (*The Pure One*, dir. Kamal Amrohi, 1972) to Hema Malini in *Dream Girl* (dir. Pramod Chakravorty, 1977). As the titles of these classic films suggest, the conjunction of a beautiful voice and a beautiful image created impossibly idealized representations of women. Even if a character was derided as a "fallen woman" within the diegesis, as was the case with the courtesan Sahibjaan in *Pakeezah*, the fact that she sang in Mangeshkar's voice confirmed her impeccable moral stature. The aural identity projected through Mangeshkar's voice augmented the identities on screen by "cleansing" them of potentially questionable or nonnormative qualities, reassuring audiences of the fundamental goodness of the characters.[30]

But what sets apart the Indian case from Hollywood is the institutionalization of playback singing, and the place of privilege accorded to Mangesh-kar within that institution. By 1955, playback singing became the norm for *all* commercial films and was not just used for a specific genre or subset of films. This meant that audiences were taught to accept that there were *at least two* sources for the vocal sound in song sequences: the character mouthing the lyrics in the film's diegesis and the "invisible" playback singer, whose voice was instantly recognizable. For Neepa Majumdar, this is one of many ways in which "there is a stretching of the relationship of sound and image in Indian cinema."[31] Or, put differently, Indian cinema's audiovisual contract allows sound and image to be disarticulated and rearticulated in multiple ways.

## Clause 3: Desirable Disjunctures

Playback stardom requires that audiences recognize and relish these varied aural and visual discordances. They are hardly seen as "disjunctures," in that they are not considered negative or problematic. These are recognizable and *desirable* disjunctures. Whereas playback singing (and dubbing more gen-erally) demands synchresis and lip-synching—technologies that attempt to smooth over any telltale signs of the disconnect between sound and image—playback *stardom* requires that we acknowledge those very technologies. In other words, the cinematic institution of playback simultaneously causes, requires, and erases various disjunctures, even as it fosters a meta-level under-standing of these processes.[32] As I explain later in this chapter, the increased visibility of singers on televisual and digital platforms in recent years is crucial in keeping alive Hindi film audience's investments in playback. In previous decades, it was not visibility so much as voice recognizability—the audience's ability to identify the singer in a song sequence and not confuse her voice with that of the screen actor or other singers—that cultivated the desire in/ for the disjunctures I describe. Voice recognizability leads audiences not just to link the singing voice and the synchronous image of the dancing body, but to *relish* the split between the two. It is these disjunctures—between speech and song, and between sound and image—and their simultaneous avowal and disavowal, that make playback stardom possible. Thus, far from just being beguiled by Mangeshkar's voice or by various actresses' charms in song-dance sequences (as many fans and critics would have it), Indian film audiences are in fact participating in a complex audiovisual contract, one that demands that we keep at bay certain kinds of knowledge about cinematic technology while embracing others.[33]

## Clause 4: Paratexts and Public Discourse

The conjoining of sound and image in the audiovisual contract implies that these elements work together to render a cinematic sequence meaningful. But there is a further complication that Chion misses: the dynamics of aural stardom are so powerful that the meanings attached to a voice depend not just on the image to which it is attached, but also on ostensibly nonfilmic information about both performers (singer and actor). Such information circulates in print and digital media, on television and radio, and in the material culture surrounding media industries—everything from posters of films (and film stars) to cassette and CD covers. Paratexts, and public discourse more generally, shape how audiences put together sound and image into a meaningful relationship. The gendered and sexualized discourse surrounding star singers and actors complicates audiences' assessment of the morality of these performers and the characters they play.[34]

In underscoring the importance of paratexts, I am building on what Gerard Genette demonstrated for literature and what Jonathan Gray established in the case of cinema and television.[35] Whether in India or elsewhere, paratexts play a "constitutive role in creating textuality."[36] They do not just generate hype. They matter, more crucially, at the level of the audiovisual contract. Just as soundwork cannot simply be construed as "added value" for a film, paratexts are not mere vehicles for "extra" information.[37] I make my case below through an analysis of Ila Arun, a pop and folk singer who shot to fame in the 1990s. Arun perfectly illustrates how a singer's public persona—the way she looks, the way she presents herself, her other performances (on- and offscreen), any gossip that circulates about her—is at least as important as that of the actor and the vocal performance itself.

What is key, moreover, is not just that fan discourse shapes how we interpret an audiovisual text, but that only *certain* kinds of information are mobilized in the process. In Lata Mangeshkar's case, the fact that she never married gets folded into the rhetoric about her saintliness, rather than, say, casting her as queer or as a "public" woman.[38] Similarly, Ila Arun's stage career and her ethnicity and class status had to be eclipsed in order for her to emerge as an "authentic" folk voice. Listening to the audiovisual contract with a feminist ear unearths such contradictions. It demonstrates that Bombay cinema's audiovisual contract requires a willful ignorance on the part of audiences about certain aspects of their beloved stars' lives, even as it asks them to keep in play other kinds of knowledge and gossip. Desire requires, fosters, such disjunctures.

## Clause 5: Engendering Cinema and Nation

Hindi cinema's audiovisual contract suggests that we read cinematic representations of women in relation to the discourse of nation. In historian Partha Chatterjee's classic formulation, certain Indian women were aligned with spirituality, tradition, and the "inner domain" of culture during the anticolonial struggle.[39] While this argument has been amply critiqued and qualified over the years, the broad contours of Chatterjee's intervention remain instructive in thinking about the problem cinema once posed for the national imaginary. In placing even the most modest and normative of women in the "outer," public realm, cinema threatened to destabilize the symbolic status accorded to the figure of woman. For Sanjay Srivastava, the success of Mangeshkar's "pure" and "girlish" voice lay in the fact that it contained the aural and visual presence of women in cinema.[40] The gendered anxieties registered in Bombay cinema's notion of "good-girl" and "bad-girl" voices make all the more sense when we remember that it was in the early years of the nation that Mangeshkar consolidated her status as the hegemonic voice of Indian femininity. I demonstrate in this chapter that this clause articulating gender, cinema, and nation together retained its power for a long time. Sociocultural ideas about nation and femininity were critical to the reception of not just Mangeshkar's voice but others as well, including those that emerged in the 1990s.

## Clause 6: Somatic Clause

The history of Mangeshkar's ascendancy is, in part, a history of how Bombay cinema alleviated the "threat" of women's bodies in public. But what exactly made the body so dangerous? What assumptions constituted the aural and visual presence of women as a threat? The answers lie in the "somatic clause," my term for two interrelated ideas about the body that were integral to the audiovisual contract well into the 1990s. First, this clause of the "old" audiovisual contract regarded the body—whether audible or visible—as the home of vice. To grasp this association one has to simply recall the many "cabaret" songs of the 1960s and 1970s in which Helen, ever typecast as a Westernized woman and vamp, danced to Asha Bhosle's breathy and sensuous voice.[41]

This notion of the body-as-vice tapped into a more global tendency to ignore the materiality of the singing body in cinema. Discussing song dubbing in Hollywood musicals of the 1930s and 1940s, Marsha Siefert observes that "the technological separation of the song from its singer meant that the image of singing did not have to reflect the physicality of its bodily production."[42] Siefert links this erasure to Rick Altman's argument that technological and technical developments in 1930s cinema strove "to reduce all traces of the sound work from the soundtrack," reflecting a broader bourgeois tendency to efface all signs of labor.[43] Innovations like the use of soundstages, camera blimps, and directional microphones, as well as "inaudible" sound-editing practices (such as cutting to sound and raising dialogue levels while reducing "background" sounds), were integral to the development of classical Hollywood style. Thus, the erasure of bodily labor was incorporated into the very form of sound cinema in the United States.

These insights about the intersection of gender and class in cinematic soundwork apply to the Indian context as well. Playback as a system was designed to hide the fact that voices emerge from bodies and that singing entails labor. Add to this the story that historians of music and dance in South Asia tell of zealous reform movements that sought to defend and "purify" Indian society by erasing the physicality of the body and its caste connotations from the ambit of national culture in the early to mid-twentieth century.[44] The immense cultural investment in Mangeshkar's "disembodied" voice comes as no surprise given this complex of technological, social, and ideological forces devaluing women's bodies.

Second, at the heart of the somatic clause was the concept that voice—the singing voice, in particular—expresses something deeper and truer than what is visible on the surface of the body.[45] This understanding of voice as essence hooked into a foundational conceit of Western modernity, "the idea of voice as guarantor of truth and self-presence, from which springs the familiar idea that the voice expresses self and identity and that agency consists in having a voice."[46] I take up the challenge of dismantling this investment in the rational, linguistic "content" of speech over its sonic, embodied aspects in chapter 3. I demonstrate there that such a binary conception of form and content (of materiality and meaning) is as unhelpful in understanding the speaking voice in cinema as it is in unpacking how the singing voice signifies—my task here. A profoundly modern cultural institution, Indian cinema shares some commonalities with Euro-American conceptions of voice and subjectivity; however, ideas about voice that gained currency on the subcontinent were not merely derivative of the West.[47] The voice-equals-essence construction I'm elaborating here does not refer to an individual's interiority, agency, or selfhood. It is, instead, the voicing of a particular *subject position*. Per Hindi cinema's "old" audiovisual contract, the material sound of a woman's singing voice was an audible sign of the archetype the character embodied on screen.

What I find striking is that the somatic clause reflected a prioritization of the aural and the musical over the visual.[48] Indeed, the somatic clause existed in tension with the broader notion of the audiovisual contract in that this clause implied that sound mattered *more* than image. Consider how the pristine sound of Mangeshkar's voice "cleansed" the accompanying images.[49] If there was anything risqué about the biographies or performances of the actors in the songs, it did not stick to the star singer. What this tells us is not just that Mangeshkar was lionized but that voice *itself* was considered trustworthy. Voice was the repository of the true self, where one's cultural and moral essence could be located. So if a character's singing voice sounded bodily, she was considered immoral and not "Indian" enough. If her singing voice sounded saintly and disembodied, those positive qualities of voice attached to her.[50]

As time passed, ideas about the body and voice changed, as did the sound-image relationship in Hindi cinema. Television in the postliberalization period was a crucial site in which these changes took form. In what follows, I lay out how the overlaps and connections among various media industries—that is, the interaural and interocular fields in which films operate—led to a reimagining of gendered norms surrounding vocality and visuality.

## Singing on Television

The sound of women changed in Bombay cinema from the beginning of the 1990s. It was in the early years of this decade that the Indian government, in a bid to "open" the nation to the world, instituted a series of neoliberal reforms. In a striking departure from the state-led model of development that had driven the economy since Indian independence, the reforms ushered in a consumer economy flush with private and foreign capital. These new "liberalization" policies had a profound impact on the cultural and media landscape of the nation. Where once there had been a single state-run broadcaster, Doordarshan, there appeared in 1991–92 a plethora of cable and satellite television channels. Much of the programming on these new channels was film-based. Besides broadcasting films, these new channels featured countdown shows, quiz shows, and talent competitions revolving around film songs, all of which were part of the "re-sounding" of public culture in this period and helped Bombay cinema recover from the doldrums of the 1980s.[51]

That music was the key to audiences' hearts and pockets was not a new lesson for the industry. The Hindi film-song medley shows *Chhayageet* and *Chitrahaar*, and similar shows featuring "regional" film music, were among the most popular shows on Doordarshan. These shows built on the success of *Binaca Geetmala*, a countdown program hosted by Ameen Sayani on Radio Ceylon (and later All India Radio) for four decades. And yet, film music consumption had rapidly declined over the course of the 1980s, going from 90 percent to 40 percent of recorded music sales, due to the "cassette culture" that flourished in this period.[52] The rapid proliferation of cassette technology restructured the commercial music industry, such that nonfilm musical genres began to undermine film music's de facto status as popular music. Gregory D. Booth's pathbreaking ethnography of Bombay film musicians evidences that these years of apparent decline for cinema were in fact a crucial period of transition, when the industry was laying the groundwork for the modes of film- and music-making that would come to characterize "New Bollywood."[53] The old system of recording a film song in one take (with singers performing alongside a large orchestra) was being replaced by more segmented practices of recording and editing. Recording studios outfitted with newly available programmable synthesizers and large multitrack recording consoles facilitated a gradual shift from monaural to stereo sound.[54] While the 1980s are remembered as a relatively insipid period for Hindi film music, the late 1980s and early 1990s gave us several hit Hindi soundtracks, including *Tezaab* (*Acid*, dir. N. Chandra, 1988), *Qayamat Se Qayamat Tak* (*From Disaster to Catastrophe*, dir. Mansoor Khan, 1988), *Maine Pyaar Kiya* (*I Have Loved*, dir. Sooraj Barjatya, 1989), *Dil* (*Heart*, dir. Indra Kumar, 1990), *Aashiqui* (*Romance*, dir. Mahesh Bhatt, 1990), *Saajan* (*Beloved*, dir. Lawrence D'Souza, 1991), and *Roja* (dir. Mani Ratnam, 1992). The audible return of melodious music in these romantic dramas and the shifting technological and production terrain make this a crucial period in the history of Hindi film music and soundwork more generally.[55]

To this narrative of musical and technological transformation I want to add an appreciation of television's role in shifting audience expectations of Hindi cinema. Over the course of the 1990s, distinctions between film and nonfilm music—whether in terms of artists, genres, performance styles, formats, production practices, or distribution and consumption circuits—

gradually disappeared. As a singular venue for showcasing both film *and* nonfilm music, television in the 1990s was instrumental in transforming how audiences perceived singing and dancing bodies, and what they expected to hear and see on screen. In short, television transformed Bombay cinema's "old" audiovisual contract.[56]

How did this come to be? For one, the innovative formats of 1990s television shows and their anchors' novel styles and gimmicks extended the reach and popularity of the Hindi film song like never before. For example, Zee TV, the first predominantly Hindi television channel, managed to turn the widely played film-song game *antakshari* into a televised quiz show.[57] Annu Kapoor, a prominent film and theater personality with deep musical knowledge, hosted *Antakshari—the Great Challenge* (later renamed *Close-Up Antakshari*) for over a decade. Zee also ran a music countdown show called *Philips Top 10* which interspersed film songs with comic skits by actors Pankaj Kapoor and Satish Kaushik. *Superhit Muqabala* on Doordarshan, was hosted by the zany DJ and rapper Baba Sehgal. There was also comedian Javed Jaffrey's *Videocon Flashback* on Channel [V], which arguably did more than any other show to (re)introduce the youth to older Hindi film songs.

Apart from drawing middle-class and young audiences back to Bombay cinema, television in the 1990s provided a pathway for younger singers to enter the industry. *Meri Awaaz Suno* on Doordarshan and *Sa Re Ga Ma* (later called *Sa Re Ga Ma Pa*) on Zee were the earliest music reality shows on Indian television.[58] Often, the hosts and judges of these televised competitions were film and music heavyweights. For example, *Sa Re Ga Ma* was hosted by singer Sonu Nigam and *Meri Awaaz Suno* by Annu Kapoor (who would go on to host *Antakshari*). *Meri Awaaz Suno* was a collaboration of Doordarshan, Lata Mangeshkar, and the film producer Yash Chopra; judges included famous singers from the film and classical realm including Mangeshkar herself, Manna Dey, Bhupen Hazarika, and Pandit Jasraj. The show was thus a platform for budding artists to win the approval of the old gatekeepers and catch the attention of music directors and talent scouts. Singers like Sunidhi Chauhan and Shreya Ghoshal won these competitions in part because they were able to imitate Mangeshkar. While these artists would go on to experiment with different styles and genres, their entry into the world of playback singing rested on their ability to match the existing aural ideal, and on the interaural connections between media industries. Just as gramophone and radio had served previous generations of film singers, television generated a fan following for these young singers that opened doors for them both inside and outside film circles. By exposing Indian audiences to new voices, it also taught us to listen differently than we had in the past.

## Indipop Music Videos

Even as audiences were (re-)embracing Hindi film songs, the sound and look of this music was itself changing. Television in the 1990s was a platform for not just film songs but also Indipop, regional, and classical musics, and fusions of all of these genres. It thus extended the nonfilm music industry's gains from the cassette revolution of the previous decade.[59] As I elaborate further in chapter 2, the influence of these different musics on Hindi film soundwork was profound. Hindi film songs became more "heterogeneous" as they borrowed from the plethora of musical and visual styles that were being popularized by television.[60] The industry also drew nonfilm artists into its orbit. For example, it was television that made legible Ila Arun and her "ethnic" Rajasthani repertoire. Many Indipop artists who got their break in those heady years of postliberalization—music directors Shankar-Ehsaan-Loy, for instance—would also go on to become Bollywood fixtures. One might frame this as a boom-and-bust story, a tale of how the behemoth that is the Bombay film industry neutralized the threat that pop music posed to its hegemony. But to do so would be to ignore the fact that both Hindi film soundwork and the audiovisual contract that sustained it for decades underwent radical metamorphosis. The television and music business wrought changes not just in the "old Bollywood sound," as Gregory D. Booth argues, but, even more fundamentally, in the relationship between sound and image in cinema.[61]

The emergence of music videos is an important part of this story. In his 1999 epilogue to *The Voice in Cinema*, Michel Chion identifies the music video as a revolutionary form:

> From the extreme close-up of lips, implacably accompanying the song in perfect synch, to the movement of objects and other visual forms synched to the articulation of a text (as in certain Peter Gabriel videos), not to mention all the possible relationships between the image of a mouth or some other movement articulated in the image, and a sung text on the soundtrack, the music video has been a laboratory, a place to explore in truly interesting ways the relations between voice and image. The cinema has benefitted from it.[62]

Chion's breathless praise for the music video is well warranted. There is no question that the representational strategies of this form have infused new life into cinema. That said, many of the innovations Chion describes were underway in Indian film songs well before the arrival of music videos. Put differently, if we think about the audiovisual contract beyond the confines of Euro-American cinema, we see that Indian filmmakers have been playing with, and multiplying, the relationships between sound and image ever since the institution of playback in cinema. The true intervention of music videos in the postliberalization period—what they did that so profoundly rehauled the audiovisual contract—was to reimagine the figure of the singer, especially the woman singer.

Music television afforded singers a kind and level of visibility that were entirely new. The music industry's strategy of promoting albums through slick, often extravagant music videos meant that expectations for singers began to change. Their bodies could no longer be invisible; their voices could not be construed as "disembodied" entities.[63] For Peter Kvetko, "reintegrating this 'disembodied voice' is . . . at the core of how Indipop performers and marketers have understood their work from the 1990s to the present."[64] The visual presence of the singer is critical to this formulation. Indian cinema's much-loved disjuncture between singing and acting (clauses 2 and 3) was highlighted and complicated as more and more singers appeared as themselves—as *singers*—in music videos. To be clear: star playback singers did perform in live shows throughout the 1970s and 1980s; however, since those shows were not broadcast, the vast majority of audiences rarely *saw* those artists in the act of singing. Televised classical, light-classical, and pop music performances were a staple on state television in the 1980s. But the difference between those Doordarshan shows and music videos on satellite television of the 1990s was stark. The latter format clearly presented singers as doing more than voicing lyrics.

Singing was rendered a new kind of performative venture in music videos. Singers' gestures, dance moves, and role in the narrative mattered in ways that they hadn't in cinema, previous televised formats, or live shows. Artists were not stiff or constrained in their movements, as Lata Mangeshkar famously was in her stage appearances. As my close readings of the "Afreen Afreen" and "Q Funk" videos in chapter 2 illustrate, there was an emphasis in the postliberalization period on rhythm, sexuality, and the body. Many a music video included famous models and budding actors in cameo roles alongside the singer. Many showed young people dancing in clubs or at concerts, often as part of the singer's adoring posse. Indeed, it became increasingly clear that singers needed more than just vocal talent to find success.

At the forefront of the Indipop movement were women like Alisha Chinai, Suchitra, Sharon Prabhakar, Suneeta Rao, and Shweta Shetty. Cultural expectations about vocal and visible performances of femininity were clearly in flux at the time, and these women artists benefited from—and sped along—the changes. Even as the Mangeshkar ideal persisted in Hindi cinema, "vocal timbre and delivery among Indipop's 'divas' . . . [could] be bluesy and shouting (as in Shubha Mudgal's hit 'Ab ke Saawan'), forcefully-spoken (as in Alisha's verses in 'Made in India') or gospel-inspired and soulful (the singer, Mehnaz, is perhaps the best example)."[65] This wide range of voices on music television signaled a shift in normative conceptions of gender and sexuality. The audible diversity was accompanied by dramatic changes in visual representations. In addition to sexualized and Westernized (but not debased) images of women in music videos, one saw more women clothed in male garb. In "Johnny Joker" (1993), Shweta Shetty performs in a suit. Likewise, in all her pop videos, Falguni Pathak is dressed in butch clothing.[66] So if, as Shanti Kumar argues, 1990s television made the national community "un-imaginable"—that is, beyond the limits of what was deemed visible and possible in the past—this was especially the case for Indian womanhood on music television.[67]

A case in point is Alisha Chinai's 1995 album *Made in India*. Popular with the young and old alike, it was the first massive hit by an Indipop singer and became—and for years, remained—the highest grossing pop album.[68] The titular music video features the singer in the role of a discerning Madonna-esque diva looking for a lover "made in India." The scenario of an Indian woman choosing her own partner without the presence or influence of family, the emphasis on a woman's sexual desire, Chinai's fluid transitions between Hindi and English in the lyrics, and her versatile vocal style ("deep and strong" chanting in some places, "open" and "smooth" singing in others)—all this and more makes "Made in India" an excellent example of the way Indipop's visual and aural experiments cast women as confident, desirous, cosmopolitan figures.[69]

## R. D. Burman and the Remix Boom

The shift in cinematic, musical, and cultural norms in the 1990s was also fueled by the remix boom, which repackaged older Hindi film songs—and

music director R. D. Burman's work, in particular—for a new generation of
fans.[70] Everyone in the remix business—from Bally Sagoo, who first popularized the genre among urban middle-class audiences with *Bollywood Flashback* (1994), to Indipop groups like Bombay Vikings, Colonial Cousins, and
Instant Karma—shored up their good intentions and musical expertise by
presenting themselves as R. D. Burman fans.[71] Speaking of *Rahul and I* (1996),
her tribute album to R. D. Burman (her late husband), Asha Bhosle notes
that the idea for the project started with him: "he thought that we ourselves
should do trendier versions of these songs so that for today's generation, these
songs remain associated with us."[72] I regard the remix boom as extending R.
D. Burman's posthumous comeback.

R. D. Burman's oeuvre was fundamentally rhythmic, and thus eminently
catchy and danceable. Explaining what distinguished the famed music director from his predecessors and contemporaries, Gregory D. Booth notes:
"[He] more clearly conceptualized and produced [songs] as both parts of a
film soundtrack and as pop songs. . . . Burman and his collaborators pur-
sued a range of innovations in sound recording both for film and record that
not only made the rhythmic details of this music sharper but also made it
possible for those rhythmic details to be heard clearly on recordings."[73] So
pronounced were his rhythmic innovations that they enabled more physical
choreography.[74] In many of his song-dance sequences, dancers' movements
closely mirrored the complex, variable rhythmic patterns in the music. R. D.
Burman's compositions also incorporated more corporeal sounds than ever
(Ah! HA! Ooo-ooo!). This was not just the case when *he* sang, but also for
the parts assigned to his favored singers, Kishore Kumar and Asha Bhosle.[75]
Kumar's yodeling skills and other vocal antics are as legendary as Bhosle's
breathy vampish voice in her cabaret songs.[76] For Biswarup Sen, R. D. Burman's collaborations with Kumar were emblematic of a "'second revolution'
in Hindi film song" (the first, he argues, happened in the 1930s). Film songs
in the Kishore-RD era "proposed radically new versions of pleasure, sexuality, and desire: they celebrated the *body* by invoking new styles of movement, liberated the voice from the constraints of formal singing, and brought
into play an accelerated notion of being."[77] Sen does not elaborate how Hindi
film songs of this period "liberated" the singing voice, but it is clear from his
analysis (as well as Booth's work) that R. D. Burman compositions encour-
aged singers, actors, and audiences to move their bodies—not just their vocal
chords—in new ways.

The return of R. D. Burman via the remix boom entails, among other things, the return of *bodily* elements in vocal performance. Music videos of 1990s remixes foregrounded the body and sexuality, leaving them open to the charge of vulgarity.[78] You'll remember that the somatic clause of the "old" audiovisual contract equated the body with all things bad and dangerous. This is precisely what made R. D. Burman's work so edgy and popular, both in the 1970s and when it was picked up again in the 1990s.[79] I elaborate on the audible presence of the body in later sections of this chapter. For now, suffice it to say that R. D. Burman's musical experimentation elicited new ways of moving, singing, and listening to Hindi film songs. This made his songs especially valuable for artists seeking to shake up the music scene in the 1990s and early 2000s.

In sum, I am arguing that music programming on postliberalization television did not just popularize new artists and musical styles; it introduced audiences to new modes of bodily performance. The dramatic growth in the beauty, fashion, and fitness industries around this time also meant that Indian consumers encountered bodies—women's bodies in particular—in new and different ways. These various developments *outside* the putative boundaries of cinema eventually transformed notions of listening and voicing in the Bombay film industry.

Shikha Jhingan places the moment of rupture in Hindi cinema's sonic ideal in the 1980s, when Pakistani singers Nazia Hassan, Noor Jehan, Salma Agha, and Reshma traveled to India (both physically and via "pirate" media circuits), triggering affective and aural memories of a different time and space, and engendering more flexible, expansive notions of belonging.[80] Jhingan foregrounds the "new modes of listenership" fostered by the rise of both cassette technology and *mehfils* (salon performance), a point I explore in chapter 2 in relation to qawwalis. The *mehfils* she discusses were small, private concerts organized by nonstate institutions and music lovers who took advantage of a calm in cross-border relations to invite Pakistani singers— many of them women—to perform in India. These much publicized but intimate performances "brought to life the relationship that a singer-actor had to her own voice, a live corporeal performance."[81] I cannot agree more with Jhingan's assessment of the shift such performances effected in audiences' understanding of the singer's relationship to her voice. My own emphasis, however, is on the 1990s, for it is then that the relationship between the sound and image of women's bodies was being reconfigured *on screen*—first on television and then on film. Television, in effect, extended the work begun in the era of cassette tapes and live *mehfils*.

Whether one dates the changes to the early 1980s or the 1990s, what is remarkable is how gradual the process of displacing the "nightingale of India" from her high perch was. Even after Mangeshkar stepped out of the limelight, her voice continued to be regarded as the ideal for women in Bombay cinema.[82] The waning of the Mangeshkar monopoly throws into sharp relief the rapid and dramatic shifts in the realms of television and nonfilm musics. Television pushed the Hindi film industry to make room for other singing voices, but those voices that sounded overtly sexual or irreverent were rarely assigned to the heroine. The "good girls" of Hindi cinema began to dress and dance in more provocative ways, but they still sounded pristine. In other words, the somatic clause's association of the body with vice persisted in the aural realm, even as visual representations of women began to shift. The next section of this chapter illustrates this "aural lag" by following the voice of Ila Arun over the course of the 1990s. Charting how popular but nonnormative, "ethnic" voices such as Arun's were deployed in this decade of flux points up the gendered implications of the audiovisual contract, both in its "old" iteration and in the form it would take in the new millennium.

## The "Ethnic" Voice and the Aural Lag

### Ila Arun's Banjarin Aesthetic

Ila Arun's name is synonymous with Rajasthani folk-inspired tunes.[83] Although Arun comes from a theater background and has acted in several films, her fame rests squarely on her vocal persona. Her songs enjoyed wide circulation via the various satellite and cable channels newly available to Indian audiences in the 1990s, and through well-established circuits of the cassette industry. In many of her albums and music videos, including the hits "Vote for Ghaghra" (Vote for Skirt) and "Bicchuda" (Scorpion), Arun presented herself as a brazen, pleasure-seeking woman. The distinctive coarseness of her voice, as well as her full-throated style, uninhibited vocal presence, and suggestive dance moves, earned her the title "Rani of Raunch" (Queen of Raunch).[84] The sexual and ethnic otherness signaled by this pop journalistic label was heightened by Arun's use of a rustic idiom in her songs. The language of the lyrics gave her voice a raw, earthy feel, a quality that signified not only rural India but also assertive sexuality. Arun's first hit as a playback singer was "Morni Bagama" (Peahen in the Garden) from *Lamhe* (*Moments*, dir. Yash Chopra, 1991), but it was the notoriously popular "Choli Ke Peeche" (What's behind the Blouse) from *Khalnayak* (*Villain*, dir. Subhash Ghai, 1993) that cemented her status as the quintessential "ethnic" voice in Hindi cinema.

The adjective "ethnic," as applied to her voice, stands not for a specific ethnic group so much as an exotic "other" native to North India. In most parts of the country, the mainstream media positions urbane, Hindi-speaking North Indians as quintessential national subjects. People of other caste, class, and ethnic groups are marked, and sometimes mocked, as being different. Ila Arun's sartorial aesthetic, as much as her voice, language, and music, highlights such difference. Her voice was embodied on screen by women dressed in traditional Rajasthani (particularly, *banjarin* or "gypsy") attire—colorful, heavily embroidered *ghaghra-cholis*, oxidized silver jewelry, and intricate bindi patterns on the forehead—singing unabashedly of desire and sex.[85] Ila Arun herself sports this look in all her public appearances, folk-pop music videos, and her breakthrough film song, "Morni Bagama." While this "ethnic" look was all the rage among middle- and upper-class Indian women in the 1990s, the aesthetic it references is that of rural, implicitly lower-caste and poor, women in the interiors of North India. As in other parts of the world, loudness and brashness are also qualities associated with lower-class women in the subcontinent. Ila Arun's voice thus represented a glamorized conflation of ethnic, caste, class, and sexual othering. It stood for all the nonhegemonic and immoral connotations that had been purged from Lata Mangeshkar's voice. These entrenched sonic associations mean that any attempt at what Irina Leimbacher calls "haptic listening"—prioritizing the textural qualities of voice over lexical content—risks rehearsing the hierarchies that cast Ila Arun as the "ethnic" voice in the first place.[86]

The emergence of this "ethnic" voice in the 1990s marked a shift in the aural representation of women in Bombay cinema. Asha Bhosle's "bad-girl" voice and the sexually adventurous styles of Indipop singers discussed in the previous section called up Westernized Indian women. The "ethnic" voice, by contrast, was a bawdy and bodily voice firmly rooted in India. Importantly, even though she was allowed into the world of playback singing, this "other" woman was not granted a starring role—at least not at first. Her voice was coded as *so* different that it required translation, both linguistically and musically.

Consider "Morni Bagama," in which Ila Arun not only provides playback but also makes an appearance as a *banjarin*, a member of a nomadic group native to Rajasthan. The song opens with a panorama of the desert, with a woman, followed by a caravan, gradually coming into view at the center of the shot. Similar iconography suffuses Nusrat Fateh Ali Khan's 1996 song "Afreen Afreen," which I discuss in chapter 2.[87] What is striking about "Morni Bagama" is that although the anonymous *banjarin*'s gestures imply that she is the one singing, the immensity of the landscape and the sounds of the howling wind—like a deep breath at the end of each line—link the singing voice to the land, as much as to her. Having embodied Ila Arun's earthy voice in the figure of the *banjarin* and in the land itself, "Morni Bagama" shifts the setting, melody, and mood of the song. Gathered at night around a campfire, the *banjarin* and her fellow musicians begin performing a popular Rajasthani folk song about love and longing. This is when the film's protagonists, Viren (Anil Kapoor) and Pallavi (Sridevi), encounter them. Seated some distance from their camp, Pallavi gives her city-bred friend Viren an explanation of the Rajasthani lyrics before launching into a Hindi version of the song herself. The camera centers on Pallavi, reducing the folk musicians to distant figures on the horizon. Not surprisingly, the singing voice attached to the heroine is that of Lata Mangeshkar. Now that the "other" woman's voice has been appropriately translated and contained, the song can fuel the romantic fantasy of the hero. The *banjarin* re-enters the song (aurally and visually) periodically, but each time, her lines are translated into Hindi by Pallavi. Musical, linguistic, and visual codes in "Morni Bagama" thus render the *banjarin* an exotic native figure marginal to the film's diegesis.[88]

A few years later, in *Khalnayak* (1993), the voice and figure of the *banjarin* enter the performance space of the Hindi film song on more equal footing and with more sexual overtones (see video 1.1 https://doi.org/10.3998/mpub.11713921.comp.1). In the infamous and well-loved sequence "Choli Ke Peeche" (What's behind the Blouse; "Choli"), the heroine Ganga (Madhuri Dixit) performs a sexualized number for the villains while disguised as a dancer in a *banjarin* troupe. Ganga is granted—and thus protected by—a voice close to Mangeshkar's in pitch and style, that of singer Alka Yagnik.[89] The other lead dancer is Champa (Neena Gupta), and she is assigned Ila Arun's voice (see figure 1.1). While the song lyrics (and, to a lesser extent, the choreography) elicited the ire of self-appointed "guardians" of Indian culture, few public commentators—including those who defended the song for its folk-musical origins—remarked on the work that Ila Arun's voice does. This is surprising because, as Monika Mehta argues, the song's frisson rests in part on the star personas of its four women performers: the actors Neena Gupta and Madhuri Dixit, and the playback singers Ila Arun and Alka Yag-

Figure 1.1. Champa (Neena Gupta, with Ila Arun as her playback voice) dancing as a *banjarin* in "Choli Ke Peeche," *Khalnayak* (dir. Subhash Ghai, 1993).

nik.[90] Moreover, it is Ila Arun's commanding, bodily voice and Neena Gupta's provocative gestures (rendered in close-up) that open the song. As in "Morni Bagama," the "ethnic" woman is not granted a central position in this song-dance sequence; however, she is the first to sing here. It is she who first poses the potentially raunchy question, "Choli ke peeche kya hai?" (What's behind the blouse?).

The bold, playful attitude and sexual connotations audible in the opening line are tempered somewhat as Ganga begins singing. Gradually raising her veil, Ganga voices the sentiments of the ideal Indian woman: "Choli mein dil hain mera, chunri mein dil hain mera / yeh dil mein doongi mere yaar ko" (My heart is in the blouse, my heart is in the veil / I'll give this heart to my love). Except for a few fleeting moments, playback singer Alka Yagnik's vocal performance for Ganga hews close to the "pure" and "smooth" Mangeshkar ideal. The vocal burden of difference and desire thus falls on Ila Arun. While Arun's voice does not require translation in this song as it did in "Morni Bagama," it still needs to be properly contained. It is put in its place as the main character appropriates the musical style, performance aesthetic, and clothing associated with it—all for the noble cause of rescuing the hero. This is not to say that "Choli" loses its sexy attitude once the virginal Ganga delivers her response to Champa. All of the dancers' moves are suggestive, as are the villainous onlookers' leering responses. But the heroine's chaste voice and lyrics push against the bawdy, bodily voice of her friend and the sexualized visual and dance choreography of the entire song.

Fast-forward another five years to *Dil Se* (*From the Heart*, 1998), the last film in director Mani Ratnam's terrorism trilogy. Here, in the film's most famous song, the sartorial and musical aesthetic of Rajasthan and the voice of the "ethnic" woman take center stage. In "Chaiyya Chaiyya" (Shake It), the mysterious woman (Malaika Arora) who sings and dances with the hero Aman (Shah Rukh Khan) atop a train is irrevocably "other." We do not know who she is or where she comes from; her presence in the northeast of India is never explained. But her voice in this song does not need to be accompanied, translated, or tamed by that of the heroine. Notably, the "ethnic" voice is rendered here not by Ila Arun but by playback singer Sapna Awasthi. It is now a recognizable type that can be voiced by other singers. Awasthi's voice works alongside the Punjabi and Islamicate idiom of the song as a marker of difference. As such, it is an important part of the film's broader project of staging the confrontation of hegemonic national identity with various kinds of difference, some assimilated and accommodated with the nation, and others defiantly antinational.[91] That the "ethnic" voice occupies a more central position in the 1998 film and that it is not just associated with Ila Arun are signs of the rapid changes taking place in the realms of film, music, and public culture in India in the postliberalization period.

The arc I have charted from "Morni Bagama" (1991) to "Choli" (1993) to "Chaiyya Chaiyya" (1998) spans less than a decade, and yet it marks a dramatic shift in representations of women and vocal performance norms in Hindi cinema. What is interesting is that much of the "old" audiovisual contract remained in place during this time. Audiences still expected a mismatch between singing and speaking voices in cinema, and dubbing practices, in song sequences and otherwise, continued apace (clauses 1 and 2). The explosion of new musical formats, media, and venues for musical consumption made audiences in the postliberalization period all the more appreciative of the sound/image split and invested in scurrilous gossip about their favorite singers (clauses 3 and 4). Ila Arun provides a striking example of the way the changing dynamics of stardom in this period *intensified* the paratexts and public discourse clause (clause 4) of the audiovisual contract. Her success rested not just on her vocal talent and the widespread circulation of her music videos via television and cassette (and CD) culture, but also on the discourse about her as the "Rani of Raunch." This discourse mobilized intersecting ideas about nation, gender, sexuality, and ethnicity (clause 5). The fact that these identity categories were linked to the sound and image of Arun's body suggests that the somatic clause (clause 6), too, retained some of its power. That Bombay cinema of the 1990s was still invested in the notion of voice-as-essence is evident in the fact that Ila Arun could *only* sing for marginal characters. The coarse and "open" sound of her voice embodied otherness to such an extent that she could not represent the ideal Indian woman. The rustic tongue and sexual connotations of her performances confirmed her status as the "ethnic" voice. That said, Arun's popularity also rested on the fact that the other part of the somatic clause—the equation of the audible and visible body with immorality (body-as-vice)—was being revised.

## Bodies on Display

By the time the "ethnic" woman became prominent in the 1990s, two other nonnormative figures, the vamp and the *tawaif* (courtesan), had receded from the screen, their performative functions largely taken over by the heroine. As several scholars have noted, the virgin/whore dichotomy that had long structured the aural and visual representation of women in Hindi cinema began weakening as early as the 1970s.[92] Westernness gradually ceased to be a taint for women, and this meant more latitude in the representation of the ideal Indian woman. As "the display of the body and the body-in-performance [became] integral to the spectacle" of Bollywood, heroines began starring in "item numbers."[93] These catchy, highly choreographed and sexualized song-dance sequences became a key element of Hindi cinema in the late 1980s and early 1990s, and are a mainstay of big-budget films today.[94] One of the first item numbers was "Ek, Do, Teen" (One, Two, Three) in *Tezaab* (*Acid*, dir. N. Chandra, 1988), which gave actress Madhuri Dixit her first big break.[95] Dixit, you will remember, played the chaste heroine masquerading as a vamp in another item number, "Choli." While "Choli" courted the most ire, it was just one among many song sequences that showcased women's bodies, via their gestures and movements, vocal sound, and appearance. Some of these songs, like "Jumma Chumma De De" (Jumma, Give Me a Kiss) from *Hum* (*Us*, dir. Mukul Anand, 1991), are easily recognizable as item numbers. They are, to use Usha Iyer's dance-centric terminology, "production numbers" that center dancers performing choreographed moves in a proscenium-like public setting.[96] Others, such as "Kaante Nahi Katthe" ([Time] Passes Slowly) from *Mr. India* (dir. Shekhar Kapur, 1987) and "Dhak Dhak Karne Laga" (My Heart Goes Thump Thump) from *Beta* (*Son*, dir. Indra Kumar, 1992), are not item numbers per se. These production numbers were framed as (ostensibly) private fantasies of the hero and/or heroine. Yet, in all these songs, heroines danced as provocatively—and, in some cases, as publicly—as vamps did in earlier films. Rules about gender, sexuality, and bodily performance were clearly beginning to change.

While item numbers predated the rise of satellite television by a few years, their proliferation and institutionalization were tied to the broader experimentation in media formats underway on television in the 1990s. As film songs gained wider circulation via cable and satellite television, they had to compete for audience attention with the remarkable array of musical and dramatic performances now available on television. Previously, racy dance numbers lured audiences back to the cinema for "repeat viewings"; now, item numbers hooked fans to television screens. Item numbers offered a sexualized commodity spectacle that was different from, but as tantalizing as, the music videos of the Indipop and remix industry. Ila Arun's extrafilmic work popularized a bodily voice that worked well for item numbers, and this allowed her to break into the Bombay film industry. On the one hand, the fact that voices such as Arun's were reserved for minor characters performing item numbers (and not heroines) extended Mangeshkar's monopoly. On the other, the very fact that such "ethnic" voices were viable in the playback industry was a sign that Mangeshkar's position as the voice of Indian womanhood—and the somatic clause of the audiovisual contract that sustained that notion—was crumbling. Working in tandem with other sexualized performances (in music videos, fashion shows, and beauty pageants), item numbers pushed the bounds of propriety for women. As such, they were important sites in which the transition away from the "old" audiovisual contract was being worked out.[97]

The transformation of women's soundwork and bodily performance in the 1990s was not limited to Hindi films and television. It was part of a broader cultural shift in perceptions and discourses about the body in India. Shoma Munshi writes that the postliberalization period witnessed "a new confidence . . . [and] an obsession with the body, arguably to an extent not seen before, where the 'desirable' body [was and] is now on display through the constant circulation of images in the media."[98] If, in earlier decades, cinema represented a threat because it made women's bodies public, sweeping transformations in the media landscape and the phenomenal expansion of bodywork industries (particularly beauty, fitness, and fashion) in the 1990s did away entirely with the notion that the place of the ideal woman (and her body) was in the private sphere. In 1994, two Indian models won international beauty pageants: Aishwarya Rai was crowned Miss World and Sushmita Sen Miss Universe. Public ambivalence, feminist and otherwise, around beauty pageants dissipated quickly, and the two women's success was hailed as a *national* victory. As if overnight, modeling and acting came to be seen as viable, respectable professions for middle-class women. (Both women, but Rai in particular, would go on to become Bollywood stars.) More generally, there emerged the idea that the modern Indian woman is one whose "worked-out, taut body . . . [is a] statement to the world that its owner cares for herself and how she appears to the world."[99] While women did not adopt the "ultrathin" body wholesale, that ideal was (and remains) a very attractive prospect, particularly when articulated with the notion of the "new Indian woman."[100] As numerous studies on gender, media, and globalization show, this construct constitutes not a break from the past so much as a rearticulation of tradition and modernity.[101] But what was most certainly new about this ideal in the 1990s was the centrality of beauty and the body.[102] This conception of women's bodies was (and is) at odds with the body-as-vice subclause of the audiovisual contract. The body-on-display began to carry a positive valence: it came to signal not hypersexuality so much as a modern, cosmopolitan Indian identity.

I have been arguing that the sound and look of women's bodies in Bombay cinema changed in two ways in the 1990s: first, more sexy and bodily playback voices came to be heard, and second, "good" girls began to dress and move more provocatively. These two developments were disconnected in that those "other" playback voices (such as Ila Arun's) were not attached to the newly unrestrained dancing bodies of the heroines. Thus, changes in the representation of women—or, more precisely, changes in the *logic* underlying cinematic representations, the audiovisual contract—were mainly happening in the visual realm of performance and not in the aural realm. The somatic clause (clause 6) is critical to understanding this aural lag. According to the somatic clause, the body signaled vice, and the singing voice represented the "truth" of the character. This explains why we heard voices that sounded very much like Mangeshkar's in item numbers of the 1990s that featured heroines. Although Madhuri Dixit's risqué dancing ushered in a new era for the heroines of Bombay cinema, these "good" women still sounded wholesome. They continued to be assigned voices similar to Mangeshkar's because the association of the body with vice persisted in the aural realm. Thus, negative connotations of the body were dissipating much faster in the visual realm than in the aural one. I might go so far as to say that it was the continuity in *voice* that allowed for the pushing of boundaries in other aspects of women's performance in Hindi cinema. Further, if the essence of Indian womanhood lay in voice, then allowing the heroine to sing in Ila Arun's voice was a dangerous prospect. All in all, it would take another decade for the somatic clause to be recoded entirely and for an altogether new conception of body and voice to emerge in Bombay cinema.

For listeners accustomed to Hindi cinema's hegemonic feminine voice, women's playback today has a very different, much more visceral feel. In the next section of this chapter, I lay out recent changes in the industry that have allowed for the "new acceptance for lower octaves and meatier tones."[103] Since this aural and visual revolution aligns with the emergence of New Bollywood in the first decade of the twenty-first century, I refer to it as "millennial soundwork." The revised conception of women's vocal labor I describe dovetails with shifts in the understanding of the body in Indian public culture.

## Millennial Soundwork

The vocal diversity that emerged on 1990s television now suffuses Hindi film soundwork. Indipop may no longer be distinguishable as a discrete industry or genre, but that is because it and other musical genres that came alive in the postliberalization period left a profound impact on the sound of Bombay cinema—particularly the sound of *women* in this cinema. Coming from a variety of musical backgrounds and dabbling in a wide range of styles, today's singers sound very different, not just from Lata Mangeshkar and Asha Bhosle, but also from one another. Often, their fluency with multiple musical genres makes them sound quite distinct from one song to the next. While singers are sometimes praised for their "distinctive" voices, it is clear that voice recognizability and consistency are no longer valued. The self-sameness that marked the ideal Indian voice in Hindi cinema for almost five decades is nowhere to be heard. In short, diversity and experimentation, not voice monopoly, characterize women's playback singing today.

If there is one defining feature of this rich and varied vocal landscape, it is that singers do not shy away from the sound of the body. Contemporary playback singers are not just permitted to "display" the body; they are expected to do so. Their voices are valued *precisely* because the body—different kinds of bodies, different bodily states—is now audible in their performances. They are also more visible than ever as singers. To frame these changes in terms of the audiovisual contract, the somatic clause has been transformed such that the body—a woman's body, in particular—is no longer a seat of vice. It is instead a music-making entity, and it is *visible* as such in a variety of paratextual forms. The new visibility accorded to women's musicking bodies through YouTube channels, making-of videos, and television shows highlights the labor of singers in Bombay cinema.[104] In this new iteration of the audiovisual contract, sound and image are hyperembodied; that is, the proliferation of bodily voices and images generates all sorts of composite texts. While the somatic clause has crumbled, other clauses of the audiovisual contract have grown in importance. Disjunctures between sound, speech, and image are more apparent, and more desirable, than ever before. Now that voice is no longer a pure, disembodied construct, the hierarchical relationship between voice and body has also lost force.

If women's singing voices sound more complex and fleshed out today, it is, in part, because the audible presence of the body is not equated with sex. "Yahi Meri Zindagi" (This Is My Life), Aditi Singh Sharma's wistful teenage track in *Dev D* (dir. Anurag Kashyap, 2009); "Bhare Naina" (Tearful Eyes), Nandini Srikar's dirge in *Ra-One* (dir. Anubhav Sinha, 2011); "Khaabon Ke Parindey" (Dream Birds), Alyssa Mendonsa's romantic bossa nova tune in *Zindagi Na Milegi Dobara* (*One Life to Live*, dir. Zoya Akhtar, 2011); "Dhadaam Dhadaam," "Ka Kha Ga," and other jazz numbers by Neeti Mohan (and Shefali Alvares) in *Bombay Velvet* (dir. Anurag Kashyap, 2015); and "Jag Ghoomeya" (Roamed the World), Neha Bhasin's version of the love song from *Sultan* (dir. Ali Abbas Zaffar, 2016), are examples of the diverse ways in which recent Hindi films sound out women as bodily subjects. This audibility opens up affective possibilities that were impossible for decades. The delinking of body and sex—the undoing of any *necessary* association between women's bodies and sex—means that the immoral connotations attached to the sound of the body are dissipating. Importantly, we hear the body in the heroine's voice, not just in marginal characters' singing voices. The lead voice no longer needs to distance itself from the body or veil itself in chastity.

Unlike the previous generation, few of today's singers were dubbing artists who got their start mimicking Mangeshkar. They came to film music through other routes and have no investment in maintaining Bombay cinema's old vocal ideal. Take Shefali Alvares, for example. Daughter of jazz vocalist Joe Alvares, she grew up listening to everything from Motown to gospel to *The Sound of Music*, and sought a career in jazz. She began performing alongside her father and eventually formed the rock-funk band Distil Soul, in which she continues to perform. Her entry into Bollywood was somewhat fortuitous, occasioned by a 2010 call from music director Pritam Chakraborty's office saying he was "looking for new voices."[105] Rekha Bhardwaj is a classically trained Hindustani singer who struggled to get a break in the 1990s, despite her connections to the film world through her husband, Vishal Bhardwaj. Her first hit was "Namak Ishq Ka" (The Salt of Love), her "folk" item number for *Omkara* (dir. Vishal Bhardwaj, 2006). The appeal of Alvares's and Bhardwaj's voices lies in their rootedness outside Bombay cinema.[106] Different musical styles discipline singers differently, such that their voices bear the marks of their musical background. The vocal range, pitch, and texture of singers specializing in nonfilm musics are critical to the film industry in the new millennium.

Contemporary singers move effortlessly across musical genres and media. A number of them—Shreya Ghoshal, Mahalakshmi Iyer, Shruti Pathak, Shilpa Rao, and Monali Thakur, for example—are classically trained. Others, like Harshdeep Kaur, Jaspinder Narula, and Kavita Seth, specialize in Sufi music. Some, like Rekha Bhardwaj, are accomplished in both genres. Still others, like Suman Sridhar, are known more for their nonfilm musical work than playback. No matter their training and specialty, these singers' musical identities are not limited to cinema. They sing ad jingles, form bands, compose music, and record albums unrelated to films. Even those who go directly from winning televised music competitions to singing playback cultivate their talents (and fan base) by performing in live shows, on television, and on radio. Many artists garner a following online as well, posting audio and video recordings on YouTube and SoundCloud. Live gigs and online projects often take up more of their time and energy than films. In short, Bombay cinema has become just one among many contexts in which singers ply their vocal skills.

This interaural, intermedial musical landscape is a result of—an *amplification* of—changes set in motion in the 1990s. The explosion of music venues, platforms, and formats in recent years has meant that music-making is a viable career whether or not one hails from a musical family. In straddling diverse musical domains, contemporary singers are following the lead of people like Shubha Mudgal and the Colonial Cousins (Hariharan and Leslie Lewis), who were among the first to breach the classical/pop divide through their fusion albums.[107] Their border-crossing work had a profound influence on those artists who came of age during the postliberalization period. For example, Harshdeep Kaur tells of how hearing Mudgal made her realize that "a raw voice also had its own personality," and that one did not have to sound like Lata Mangeshkar to be a good singer.[108] One pioneer of the current generation of playback singers is Sunidhi Chauhan. She won the first season of *Meri Awaaz Suno*, India's first televised music competition, in 1996, by showcasing her precocious ability to sing like the grand dame of Hindi playback. In more ways than one, that win was a point of departure for Chauhan. She would go on to sing in a variety of idioms and timbres over the course of her career, and her bold vocal choices opened the door for other singers.

The last two decades have also seen the rise of a new crop of music directors, including A. R. Rahman, Shankar-Ehsaan-Loy (SEL), Vishal-Shekhar, Amit Trivedi, Pritam Chakraborty, and Sneha Khanwalkar. The men—and they are overwhelmingly men—who now dominate the Bombay film-music scene are always in search of a fresh and distinct sound. Like today's singers, they are not the product of the Hindi film industry, at least not exclusively so. For example, all three members of SEL come from nonfilm contexts.[109] Shankar Mahadevan was an engineer who had trained in Carnatic music and freelanced as a singer. Loy Mendonsa and Ehsaan Noorani both worked in advertising and television, which is how they met Mahadevan. Mendonsa's musical passions are wide ranging, as evidenced by the "sounds [he] would wake [his daughter, singer Alyssa Mendonsa] up to every morning, from Betty Carter to Herbie Hancock and Stevie Wonder."[110] Noorani is an accomplished guitarist who names the blues as his primary love, even as he has been influenced by many other genres, from rock to pop to electronic music.[111] Given that the norms surrounding a "good" voice differ across musical worlds, and that the 1990s whetted listeners' appetites for different sounds, it is not surprising that contemporary music directors have invited a wider range of vocalists into their studios.

All the more important is that music directors today operate with a wholly new conception of voice. A. R. Rahman was a pioneer in his treatment of "the singer as an *instrument*. . . . [To him,] a singer [is] not a voice to be identified, but one of the many instruments that contribut[e] to a song."[112] Other music directors may not be as explicit about their philosophy of voice, but their compositional and production choices betray a similar understanding: "Now, with other composers who extensively use programming, like Pritam Chakraborty and Amit Trivedi, voices like Alvares's in 'Subha Hone Na De' or Mendonsa's in 'Uff Teri Adaa' are machine-tuned to make them sound more clubby; with a folk voice like Bhardwaj's, the natural scale of her voice can be shifted to suit the undertone of a particular song."[113] The extensive use of technology allows for the manipulation of voices during the composition, recording, and postproduction process. Music directors and engineers work not so much with playback artists as with sonic fragments produced by singers and other musicians' instruments. As dramatic as this conceptual shift is for music directors' work and stardom, it has equally important implications for singers. The singing voice is no longer construed as a manifestation of an authentic inner self or cultural essence, as the somatic clause of the "old" audiovisual contract held. Rather, in more postmodern vein, voice is treated as a variable bodily technology.

The visual representation of contemporary playback singers further reifies this notion of voice as instrument. Whether in making-of videos, music reality shows, "unplugged" performances posted on YouTube, or shows such as *Coke Studio* and *The Dewarists* which feature live studio recordings, singers are typically depicted in front of a microphone surrounded by other musicians. Close-ups of the singer are intercut with those of their fellow artists' hands and musical instruments. Mics and headphones abound, never letting us lose sight of the fact that technology is a critical part of the music production process. If the image of a woman standing with a mic is ubiquitous, so too is that of a man (the music director) sitting at the soundboard or computer, directing the singer.[114] These paired images tell us that it is not just musical talent that makes a song; it is what the music director as technician does with their sound that makes a song.

To be clear: my argument is not about the newness of technology. It is, rather, about how three key terms—voice, body, and technology—are articulated anew in Bombay cinema's millennial soundwork. The Indian audiovisual contract has never demanded a complete erasure of technology. As Neepa Majumdar astutely observes, Mangeshkar's collaborators routinely "emphasize[d] her affinity for the microphone. She exist[ed] only as a recorded voice, a voice mediated by technology."[115] If on the one hand, voice was equated with essence (hers was the essence of "Indian womanhood"), on the other, that voice was understood to be a thoroughly mediated entity. So pronounced was the idea that body-equals-vice that Mangeshkar was (had to be) "disembodied in the very act of recording her voice." Millennial soundwork more thoroughly entangles the categories of voice, body, and technology. It makes the connections between them both audible and visible. Today, the singer's voice does not just sound bodily, it is visualized as a musical technology that she and, more importantly, the music director manipulate.

## Women's Musicking and the Somatic Clause

The shift to thinking about voice as a musical instrument of the body must be understood as part of a broader recalibration of the body in Indian media and public culture. As might be expected, the transformations set in motion with the expansion of bodywork industries in the 1990s have continued apace. The new Indian woman's glamorous, fit, well-groomed body is a sign of her robust sense of self; her poise and confidence announce her place in the world. Equally, this body is a sign of her aspirations, her desire to be a global, cosmopolitan, and wealthy subject. Such aspirational desires are naturalized in public discourse, and much ink is spilled on how to attain and maintain a fit, beautiful, and "classy" Indian body. Thus, the body is newly imagined and *made visible* as a self-making technology.

As a gendered and classed project, bodywork in contemporary India emphasizes how one appears to others. In her ethnography of the new Indian middle class, Meredith Lindsay McGuire writes of personality development and enhancement (PDE) courses, which teach upwardly mobile Indians "how to sit, how to stand, how to talk, how to conduct [oneself]" in the new spaces of conspicuous consumption in urban India.[116] The "kinesthetic pedagogies" employed in PDE courses clarify that "the production of the new middle class entails the production of a new middle class body."[117] It is through bodily performance, through the cultivation of new bodily dispositions, that one announces one's modern, middle- and upper-class Indian identity.[118] Of course, the body has long been imbricated in the production of social identities in India. What seems different in the last twenty years is the more overt emphasis on the *display* of the body. If, as Christopher Pinney has argued, the constitution of the "universal" Indian subject in the early twentieth century entailed perspectival pedagogy—teaching subjects to *see* in a new way—then this project continues a century later in the conscious cultivation of the desire to *be seen*.[119] The architecture and social norms of shopping malls and coffee shops like Barista, where the young and affluent socialize, ensure that "one is *seen* consuming and that one can *watch* others consume."[120] So, if the audiovisual contract coaches audiences in how to listen to women's onscreen voices, that disciplining of ears and eyes is part of a broader bodily education in enacting gendered, sexual, and classed norms. In what follows, I demonstrate that the public visibility of bodies and the emphasis on the labor of certain bodily projects have critical implications for Hindi film soundwork in the new millennium.

If beauty, fitness, and PDE regimens are means of bodily display, then using one's voice (in the Hindi film song) has become another way of doing so.[121] Matthew Rahaim's term "the musicking body" may be of use here.[122] Rahaim uses it to clarify the importance of spontaneous gestures in Hindustani (North Indian classical) vocal practice. The musicking body is one that moves as it makes music: it is a "trained body in action, engaged mindfully in singing and/or playing an instrument."[123] In this formulation, singers' unchoreographed gestures are not supplements, ornamental or otherwise, to vocalization. Rather, they constitute "a stream of melody parallel to voice . . . [that] complements vocal action without duplicating it, revealing knowledge about the shape, texture, and motion of melody" gleaned through years of study under specific teachers.[124] The musicking body is cultivated over time through emulating one's teacher—thus it involves making the "paramparic" (i.e., of one's vocal lineage or tradition) body come alive in the moment of performance. The musicking body is a visible manifestation of the singer's musical lineage and training, and thus his expertise. The norms and composition practices of Hindustani classical music are distinct from those of the Hindi film industry, notwithstanding the genre-crossing ethos of the industry today. Also, crucially, Rahaim's unmarked musicking body is primarily a *male* body. As one of Rahaim's fellow music students (a woman) points out, the expansive repertoire of gestures available to men is not accessible to women performers.[125] Her personal experience matches the historical insights offered by music and dance scholars who have documented how the interconnected discourses of colonialism and elite nationalism were brought to bear on women performers (*tawaifs*, *devadasis*, and others) in the early years of the twentieth century as part of social reform movements. Any discussion of the body in performance must deal with the gendered dimensions of the colonial and nationalist histories of music, dance, and film in India. I take up the term "musicking body" here to illuminate the revised terms of Hindi cinema's audiovisual contract and the gender politics audible and visible today.

Applied to playback singing, the musicking body describes the dramatic shift away from the "old" somatic clause, which deemed all aural and visible manifestations of the body potentially threatening. To conceptualize the woman singer as a musicking body is to acknowledge the place of the body in *all* musical performance, not just in vamp or *tawaif* songs. It is to grant that the singer's body is as important as that of the actor who lip-synchs the lyrics and dances to them. Most crucially, the musicking body overwrites older, derogatory references to carnality and immorality with an emphasis on the creative, artistic labor of the singer. That the body is more audible than ever in Hindi playback singers' voices is attributable, at least in part, to the fact that such bodily sounds are not written off as illegitimate and immoral. A woman performing non-"classical" music or dance in public is no longer an anomaly. She does not pose the symbolic threat that Mangeshkar did in her early years and thus does not need to walk the line between virgin and vamp in the same way. She can sing in a variety of styles and timbres, and her vocal labor is now assessed very differently. The new visibility of her musicking body has closed the aural lag that characterized Hindi cinema of the 1990s.

Contemporary playback singers think of themselves as artists who are "creative and emotionally invested in [their] music."[126] They cultivate a musical repertoire and career that far exceed the bounds of cinema. Of the many kinds of music-making they engage in, their collaborations with other artists are of particular note, as Amanda Weidman observes. The act of "jamming," Weidman writes, "is what confers value; it is considered the place where one's true musical self emerges."[127] If, in the Hindustani music context, the musicking body is a visible and performative marker of a singer's lineage, in the context of Bombay cinema's new soundwork, it marks singers' commitment and creativity. Playback singers are at pains to fashion themselves as artists committed to music as a whole. Where once the consistency of Mangeshkar's voice was lauded, now versatility and flexibility are prized. These are the qualities that confirm one's musical expertise. In arguing that contemporary playback is construed as the product of musicking bodies, I do not mean that musical expertise was irrelevant in Mangeshkar's time. She was, after all, *revered* for the precision in her voice. The same goes for P. Susheela, the "Lata Mangeshkar of South India."[128] But note my use of "revered" here. What I am arguing is that virtuosic music-making by playback singers is no longer treated as a divine gift—whether a gift bestowed on the singer by god, or gifts bestowed on us, the listeners, by the goddess-singer. It is, instead, something the singer cultivates and performs in different spaces, platforms, and genres. Playback singing is labor she makes visible in myriad media forms and contexts.

One visible measure of this shift to the notion of women's musicking bodies is the fact that a film song is at least as likely to be linked to images of the *singer* performing the song in various contexts as it is to images of actors lip-synching and dancing (i.e., song picturization) (see figure 1.2). Even as aural stardom and voice recognizability are blunted today due to the sheer number of artists crowding the field, singers enjoy much greater visibility in

Figure 1.2. Neeti Mohan singing a version of her song "Nainowale Ne," from *Pad-maavat* (dir. Sanjay Leela Bhansali, 2018), on a music video for the album *T-Series Acoustics*.

the public sphere. As "Female Singers' Adda" demonstrates, stardom rests not just on singers' vocal talents (or their association with particular actors) but also on their visual presence on various media platforms and on audiences' knowledge of the range of their musical skills.[129] They render songs in music videos; in staged shows; in interviews recorded for television, radio, or YouTube channels; and in making-of videos. This last genre shows singers in recording studios as they practice, and play with, melodic and rhythmic variations on their lines. A quick YouTube search shows us just how widely available still images and video clips of singers performing their hit numbers are. Such paratexts ensure that the musicking body of the singer is no longer invisible.[130] These new kinds of paratexts affect not just clause 4 of the audio-visual contract but clause 2 as well: sound and image now stand in a different, more dynamic relationship to each other than they did in the past.[131]

The heightened visibility accorded to women's musicking is occurring in conjunction with the "retreat of the song sequence into the soundtrack."[132] That is, fewer songs are lip-synched today, and "songless" films are considered more realistic.[133] This means that although we *hear* and *see* more of women's bodies in cinema, the two—the sound and image of women's bodies—are not necessarily fused in song picturization. This might seem like a process of disembodiment, detaching the singing voice from the image of the acting body, but it is in fact a kind of *hyperembodiment*. Now, more than ever before, a single song (and a single voice) is attached not just to images of glamorous actresses lip-synching in song-dance sequences, but also to *other* bodies—those of singers, both professional and nonprofessional—performing the song in diverse nonfilm venues and platforms. Recall that Bombay cinema's audiovisual contract has always allowed cinematic sound and image to be disarticulated and rearticulated in multiple ways (clause 2). What we witness in millennial soundwork, then, is an *intensification* of a process that was already in place. During the Mangeshkar era, a single ideal voice was paired with scores of ideal images in song sequences. Film songs have long been remembered and marketed using the names of star actors, music directors, and singers. The difference now is that the songs are attached not just to singers' names but also to moving images of them, their musicking bodies.

## The Labor of Vocal Performance

That we see the body (of the singer) as she sings is a significant departure from conventions of playback institutionalized not just in India but around the world. Let us return to Marsha Siefert's comments on how the physicality of singing was erased as song dubbing became institutionalized:

> The technological separation of the song from its singer meant that the image of singing did not have to reflect the *physicality of its bodily production*. The physiology of singing (wide open mouth, unusual or extreme facial expressions, visible signs of breathing) and its physicality (strength, endurance) is no longer necessarily visible. The [actor] could dance, do acrobatics, or otherwise move around with only minimal lip movement to produce consistent, clear singing. In addition, the microphone, necessary to achieve clarity and presence expected from the popular music sonic ideal, was also visually absent. Thus larger than life singing with minimal body effort or accompanied by dancing with no technological requirements came to appear natural and more like speaking.[134]

In other words, one could not tell from watching Hollywood musicals—or Hindi films, for that matter—that singing and dancing involved bodily labor. Nor was it evident that singing for the screen required technological equipment. In the case of Bombay cinema, the "old" audiovisual contract fostered awareness of playback singers and the cinematic technology that made them aural stars (clause 3). Yet the physicality of their vocal labor was never on display, allowing Mangeshkar and other singers to navigate the gender, class, and caste politics of that era. If, as Rick Altman suggests, the technological silencing of all traces of soundwork stemmed from a "standard trait of bourgeois ideology"—the erasure of labor—then what do we make of the return of certain kinds of bodily labor to the screen in India today, at a moment when neoliberal projects of all kinds flourish?[135]

The bourgeois tendency in India of the new millennium is to emphasize projects of self-making. Much that was absent from film songs in the past— the physiology of singing, the microphone, the image of the singer herself—is present in the aural and visual culture of Bollywood today. Now, the emphasis is on seeing and hearing the body, and on seeing some of the bodily labor and technology it takes to produce a song. This, I am proposing, is akin to, and a version of, the visible bodily labor of producing the new Indian woman and the new Indian middle class. In chapter 2, I discuss how visual representations of Sufipop extend the postliberalization emphasis on the individual (Indipop) star. Below, I develop the related argument that the newly visible labor of singing on television and digital platforms has transformed what it means to be a woman singing playback in Bombay cinema.

Seeing women singers at their task is crucial to the reconfiguring of the old somatic clause, which equated the voice with essence and the body with vice. In the contemporary moment, we witness women engaging in a new kind of performance for cinema. In award shows, playback artists dress and move in much the same way that actors do on screen. The sheer visuality of these stage performances, Monika Mehta argues, "underscores the relatively new expectation of playback singers (especially female playback singers) to develop a compelling stage presence."[136] In ostensibly informal settings, too, such as when singers are jamming with their bandmates or rehearsing lines before recording them, singers are expected to move and emote visibly as they sing. This expectation stands in sharp contrast to those generated by the "old" audiovisual contract. Per the somatic clause of that contract, a respectable woman had to do all she could to erase aural and visual signs of the body, or else risk being labeled immoral. Recall the distancing of the body in Lata Mangeshkar's performances—the stillness of her body as she sang, her contained posture and expressions—and in the discourse about her. Today's singers are confronted with a diametrically opposed set of expectations, one that requires "a re-education of the body for public performance."[137] Discussing the "neo-liberal logics of voice" that operate in the South Indian playback industry today, Amanda Weidman explains that in order to seem "authentic," women singers must now match their appearance and performance to the demands of the song: they "need to be willing to some extent to 'act the part': to dress in ways that evoke the on-screen characters their voices represent in the films, and to move and gesture when they sing."[138] While Weidman's fieldwork is focused on Tamil playback, much of what she describes is evident in the Bombay-based industry as well. For instance, the notion that singers are "actors" who express the emotions described in the song lyrics is one that Hindi playback singers routinely invoke as they describe their method.[139] Previous generations of singers also conceived of their work in this way, but they were bound by the injunction to distance voice from the taint of the body and hence followed Mangeshkar in emoting vocally but invisibly.

This new understanding of playback singing as creative, bodily labor bears on the relationship between singers and music directors. It has implications for the work that goes on in the recording studio: "Time in the studio that used to be devoted to learning and rehearsing an already composed song is now more often given over to experimentation, in which the singer's role as an artistic and intentional subject is, perhaps, more acknowledged."[140] The hesitation in Weidman's language here—"perhaps"—is instructive. It speaks to the tension between A. R. Rahman and other music directors' conception of voice and that of the singers themselves. In presenting themselves as versatile musicking bodies, singers honor and highlight their vocal contributions. Valuing their work as creative artists helps them lobby for better contracts and royalties. The Indian Singers' Rights Association (ISRA), formed in 2013, recently scored a series of legal victories, with the Delhi High Court affirming the organization's right to collect royalties from commercial venues that broadcast its members' performances, as allowed for in the Copyright Act of 2012.[141] In a statement hailing this 2016 ruling, the ISRA writes: "At Last!!! Singers are NO MORE VOCAL INSTRUMENTS. Their Creativity in a Song is now recognized and they shall now start getting Royalties from the Exploitation of their Performances."[142] The statement goes on to say that this development *does not* put singers in competition with other artists and entities, including music directors, lyricists, producers, and music companies, all of whom may also claim royalties for their work on songs.

Such protestations notwithstanding, the ISRA's explicit rejection of the notion that singers are "vocal instruments" does push against the working assumption of contemporary music directors who use digital technology to isolate, fragment, and manipulate voices. Voice is, in practice, an instrument with which music directors play. This conception of voice shifts emphasis from the talent and aural stardom of the singer to the sound she produces,

the materiality of her vocal performance. It places that sonic fragment in relation to other sounds produced by other musical instruments. It also diminishes the importance of the singer to the song and its success with audiences.
If the singer is no longer a singular voice, aurally recognizable and constant
across songs, she can no longer be as big an aural star as Mangeshkar was.
She is superseded by the music director, whose role it is to create a pleasurable ensemble of sounds from the raw material that is her voice and other
musical instruments' "voices." While women's playback singing has opened
up in many ways, the division of labor described above is pretty conven-
tional. Women lyricists and music directors are still hard to find in the male-
dominated industry. Thus, even as the "old" audiovisual contract has been
substantially revised in the new millennium, gender hierarchies persist in
other ways.

One hierarchy that has come undone over the last several decades is that
between sound and image. From the late 1940s through the 1990s, voices
that sounded like Mangeshkar's cloaked the dangerous sexual connotations of cinematic images. Since voice was equated with moral and cultural
essence, singing in a "disembodied" voice protected not only film characters but also playback stars from disrepute. This prioritization of cinematic
sound (voice, in particular) over image no longer applies in Bombay cinema.
The relationship between sound and image is very different now than it was
seven decades ago, when both the nation-state and the aural ideal of Indian
femininity in Hindi cinema came into being. Today, playback voices do not
need images of lip-synching actors to be embodied. Audiences can visualize
singing voices apart from actors' bodies because singers are now very visible.
Audiences see the voice that sings. More, we can see it in the act of singing
and recording. As we begin to visualize voice differently, and as we begin to
see songs as the product of musicking bodies, the notion that voice is inherently disembodied collapses.

It would be easy to see these historical developments as being specific
to Hindi cinema of the new millennium. They are indeed so, but they also
bear on our understanding of singing voices in other times and places in crucial ways. Listening to shifts in Hindi film soundwork teaches us that the
disembodiment audible in certain voices is but one historically specific way
of framing the relationship between voice and body. It helps us refine and
extend such foundational concepts of cinema and sound studies as the voice-

body relationship and the audiovisual contract. It demonstrates how other key constructs—including soundwork, paratexts, mismatched women, and musicking bodies—work outside of the contexts in which they were first theorized. It underscores the importance of these concepts, even as I tweak them for wider applicability. Finally, my analysis in this chapter reminds us to listen to more than just films. In theorizing playback voices as an element of Hindi film soundwork, I move those voices outside the bounds of the film song. That is, I account for the ways in which other aural and visual media—paratexts such as making-of videos, but also music television more generally—shape the sound of women in Hindi cinema. Counterintuitive though it may be, visibility emerges by the end of the chapter as a critical element of soundwork. As Michele Hilmes quips, soundwork has indeed arrived at "a screen near you."[143] In the next chapter, I explore further the implications of the visibility of soundwork for listening, particularly the way listening is imagined in the Islamicate genre of the qawwali.

# Listening

Listening

## CHAPTER 2

# Re-Sounding the Islamicate

## *The Cinematic Qawwali and Its Listening Publics*

This chapter pivots from the voice to the ear—or rather, from the semiotics of voicing to that of listening. In chapter 1, I argued that interpreting women's playback voices in Hindi cinema is a multimodal affair: sound and image work together with paratextual discourses about gender, sexuality, nation, and the body to render singing voices meaningful. Here, I build on those insights about the visibility of soundwork and shifting notions of identity by attending to how one particular genre of Hindi film songs conjures listening publics. As media and sound studies scholar Kate Lacey notes, listening publics are "made up of listeners inhabiting a condition of plurality and intersubjectivity."[1] That is to say, the term does not simply describe a group of listeners; it casts *sound* as a means of forging connections and community. A listening public is a gathering that is aurally oriented. The shift from voicing to listening that this chapter enacts is, thus, also a shift from individual to collective figurations. Where previously I homed in on an individual singer or figure associated with a particular voice, here I ask how communities are called into being (or not) through soundwork.

I center my analysis on the qawwali, a Sufi poetic genre that evinces a sophisticated notion of listening and its effects. For decades, the qawwali and the ghazal have served as preeminent musical markers of the Islamicate in Hindi cinema.[2] Both genres boast a long and syncretic history in South Asia. The qawwali, in particular, emerges from philosophical and religious traditions that prioritize listening—especially collective listening—as an ethical and spiritual practice. As Charles Hirschkind notes in his magnificent study of cassette sermons in Egypt, while Roman and Christian rhetoricians dwelt on the importance of oratorial techniques, Muslim thinkers theorized listening.[3] In the Sufi Chishti order, which is influential in South Asia, listening to mystical songs (qawwalis, specifically) in the company of fellow believers is understood to be the route to the divine. Such gatherings for the purpose of cultivated, ritualistic listening are called *sama'*.[4] While there are subtle differences in the relationships that sustain qawwali performances at public *dargahs* (shrines) and those at more exclusive *sama'* gatherings for Sufi elites, what unites these sacred spaces and events is a sociality fostered by listening.[5] The centrality of *sama'* to Sufi devotional practice and the translation of that religious practice into more worldly terms in Hindi films make cinematic qawwalis a rich archive with which to theorize listening. This chapter explores how the kinds of publics the qawwali calls up—the way it imagines the relationship between listeners and singers—shift across the history of Hindi cinema.

How does one listen as a member of a public? How do we tune our ears to others in our midst? To what, and to what *ends*, do audiences listen? What kinds of ties does listening foster? What kind of community does soundwork engender? For some scholars of sound, the radical potential of listening lies in the answers to these questions. Consider, for instance, the crucial analytic distinction that Kate Lacey draws between "listening in" and "listening out." The former stresses the act of listening *to* a particular person, media source, genre, or such. By contrast, "listening out" describes "an attentive and anticipatory communicative disposition."[6] Here are the implications of this distinction:

> "To listen" is both an intransitive and a transitive verb. In other words, it is possible to listen without necessarily listening *to* anything. Listening can therefore be understood as being in a state of anticipation, of listening *out* for something. . . . There is a faith in the moment of address that there is a public out there, and there is a faith in the act of listening that there will be some resonance with the address.[7]

Lacey's emphasis on listeners' orientation to the world—"listening out" as waiting for whatever it is that will fall on our ears and emerge from/in that aural encounter—presents listening as "a form of radical openness."[8] Philosopher of sound Lisbeth Lipari similarly valorizes listening as an ethical orientation to the world. To tune our attention to that which we don't understand is a means of respecting difference and not subsuming it into the familiar: "to *listen otherwise* is to welcome the other inside, but as an *other*, as a guest, as a not-me."[9] For Irina Leimbacher, "haptic listening" is just this kind of respectful listening. Pointing to the work of experimental and documentary filmmakers, she calls for a listening that "fastens on to the affective, expressive, and musical qualities of vocalized speech more than to its referents."[10] What these utopian treatises on listening share is an investment in breaking free from the hegemonic "listening ear" (Jennifer Lynn Stoever) and the broader "aural imaginary" (Roshanak Kheshti).[11]

Whether or not all listening is as radically open and pluralistic as Lacey and other theorists suggest, the qawwali certainly calls up a public invested in "listening out" just as much as "listening in." In traditional Sufi contexts, listening to qawwalis offers the promise of spiritual ecstasy. In the more secular domain of Bombay cinema, particularly in mid- to late twentieth-century Hindi films, the qawwali offers more worldly pleasures. Thus, the cinematic audience listens with a somewhat different intent and different desires. The public gathered listens out for aesthetic pleasure as well as for spiritual, romantic, and social connection. Whereas Lacey locates such communion as potentiality (the latent possibility that defines "listening out"), I argue that cinematic qawwalis conjure publics in the very way they conceptualize listening. The nature and composition of the qawwali assembly—who is included in and invited into the group, how those assembled interact with one another and the singers, and how the aural and visual presence of the audience is rendered—have shifted dramatically over the years. These transformations, I shall demonstrate, have crucial implications for the representation of communal belonging—"communal" in both the Indian sense of religious identity and the more general sense of collectivity.

Importantly, the qawwali does not just tell us something about listening as it pertains to Sufi or Muslim characters and contexts. Cinematic qawwalis often celebrate transgressive acts of love. The critique of social boundaries that is integral to Sufi philosophy is writ large in the many qawwalis that stage (or, at the very least, comment on) the crossing of class, religious, and ethnic boundaries in romance. Other affective bonds such as friendship and kinship are also celebrated in the genre. Communities gather around the qawwali, both on- and offscreen, and those communities are not typically (or exclusively) defined by religious identity. Indeed, the notion of an expansive collective is built into the very form of a qawwali. The iterative structure, the rhythmic clapping, the troupe that follows the lead qawwals in song: all this and more make the qawwali a genre that centers one's connection to a larger group.

The qawwali ties listening to concepts such as citizenship, community, and public in a way that the scholarship on Indian cinema is only just beginning to grasp. There is, in the literature on South Asia, a growing body of work on how nation is imagined through vocality (chapter 1 contributes to that literature). There is also a rich discussion, mainly in the South Indian context, of how language politics relate to nation in cinema (see chapter 3). While ethnomusicologists have long described listening and singing as practices that bind people, this point has not been explored as much in film scholarship. Even as voice and language are now understood as part of the sound-work of nation in Indian cinema, there has not been nearly enough theorizing of listening, either in Hindi cinema or in other media. In the pages that follow, you will hear echoes of Vebhuti Duggal's and Isabel Huacuja Alonso's fabulous work on listening to the Hindi film song and the radio.[12] Both scholars demonstrate that listening has a public dimension that is as powerful as it is fraught, and that audiences routinely listen in ways that unsettle the state's attempts to fashion a national listening public. Aswin Punathambekar and Sriram Mohan also tie listening to citizenship in their discussion of how the 2012 hit song "Why this Kolaveri Di?" initiated a wave of political critique in the digital realm. #Kolaveri, they argue, condensed listening, singing, and political commentary into a powerful Twitter hashtag that became a "sound bridge" between the popular and the political.[13] In each of these examples, we encounter listeners who resist the strictures of nation and the nation-state. By contrast, in the story I tell in this chapter, the listening publics of cinematic qawwalis are more in tune with hegemonic discourses about national belonging, if in surprising ways. If I temper the utopianism of other theorists of listening, it is to reveal the historical specificity of the ways we listen and the implications thereof for gender, sexuality, religion, and nation.

In chapter 1, I outlined the transformations made possible in the sound of women's playback voices due to fundamental shifts in the music and media landscape that came to a head in the 1990s. The "'re-sounding' of the public sphere" that took place then and the concomitant rise of the Hindu right made the qawwali newly appealing to Indian ears.[14] In what follows, I demonstrate that the qawwali goes from being a secular, romantic genre in films of the 1950s through the 1980s, to a more serious, devotional form in the early 2000s. What I am calling the "classic cinematic qawwali" emphasized the wit and artistry of the singer-poet wooing his or her beloved. It celebrated Islamicate aesthetics and gendered conventions of love, even as it used a spiritual idiom to do so. In so doing, classic qawwalis invoked a listening public aligned with the romance of Nehruvian secularism.

Listening to postliberalization transformations with a feminist ear, I identify several significant changes to the sound of communal and national belonging in the qawwali. In one of its three millennial incarnations, the qawwali becomes the genre of the "good Muslim." The "dargah qawwali" features not worldly romance so much as Muslim (men's) religiosity. It emphasizes piety over poetry, devotion over delight. An appreciation of Islamicate artistry diminishes as qawwalis are used to index pivotal philosophical issues or a coming-of-age moment on screen. The revival of the cinematic qawwali in the early 2000s occurs because of two Muslim artists' prowess: the qawwal Nusrat Fateh Ali Khan and the music director A. R. Rahman. These stars' musicking also paved the way for the Sufi ethos of many film songs today, and for the expansive genre of "Sufipop." This genre veers away from the collective orientation of the qawwali and, instead, fosters what Matthew Rahaim calls an "irrelational" vocal disposition.[15] Even as Sufipop draws on Islamicate musical and literary precedents, it is largely de-Islamicized. While the genre's moorings in Sufism make it a fitting riposte to the exclusionary and violent politics of the Hindu right, it does not engender the affective investment in a syncretic, secular community in the way that classic qawwalis did.

The final transmogrification of the qawwali I explore in this chapter is the "item number–esque qawwali." These star-studded dance numbers re-embrace the genre's historical functions as a vehicle of romance. Something changes, however, as commodified and spectacular dancing bodies come to the fore. With the itemization of the genre, the social graces and elaborately gendered courtship rituals associated with the genre in its mid-twentieth-century screen iterations are rendered obsolete. Gender, romance, and the Islamicate are articulated anew. As the qawwali moves away from spirituality and male homosociality back to an investment in heteronormative romance, it no longer accords much importance to the auditor. The item number–esque qawwali does not invoke an "ethical soundscape" of any sort.[16] The diegetic audience is now figured as a group of viewers and dancers, more so than listeners. Listening, either for pleasure or for piety, gets devalued.

As this précis suggests, this chapter is not just a study of transformations in the qawwali but a study of listening across decades. The way the cinematic qawwali configures listening changes over time, which confirms what many sound students have argued: listening is not a singular thing. How we listen is historically and socially situated, part of one's "habitus."[17] Different genres and contexts elicit and cultivate distinct modes of listening and engagement.[18] My research suggests that while listening is always relational—we listen to (and for) a sound, a voice, an opinion—it does not always assume or elicit a

listening *public*. That is, listening does not necessarily or automatically position one in relation to, much less in communion with, a group. Here, I depart
from those scholars for whom listening is a utopian endeavor, holding the
promise of intersubjectivity, democracy, and equality.[19] I show that if in the
mid- to late twentieth century listening was imagined as a collective, affec-
tively charged, bonding activity, one that made "citizen-listeners" of us all,
then that listening public is no longer called forth by the film qawwali today.[20]
The various contemporary iterations of the genre call up a narrower, more
atomized audience, one that not only listens differently but also conceptual-
izes Sufism and nation—and the relationship between the two—differently.
As my example of dargah qawwalis shows, listening can be conceptualized in
ways that reinforce gendered and communal divides. In other words, listening can conjure exclusive and exclusionary publics.

As I drafted this chapter, I was keen to not simply make this a lament
about the fate of Islamicate soundwork today.[21] The question of what difference it makes to listen to qawwalis with a feminist ear was foremost on
my mind. As I note in the introduction to this book, to listen with a feminist ear is not just to listen for aural representations of otherness, but to
recognize that which casts a people or a culture as different, and to listen in
ways that challenge historical constructions of otherness that have become
aural commonsense. Just as in chapter 1, my emphasis here on the postliberalization years extends our understanding of the far-reaching and embodied
effects of the policy changes introduced in the 1990s. The early 1990s saw the
Hindu right consolidate its political and discursive power. If listening to and
singing Sufi music entails a performative resistance to Hindutva politics, as
Peter Manuel has argued, then so too does writing this chapter.[22] Notwithstanding my skepticism about the "good" Muslimness of dargah qawwalis and
the de-Islamicization of Sufipop, this chapter is my attempt to listen back to
hegemonic discourses that cast India as Hindu, and Islam as fundamentally
violent and "other." To train one's ears on a genre that was, for decades, paradigmatic of listening and nation in Hindi cinema is not a naive celebration
of Nehruvian-style secularism and syncretism. It is, rather, a pointed attempt
to listen *for* the Islamicate soundwork that gives form to the idea of India at
different historical moments. To listen to, and for, the Islamicate is to listen
differently to the sound of nation. The fact that so little has been published so
far on listening in the Indian public sphere makes the theoretical and histo-
riographical interventions of this chapter all the more urgent.

Elaborating the trajectory of the qawwali also holds a number of lessons for the study of Indian cinema and public culture more generally. Most obviously, my analysis bursts open the category of the "Hindi film song." Few would deny that Hindi film soundwork has encompassed many different genres and styles from its very inception, and that it has undergone significant shifts over the years. And yet, "Bollywood music" is still spoken of as if it is (or ever was) a single, coherent entity. Isolating and tracing a single musical genre across several decades, I fill out the story of the "evolution of song and dance" in Bombay cinema.[23] I unpack some of the more puzzling developments in the history of the film qawwali. For example, where some scholars argue that cinematic qawwalis have moved further and further away from their traditional counterparts, I account for those songs that hew close to shrine performances.[24] I also probe the counterintuitive de-Islamicization that has accompanied the "Sufi performing arts vogue" of the past twenty years.[25] As I map these shifts in the sound and look of the qawwali, I demonstrate that the changing fortunes of this Sufi form speak to broader transformations in discourses of nation, religion, and identity, as well as the business of film- and music-making in India.

The historiographic exercise I undertake in this chapter underscores the importance of interaurality. Here, as in the previous chapter, we are reminded that the television and music industries were pivotal to Bombay cinema in the postliberalization period and that they continue to shape it in the present. Equally important was the relationship between radio and Hindi cinema in the mid-twentieth century. The point is not only that extracinematic developments shape cinematic soundwork, but that underlying different "sound cultures" are distinct notions of identity, community, and belonging.[26] The traffic between disparate sonic worlds does not just produce new and interesting sounds or musical styles; it leads to conceptual friction and maneuvering of various kinds. For instance, while the qawwali laid the groundwork for the emergence of Sufipop, the latter genre operates on a wholly different set of assumptions about the ideal relationship between singers and listeners, about why one sings and for whom, and so on. Those assumptions and concepts transform what the qawwali "is" and "does," and how it is understood and received.

Last but not least, I offer this chapter as a springboard for thinking about the ways in which Islamicate culture and Muslim identity have been figured historically in Bombay cinema. Research into filmic representations of Muslim characters tells a story of tokenization, marginalization, and vilification.[27] Much of that work has focused on visual and narrative analysis. By centering Islamicate soundwork, I unsettle the persistent emphasis on visual difference—embodied in the figure of the veiled Muslim woman—in both public culture and scholarship on Islam.[28] What might an analysis of aurality vis-à-vis Muslimness in Hindi cinema entail? What does Muslimness sound like if we listen to qawwalis with a feminist ear? To what extent has the shift in the form of cinematic qawwalis over the last several decades transformed the representation of Muslimness in Hindi cinema? How does the propensity to sideline Muslim characters and experiences on screen intersect with a history of Islamicate forms such as ghazal and the qawwali? If, as I argue below, the Islamicate as we knew it has been gradually evacuated from the cinematic qawwali, what are the implications for a broader understanding of nation in Bombay cinema? Indeed, what are the implications for Hindi cinema itself, given that "its architecture [was] inspired by Islamicate forms"?[29] Such are the questions that emerge when one takes soundwork seriously.

I begin my analysis below with a section on qawwalis I think of as "classic" iterations of the genre in Hindi cinema. I discuss key aural and visual features of classic cinematic qawwalis, and the ways in which they depart from their sacred counterparts. As my subsequent close readings demonstrate, many features I identify here persist in contemporary iterations of the genre, while others undergo substantial change. To illustrate how classic qawwalis staged "loving publics" in line with Nehruvian ideals, I offer close readings of the climactic qawwali from *Barsaat Ki Raat* (*Rainy Night*, dir. P. L. Santoshi, 1960), as well as two later qawwalis, from *Amar Akbar Anthony* (dir. Manmohan Desai, 1977) and *The Burning Train* (dir. B. R. Chopra, 1980). The effusive and utopian collectivity staged in these sequences touched a chord with audiences, whose own passionate engagements with radio and the Hindi film song between the 1950s and 1970s forged bonds across social lines. With the re-sounding of public culture in the postliberalization period, audiences' listening practices changed as profoundly as did the form of the qawwali. My comparative analysis of Nusrat Fateh Ali Khan's "Afreen Afreen" music video and Rahat Fateh Ali Khan's reprise of that song on *Coke Studio* reveals how the senior qawwal's experiments transformed the genre for music television, and how the contemporary genre of Sufipop builds on, and extends, the musical, social, and political sensibilities of the 1990s. Juxtaposing Sufipop with the dargah qawwalis that A. R. Rahman composed for films like *Delhi-6* (dir. Rakeysh Omprakash Mehra, 2009), *Rockstar* (dir. Imtiaz Ali, 2011), and *Jodhaa Akbar* (dir. Ashutosh Gowariker, 2008), I read the de-Islamicization of Sufipop and the resacralization of the qawwali in Rahman's oeuvre as parallel responses in an era dominated by Islamophobic Hindutva ideals. In the final section of this chapter, I ruminate on what happens to listening—and the listening publics of classic and dargah qawwalis—when the genre becomes an item number. In the curious Indipop dance number "Q Funk," I find signs of what was to come in item number–esque qawwalis: the prioritization of dancing over listening, a self-conscious citational style that depoliticizes the Islamicate, and the rewriting of the gender and sexual politics of the genre.

## Qawwalis' Classic Features

The qawwali is a genre emblematic of the Islamicate in Bombay cinema. From the 1940s through the 1960s, cinematic qawwalis were primarily used in Muslim socials and historicals, Hindi film genres set in an Islamicate milieu.[30] The qawwalis in *Barsaat Ki Raat* (1960), *Chaudhvin Ka Chand* (*Full Moon*, dir. M. Sadiq, 1960), and *Mughal-e-Azam* (dir. K. Asif, 1960) are among the most iconic examples of the genre. As we move away from the 1960s, however, qawwalis begin to appear more frequently in non-Islamicate contexts. Masala films of the late 1970s and early 1980s feature qawwalis as wedding and party entertainment; some songs take place in the villain's den with a *tawaif* (courtesan) or a qawwali troupe performing for the brotherhood. In these later films, there is often little that is Islamicate other than the choice of musical genre and the look of the performers, who don "Muslim-style attire . . . [and gesticulate] in traditional shrine-qawwali style."[31] Irfan Zuberi and Natalie Sarrazin argue that from the 1970s onward, "devotion and zeal are re-packaged in rockstar-like movements" in the qawwali, so much so that by the turn of the millennium, the genre is disconnected "from its original roots, traditional decorum, or values."[32] While this is true to some extent, I want to carefully distinguish between Hindi cinema's classic qawwalis and more recent iterations of the genre. As diverse as they are, classic qawwalis, featured in Hindi films from the 1940s to 1980s, are similar in the way they link sonic and visual markers of the Islamicate to romance and a secular listening public.

Cinematic qawwalis replicate several key musical features of the sacred genre. Qawwali performances in Sufi *dargahs* are usually led by one or two primary qawwals accompanied by a male chorus. Jayson Beaster-Jones outlines the genre's key musical features thus: "Qawwals have distinctive voices with a very wide vocal range and, in particularly intense moments, will hold long notes at a high pitch and improvise a rapid vocal melisma (sequence of notes). The accompanying ensemble claps the beat along with the instrumentalists and contributes its collective voice in responsorial singing, especially in moments when singing/chanting a particularly powerful line of poetry that is repeated indefinitely."[33] Cinematic qawwalis approximate these musical conventions and division of labor. The repetitive nature and rhythmic intensity of qawwali make it well suited to Hindi film songs, as does its reliance on poetic tropes that enmesh the worldly and the sacred. Like artistic genres in the *bhakti* tradition, qawwalis use poetic lyrics in Urdu, Farsi, classical Hindi, and Punjabi, and speak in allegorical terms of the devotee's union with the divine.[34] The poetic text is all important in *sama'* gatherings: "musical features may enhance, but may never obscure" the lyrics.[35] Thus, for instance, the drumming and clapping are meant to support *zikr*, the chanting of god's name. In cinematic qawwalis, such rhythmic repetition is used not to remember the divine so much as to create musical hooks; the distinctive clapping also marks the film song as a qawwali.

Despite these musical and poetic overlaps, cinematic qawwalis sound quite different than traditional qawwali performances. Not only do film qawwalis feature women (often in competition with men), the men's vocal style is "more akin to crooning rather than a chest-based voice production."[36] A chest-based voice is often described as *khuli awaaz* (open voice) or *buland awaaz* (high, bright voice), and it is one that distinguishes professional qawwals from playback singers.[37] As I discuss below, it was not until the 2000s that this distinctive Sufi voice entered the sonic field of cinematic qawwalis (and Sufipop), albeit in a limited way. For much of qawwali's life in twentieth-century Bombay cinema, the genre was associated with playback singers Mohammed Rafi and Manna Dey, whose styles, while distinct in their own right, were nothing like the *buland* sound of hereditary performers like the Sabri Brothers and Nusrat Fateh Ali Khan.[38]

Most classic qawwalis are picturized not on ritual singers associated with a *dargah*, but on the hero or heroine engaged in love. The singer's love interest may be a fellow qawwal trading poetic verses on stage or one of the assembled guests. The lyrical porosity of earthly and divine love is visualized via reference to two South Asian modes of visuality: *nazar* and *drishti*. *Nazar* (lit. glance) is a paradigm that emphasizes the power of fleeting glances to both wound and thrill (lovesick) individuals. The concept, which derives from Persianate court culture, has shaped the vocabulary and conventions of Urdu poetry and, by extension, Hindi film songs.[39] A mere glance at the titles of film

Figure 2.1. Anarkali (Madhubala) singing the qawwali "Teri Mehfil Mein," *Mughal-e-Azam* (dir. K. Asif, 1960).

qawwalis from the 1960s confirms their investment in the poetics and politics of sight: see, for example, "Sharmake Yeh Kyon Sab Pardanashin," *Chaudhvin Ka Chand* (1960); "Nigah-e-naaz Ke Maaron Ka Haal Kya Hoga" and "Jee Chahtha Hai Choomloon Teri Nazar ko Mein," *Barsaat Ki Raat* (1960); "Ishqwalon Pe Zamane Ki Nazar" (The World's Eyes Are on Lovers), *Mulzim* (*The Accused*, dir. N. A. Ansari, 1963); and "Milte Hi Nazar Tumse" (As Soon as Our Eyes Met), *Ustadon Ke Ustad* (*Master of Masters*, dir. Brij Sadanah, 1963).[40] Lyrical references to eyes, sight, and *parda* (veiling) are amplified through an elaborate gestural vocabulary and cinematographic conventions that highlight the frisson of seeing one's beloved. As in other romantic film songs, close-ups and shot-reverse shot sequences depict the "play of gazes" between the lovers on stage and in the audience (see figure 2.1). Accompanying musical cues stress the intensity and transformative potential of sight, especially when it is forbidden or circumscribed.[41]

A second visual paradigm enshrined in Bombay cinema derives from Hindu religious contexts more than Islamicate ones: *drishti*, the gaze mobilized in the ocular exchange between deity and devotee. To seek a god's *dar-shan* is not only to behold the iconic idol on display but also to be *seen by* the divine. Such "mutual looking [is] . . . both reciprocal and intersubjective."[42] That is, it constitutes and links all entities involved. This visual dynamic was incorporated into Indian cinema from early on. For example, in D. G. Phal-ke's mythologicals, "deity and consort [were] depicted in an iconic mode, frontally and centered and, if depicted alive, they often [were] surrounded by attendants."[43] Alternating point-of-view shots from both the deity's and sup-plicants' perspectives emphasized the reciprocal nature of the exchanges.[44]

This iconic, frontal aesthetic is readily apparent in the staging of clas-sic qawwalis as public performances. In qawwalis as diverse as "Teri Mehfil Mein" (In Your Gathering), *Mughal-e-Azam* (1960); "Nigahein Milane Ko Jee Chahtha Hai" (I Yearn to Lock Eyes), *Dil Hi To Hai* (*It Is the Heart After All*, dir. P. L. Santoshi and C. L. Rawal, 1963); and "Parda Hai Parda," *Amar Akbar Anthony* (1977), the venue is established as a theatrical space with a raised stage or an intimate *mehfil* (salon). As I elaborate below, the relation-ship between singers and audience is articulated through response shots of listeners. The direction of the singers' gazes and the "horizontal" camera movement—alternating medium shots of the performers and tracking shots that travel back and forth between the qawwali parties and the appreciative audience—render this a scene of romantic and aesthetic pleasure. Thus, even as they draw on religious tropes, cinematic qawwalis gesture to, and extend, the secularization of the genre that has occurred in South Asia over time, through the proliferation of qawwali concerts, *mehfils*, and competitions.[45]

## Collectivity and Listening

The association of the classic qawwali with romance might suggest that it is a coupling device, like Hindi cinema's romantic duets. While the qawwali does serve such a function, the genre is, in fact, a fundamentally public and collective form. It is a group performance that, in its sacred iterations, attempts to lead those gathered to a heightened spiritual state. In its more secular iterations in mid-twentieth-century Hindi cinema, the qawwali is a performative and aesthetic experience that features collaborative music-making and listening.

Whether onscreen or off, a qawwali isn't a qawwali without a crowd. There are *always* multiple singers and listeners present; qawwalis are never sung as solo pieces or duets. The qawwali party typically includes a few distinct lead voices and a chorus that claps the beat and echoes key words, phrases, and lines. Many classic qawwalis amplify this multilayered structure by staging a back-and-forth between two groups of singers. However, even in qawwalis that do not involve competing parties, the music inevitably situates individuals in relation to others. Most cinematic qawwalis open with a sparse sound: a solo voice delivers the first lyrical line or an *alaap* with little to no musical accompaniment. This is how songs as diverse as "Sharmake Yeh Kyon Sab Paradanashin," "Pal Do Pal Ka Saath Hamara" (Our Time Together Is Brief) (*The Burning Train* [1980]), and "Arziyan" (Requests) (*Delhi-6* [2009]) begin. Alternatively, some cinematic qawwalis open with the central melody on the harmonium, percussive clapping, and tabla or *dhol* (drum) beats, and then go on to introduce the solo vocal line. All the qawwalis in *Barsaat Ki Raat* begin in this manner, as do "Jeena To Hai Usika" (Life Is His) in *Adhikar* (*Right*, dir. S. M. Sagar, 1971) and "Hum Kisise Kum Naheen" (We Are as Good as the Best of Them) of the eponymous 1977 film. In each of these examples, a plain beginning gives way to a fuller, more lush sound as other instruments and voices enter. The stark musical contrast not only points up the sound of the collective, it also embeds individual voices in that collective.

Backup singers are crucial to sustaining this sense of a supportive multitude in qawwalis. In other types of film songs, the lead voice and the chorus alternate lines or verses, with the former delivering the more personal or distinctive lines and the chorus the refrain.[46] Shikha Jhingan argues that this use of choral singing developed in the late 1940s and 1950s in the context of the consolidation of the playback system (discussed in chapter 1 of this book). As the voice of the collective, the chorus underscored the distinctiveness of playback star's voice, even as it evoked the social domain against which that vocal expression of selfhood strained.[47] But where other song types use the chorus as a social "backdrop," qawwalis grant it much greater aural and visual presence. Backup singers bolster the lead qawwals' performance with their clapping and vocal emphases *throughout* the song, not just in choral stanzas. If at times they sing along with the leaders, at other moments, they interject to echo the lead singers' words or complete their lines. Seated behind and around the primary qawwals, they are often in the same visual frame as their leaders. Thus, the qawwali ensemble envelops and anchors the soloists such that it is impossible to divorce either the individual or the romantic couple from the group. Whereas romantic duets situate the lovers as a sovereign unit, classic qawwalis affirm their coupling with a musical posse that embraces and echoes their every move.

Figure 2.2. View from the audience perspective of Akbar (Rishi Kapoor) and his qawwali party onstage singing "Parda Hai Parda," *Amar Akbar Anthony* (dir. Manmohan Desai, 1977).

If the qawwali party is one representation of the broader social world, the diegetic audience is another manifestation thereof. The collective and public nature of the genre—and the publicness of the romance staged in classic qawwalis—is amply evident in the way qawwali audiences are picturized. Unlike most romantic duets, Hindi cinema's classic qawwalis tend to be set not in empty or remote locales, but in public spaces designated for artistic performances. Whether the venue is a formal theater or a more intimate *mehfil*, the singers sit on a raised stage or platform and face row on row of guests (see figure 2.2). Frontal and tracking shots establish the spatial relationship between the singers on the dais and the audience. Thus, even when the qawwali seems addressed to a single beloved, there is *always* a larger group listening in and responding. Like the backup singers onstage, the diegetic audience is active and engaged. Those assembled sway to the music. They smile and nod in appreciation. At times, they interject with an appreciative *wah wah!* and even join in the singing. By the end of many a performance, the audience is on its feet, cheering and applauding. In short, classic qawwalis presume and gather an eager listening public.

The collectivity engendered by classic qawwalis is connected to the fan culture surrounding radio and Hindi film music. As Vebhuti Duggal has eloquently argued, the Hindi film song was, for decades, entwined with collective and public listening formations.[48] This was especially true between the 1950s and 1970s. Duggal's respondents describe gathering at neighborhood chai and *paan* shops on a weekly or nightly basis to listen to songs on the radio: "the practice of listening together generated a quotidian and public intimacy, one that was shared with friends and strangers."[49] Occurring in the public company of others, this was an intersubjective aural experience, rather than a solitary or individuating mode of listening.[50] That fans' affective investment was not just a private matter is also apparent in their spirited participation in radio listeners' clubs and the rich print culture around film songs, which included listeners' club magazines, compendiums, song booklets, and fan letters, particularly those with *pharmaishes* (listener requests).[51] Radio stations across the subcontinent received thousands on thousands of letters and postcards each week with film-song requests. Listeners waited eagerly for their names to be read on air, alongside the name of their hometown and their favorite song. The *pharmaish* enabled individual listeners and listeners' clubs located far outside metropolitan centers to place themselves in a vast "sonic-geographic imaginary" of lovers of cinema/radio/the Hindi film song.[52]

In each of the genres and listening formations discussed above, listening is a public and participatory activity. Theorizing listening as an intersubjective and public endeavor, Kate Lacey reminds us that while "audience" has come to describe any group to whom a given text or address is directed, the word's etymology grounds collectivity in the act of audition.[53] It is not just that "audience" describes a group of listeners, but that "listening . . . forms hearers into a group, a true audience."[54] Likewise, a "public" only coheres in response to a collective address. To attend to that address—to listen to what others say, write, or think (or sing!)—is to be a member of that public.[55] In recasting audiences as listening publics, Lacey restores the centrality of soundwork to group formation. She also challenges the association of listening and audiences with passivity. This idea that listening is an active process also lies at the core of traditional qawwali performances. As Charles Hirschkind puts it, *sama'* "is not a spontaneous and passive receptivity but a particular kind of action itself, a listening that is a doing."[56] In the classic qawwali sequences described above, too, listening is no passive or one-way encounter, where those assembled "merely" receive what is offered to them from the qawwals on stage.[57] Listening is instead depicted as a reciprocal affective exchange that fosters social (if not spiritual) connection. That is, classic qawwalis do not simply feature collective listening: the very act of listening binds audience members to one another and to the singer. Those present are interpellated not just as individual addressees but as a part of a "community of listeners," as active and engaged as that which gathered around radio and the Hindi film song.[58]

But, what sort of aural community is this exactly that the classic qawwali convenes on screen? Who is assumed to be part of it, and who is invited in? What work does it perform vis-à-vis the Islamicate or the nation? In what ways is this listening public about more than Islamicate culture? How, or to what extent, are these qawwalis paradigmatic of an ideal public? I answer these questions through an analysis of three classic qawwalis, "Na To Caravan Ki Talaash Hai," "Parda Hai Parda," and "Pal Do Pal Ka Saath Hamara." These examples illustrate how the classic qawwali conjures a loving public aligned with Nehruvian secularism, setting the stage for my ensuing discussion of the genre's postliberalization travels.

## Ishq Ishq! Romance in Classic Qawwalis

### The Call to Love

To understand the classic qawwali's conceptualization of listening and romance, let us consider a quintessential example of the genre: "Na To Caravan Ki Talaash Hai" (I'm Not in Search of a Caravan) from *Barsaat Ki Raat* (1960). This qawwali—which is sometimes referenced by its oft-repeated refrain, "Yeh Ishq, Ishq Hai" ("This is love, love")—is staged as a competition between two qawwali parties at the Ajmer Sharif Dargah, the famed resting place of the Sufi mystic Moinuddin Chisthi.[59] Unlike with the dargah qawwalis I discuss later in this chapter, the mise-en-scène does little to place the performance in that hallowed shrine. Instead, as with previous contests in the film, the setting is secularized. Mubarak Ali's (S. K. Prem) team is composed of his daughters, Shama (Shyama) and Shabab (Ratna); Chand Khan (Khurshid Bawra), a professional qawwal married to Shabab; and Amaan Hyderabadi (Bharat Bhooshan), a poet-singer who joins the others on stage when the lovesick Shama is unable to proceed.[60] Aptly, Shama's sickness stems from having learned that her desire for Amaan is unrequited, and that he loves Shabnam (Madhubala). For their part, Amaan and Shabnam are kept apart by her father, police commissioner Khan Bahadur (K. N. Singh), who considers the penniless poet a poor match for his daughter. These overlapping conflicts come to a head in the film's climactic qawwali, "Na To Caravan." Amaan, the film's hero, is assigned the voice of playback star Mohammed Rafi. The qawwal he must best, Daulat Khan, sings in Manna Dey's voice (accompanied by S. D. Batish). Shama and Shabab's parts, meanwhile, are sung by Asha Bhosle and Sudha Malhotra, respectively.[61] With this stellar cast of playback singers, music by Roshan, and lyrics by Sahir Ludhianvi, "Na To Caravan" stands as a veritable master class in the Sufi conception of love.

The qawwali begins with the two competing parties singing of the all-consuming and self-destructive power of love.[62] Love is the perilous attraction of the moth (*parvana*) for the flame of the candle (*shama*). Love is intoxicating. Love is obsession. Love makes one forget everyone and everything but the beloved. In the latter half of the song, as Amaan steps in to help his faltering team, love emerges as a social force as well. A harmonium melody and long solo *alaap* mark Amaan's entry, as well as a thematic and tonal shift in the qawwali lyrics. While the first two couplets are about the pain and destruction wrought by love, the rest of the song lauds love's ability to withstand obstacles. Love is not stopped by social or physical threats. Love transcends borders. Love is free; it is neither Hindu nor Muslim. Love cares little for such religious distinctions, for it is its own faith, its own code of conduct.

As Amaan sings of love's transgressive power, he weaves together references to such classic icons of romance and devotion as Laila and Qays, her *majnoon* (one who is madly in love); Radha and Krishna; Sita; and Meerabai. He also calls up Allah, Gautam (Buddha), Christ, and Moses, equating all of their religious philosophies with love. Stemming from disparate literary and mythological traditions, these references remind us that the history of the qawwali on the subcontinent is one of cultural and religious syncretism. Indeed, such a border-crossing ethos marks the song from the start: the tune of the opening couplet recalls a Punjabi qawwali by the seventeenth-century Sufi poet Bulleh Shah, "Mera Ae Charkha Nau Lakha" (My Spinning Wheel [Life] Is Priceless), famously performed by Nusrat Fateh Ali Khan (on whom more anon). "Na To Caravan" also makes reference to Bulleh Shah's *kafi* "Hindu Nahin Na Musalman" (Neither Hindu nor Muslim).[63] A series of linguistic shifts toward the end amplify Sufism's critique of rigid social boundaries. The lyrics switch rapidly from Urdu to Punjabi to Braj, even quoting a well-known qawwali attributed to the thirteenth-century mystic Amir Khusro Dehlavi, "Bahut Kathin Hain Dagar Panaghat ki" (The Road to the Well/Source [the Path of Love] Is Very Rough).[64] The Hindu folk-mythological *panaghat-lila* (woman waylaid at the well) theme is a particularly salient intertextual reference in "Na To Caravan." The speaker in the qawwali's penultimate stanza is Radha (or a fellow *gopi*), who laments the difficulty of getting water from the well as Krishna bothers her. Even as these lines are a plea for maintaining social decorum and feminine honor, the broader mythological references are to love that breaks social rules.[65]

The call to cross social boundaries—indeed, *ishq* (love) itself—comes in the form of sound. Amaan and his fellow singers draw on several interlinked aural elements (language, lyrics, and music) to dispense of borders in "Na To Caravan." Not only do the qawwals extol the virtues of love aloud and to a packed *mehfil*, Amaan explicitly casts love in sonic terms:

> *Ishq Majnoon ki woh aavaz hai jiske aage koi Laila kisi deewaar se roki na gayi,*
> Love is that voice of Majnoon that prompted Laila to ignore all barriers
>
> . . .
>
> *Jab jab Krishna ki bansi baaji, nikali Radha saj ke*
> *Jaan ajaan ka dhyaan bhulaa ke, lok laaj ko taj ke*
> Whenever Krishna's flute sounded, Radha emerged adorned
> Forgetting all that she knew and all sense of social propriety or honor.[66]

In these lines, both Laila and Radha respond to the *sound* of their lovers—to Majnoon's voice and Krishna's music. At the very moment that Amaan sings of Radha being drawn by Krishna's flute playing, Shabnam arrives at the scene of the qawwali. She is beckoned by her lover's voice, broadcast over All India Radio (AIR) Ajmer. Whereas Shabnam was previously unable to escape her father's strict supervision, *hearing* the live broadcast of Amaan's qawwali prompts her to listen to her heart.

Radio is entwined with Amaan and Shabnam's romance from the start. Shabnam's first inkling that the poet she adores is attracted to her comes in "Zindagi Bhar Nahi Bhulegi" (I Will Never Forget), which she hears him sing on AIR Hyderabad. Already a fan of Amaan's poetry, she now swoons in recognition of his lyrical description of their encounter the previous evening, the fateful *barsaat ki raat* (rainy night) of the film's title. AIR is also where Amaan finds employment when they elope to Indore, and it is his unmistakable voice on the radio that helps her father and friend identify their whereabouts. When Amaan begins singing in "Na To Caravan," the camera zooms out from a medium shot of him and his fellow singers on stage, before zooming in to a close-up of the radio. The next cut takes us to Shabnam as she recognizes Amaan's voice on air. Subsequent shots of the radio console and of Shabnam's reaction to the Laila-Majnoon line establish just how crucial the radio is to the film's denouement. The device makes the couple's forbidden romance public in a new way. Shortly after Shabnam leaves in search of Amaan's voice, her father notices her absence and smashes the radio.

It is not just the angry patriarch who would take the radio to be a vehicle of romance. Citing films like *Barsaat Ki Raat* and *Mr. and Mrs. 55* (dir. Guru Dutt, 1955), Kumkum Sangari writes that in the postindependence years, "the radio itself became an aural sign of viraha [the pain of separation]: a medium for emphasising and overcoming separation as in the filmic motif of couples joined through the agency of a song broadcast on radio."[67] Fans of Hindi film music would also recognize their own relationship to Bombay cinema and its songs in filmic representations of radio. Referring to the song that first makes a couple of Amaan and Shabnam, "Zindagi Bhar Nahi Bhulegi," Aarti Wani notes:

> The picturization of this song, the girl with the radio in a room, the voice floating in and its high erotic charge plays with the memory of the romantic meeting and touches on what is possibly experienced by many a fan of film music. The pivotal role of the radio in mediating the spaces of the studio and the bedroom as it effects the transport of sound through air replicates as it underscores the spatial economy of the Hindi film song itself.[68]

The same may be said of the radio in "Na To Caravan." It connects disparate spaces, transporting Shabnam—figuratively at first, then literally—to the scene of Amaan's qawwali performance.[69] I explore the connections between the passionate listening formations of cinema/radio/the Hindi film song and qawwalis in more detail below. For now, suffice it to say that while not all films link love, listening, and the radio as powerfully as *Barsaat Ki Raat* does, the structure of feeling of its climactic qawwali (*ishq ishq!*) suffuses the genre and, indeed, permeates Hindi cinema of the 1950s and early 1960s.[70]

## Coupling Romance and the Collective

To note the centrality of love in cinematic qawwalis of this period is not to claim that they are merely Islamicate love songs. From the earliest days of sound cinema in India, romantic duets functioned as "instrument[s] of couple-formation."[71] They cleared a sovereign space for the couple, keeping out (if momentarily) the narrative forces that threatened to block the lovers' union. While classic qawwalis are akin to romantic duets in that they are philosophical paeans to romance, they do not isolate the couple in this manner. Instead, they call up an ideal collective in which to situate transgressive romantic relationships. Recall Amaan's references to Laila-Majnoon, Radha-Krishna, and other iconic lovers in "Na To Caravan." This intertextual strategy is one that Kumkum Sangari identifies as far back as medieval romances. In those stories as in the *Barsaat Ki Raat* qawwali, love is described via reference to legendary couples, conjuring a veritable "community" of lovers: "if love is an act of elective affinity, then these acts of connection [are] analogues or synonyms of love." This intertextuality evinces not just a transhistorical conception of love but "the self-affiliating consciousness of lovers."[72] If, as Sangita Gopal argues, intimacy was the purview of the romantic duet in 1930s cinema, qawwalis of the mid- to late twentieth century imagined such intimacy unfolding in the company of others.[73] In coupling romance and the collective, classic qawwalis rendered both love and listening as public endeavors.

That romance is a social and public affair is especially evident in cinematic qawwalis staged as contests. Regula Burckhardt Qureshi writes that improvisational competitions (*muqabilas*) were popular in 1940s Bombay, particularly in Muslim neighborhoods.[74] As was the case in these live performances, qawwali *muqabilas* in film include two parties, each with a leader or two and a chorus, and the song follows a dialogic (or call-and-response) format. However, unlike the live *muqabilas* Qureshi references, cinematic qawwalis tend to have one group composed of men and one of women. Each couplet offered is an improvisational challenge to the other group. The witty back-and-forth turns the performance into a playful "battle of the sexes."[75] Many classic qawwalis draw performance elements from the *mujra* to stage a seduction or competition over a shared love interest, as is the case with the *Mughal-e-Azam* qawwali "Teri Mehfil Mein."[76] Still other screen qawwalis present a gentle mocking of heterosexual romantic conventions. Think, for instance, of *Chaudhvin Ka Chand*'s "Sharmake Yeh Kyon Sab Pardanashin" (Why Do These Veiled Women [Hide in Shyness]), where two groups of women mimic a conversation between men and women on the question of veiling, aware that there is a man spying on their festivities. Gendered play is also front and center in "Chali Chali Kaisi Hawa Yeh" (What a Breeze This Is That Blows) from *Bluff Master* (dir. Manmohan Desai, 1963), which has the hero, Ashok (Shammi Kapoor), in drag, dueling with his love interest,

Seema (Saira Bano). No matter their tone or the work they perform for the plot, classic qawwalis function as heterosexual courtship rituals in public. As such, they make audible and visible the gendered norms that make romantic coupling possible.

All three qawwalis in *Barsaat Ki Raat* are gendered contests. The first, "Nigah-e-naaz Ke Maaron Ka Haal Kya Hoga" (What Will Happen to Those Struck by Our Gaze?), ends in the victory of Chand Khan's team. The sisters Shama and Shabab manage to defeat him in the rematch that is "Jee Chahta Hai Choomloon Teri Nazar Ko Main" (My Heart Desires to Kiss Your Gaze). Along the way, Shabab and Chand Khan fall for each other and are soon married. Thus, the two qawwalis situate romance firmly in the public arena, just as "Na To Caravan" does. The sequences that precede and follow "Nigah-e-naaz" and "Jee Chahta Hai" also draw attention to the performance economy of qawwali *muqabilas*: each team in the film is sponsored by a rich businessman and hires lyricists for the contest. Thus, while the staged performances of qawwalis facilitate romance, those connections only happen in the midst of a broader community of artists and patrons.

Crucially, the community that the classic qawwali fosters is not simply a setting for romance, but is constituted by the very conventions used to represent romance in Bombay cinema. In particular, classic qawwalis leverage the poetics of sight to depict both the lovers and the audience. As noted above, visual, performative, and lyrical references to *nazar*, *drishti*, and *parda* suffuse these staged performances of courtship. In the rest of this section, I analyze "Parda Hai Parda" and "Pal Do Pal Ka Saath Hamara" to elucidate how these conventions of onscreen desire help flesh out the loving relationship between singers and the public. These songs cast collective listening as the means to achieving a secular and syncretic community. They demonstrate that as late as 1980, the Nehruvian ideal persisted in the listening public of classic qawwalis.

*Amar Akbar Anthony*'s (1977) "Parda Hai Parda" (These Veils [between Us]) is as famous a film qawwali as "Na To Caravan," albeit far less serious in tone (see video 2.1 https://doi.org/10.3998/mpub.11713921.comp.2). A quintessential 1970s masala film, *Amar Akbar Anthony* follows three brothers, separated in childhood and raised in different faiths, as they reconstitute their family unit. They must not only find one another and their parents, but also court their wives-to-be. The youngest brother, Akbar Illahabadi (Rishi Kapoor), is a professional qawwal, and "Parda Hai Parda" is one of his many public attempts to woo Salma (Neetu Singh).[77] As the title and refrain indi-

cate, the song revolves around Akbar's desire to remove the barriers—both
visual and social—between him and his beloved, who is seated in the front
row beside her disapproving father. Following convention, Akbar does not
refer to her by name, opting instead for generic descriptors like *pardanashin*
(the veiled one) and *husnvale* (the beautiful one), which veil her identity and
give his pleas wider resonance. Multicolored scarves and *dupattas*, a mirror,
a rose, a bottle of alcohol, and a lit matchstick serve as props as he spins
metaphor after classic Islamicate metaphor about love. Akbar's performance
is rendered via Hindi cinema's classic frontal aesthetic. Over and over, he
directs his gaze at Salma and enacts the unveiling he sings of through his gestures. Close-ups of Salma's bashful and pleased expressions are intercut with
those of Akbar, confirming that she reciprocates his feelings. Akbar's lyrical
pleas have their intended effect: thwarted at first by her father, Salma unveils
herself and walks up to the stage to place her hand on her lover's lips. This
metaphorical kiss brings the audience to its feet, and the qawwali ends with
much collective cheering and singing.

"Parda Hai Parda" is an illustrative example of how the combined seman-
tic power of *nazar* and *drishti* fosters romance in classic qawwalis. But note
how the song deploys cinematic techniques and tropes of desire to mark not
just couplehood but broader affective bonds as well. Throughout his performance, Akbar is oriented toward the camera and the audience. The estab-
lishing shot of the entire venue and alternating low- and high-angle shots,
from the audience's and Akbar's perspective, respectively, locate the qawwali
party on stage—at a higher position than those gathered for the show. This
shot composition and sequencing are very similar to those used in scenes of
devotees seeking *darshan*.[78] Akbar's frontal orientation and frequent direct
gaze into the camera render the audience *as a whole* as the addressee. His
gestures invite not just Salma and his backup singers but all those present to
engage in the musical conversation. Point-of-view shots from the audience
perspective, meanwhile, confirm its rapt attention on Akbar. Eyeline matches
and zooms visualize not just the object of the singer's and audience's gaze, but
the *bond* between them. Further, it is not just Salma who responds to Akbar's
overtures; other women seated beside her also attempt to raise their veils.
Akbar's brother Anthony joins in the clapping and singing, and is soon followed by the rest of the audience. Thus, in "Parda Hai Parda" as in other qawwalis of its ilk, the appreciative audience and the qawwals are bound together
in love. The singer is no distant god, but a dear artist who courts the audience
through song. While the qawwal sings of longing, what is (also) rendered
visible and audible is *belonging*.

"Pal Do Pal Ka Saath Hamara" (Our Time Together Is Brief) from *The Burning Train* (1980) goes a step further by dissolving the border between performers (backup singers) and the listening public. While this song does not use the language of *nazar* and *parda* to the extent that prior qawwalis do, it nonetheless mobilizes the intersensorial aesthetics of sight in its representation of the public. The "burning train" of the film's title is an express train that is sabotaged on its inaugural journey by a jealous railway engineer. As the train hurtles toward disaster, the unwitting passengers engage in an impromptu qawwali performance, turning the narrow compartment into a *mehfil*.[79] Ravi (Jeetendra) begins his song and dance in the aisle, with his fellow singers seated on either side. The *mujrewali* Ramkali (Asha Sachdev) and the men and women in her qawwali troupe are distinguished by their colorful Islamicate stage outfits and the fact that they stay seated for the duration of the song. That is, their appearance and performance match those of their counterparts on stage in other classic qawwalis. The passengers on the train constitute the diegetic audience for "Pal Do Pal." Standing by their seats and spilling into the aisle, they occupy the background of the frame and surround the singers. The spatial and sartorial distinction between the backup singers and audience means little in terms of musical labor, though, as everyone present claps the beat in unison and sings the refrains. The audience is thus an extension of the qawwali troupe, creating one big musical community. Like other classic qawwalis, "Pal Do Pal" maintains a frontal orientation, with the camera tracking up and down the aisle as it follows the movements and gaze of the primary singers: Ravi; his love interest, Madhu (Neetu Singh); and Ramkali. The camera also makes note of various couples—some young and some middle-aged, some married and some not—as the partners exchange meaningful looks or sing to each other. Unlike the *Barsaat Ki Raat* and *Amar Akbar Anthony* qawwalis discussed above, there is little that is specifically Islamicate about this song situation. The passengers' varied attire and mannerisms suggest a great diversity of age, faith, profession, and stature. The qawwali is the tie that binds. It makes singers and listeners of all the passengers, forging them into a doting public and a microcosm of India.

## Loving Publics—or the Public as a Lover Who Listens

In bringing a feminist ear to three classic qawwalis, I have argued that the romance of classic qawwalis binds more than just the lead lovers. Love is public. Lovers are in public, and the beloved is the public. Listening is public. The public is a lover who listens.

Classic qawwalis' public-as-a-lover-who-listens formulation makes perfect sense if we attend to the intermedial—particularly, *interaural*—formations that shape listening in South Asia. Let us tune in once more to Vebhuti Duggal, who reminds us that the participatory audience culture exemplified by the radio *pharmaish* has deep roots in the subcontinent. Audience members at *kavi sammellans* or *mushairas* (poetry symposia and gatherings) and classical music concerts routinely request artists to perform their favorite pieces. When fulfilling the *pharmaish*, the artist might name the requestor or dedicate the performance to that individual. The *pharmaish* is thus a "sign of mutual [and public] recognition . . . between the audience and the performer."[80] Duggal observes that in many a film-song *pharmaish* and in the print culture associated with it, this affective investment was expressed in the idiom of love. Sometimes, this love took the form of friendship, with both the radio and the listener imagined as friends.[81] At other times, this love was more clearly tinged with desire and longing: the film song was the beloved and the listener the *deewana* (besotted). Radio announcers used terms like *deewanapan*, *deewangi* (obsession), and *junoon* (craze) to describe listeners' relationship to film songs, as did listeners themselves.[82] The announcers' language also conveyed their deep affection (familial, if not romantic) and respect for listeners. For instance, the star radio compere Ameen Sayani always opened his broadcasts thus: "Behenon aur bhaiyyon, aap ki khidmat mein Ameen Sayani ka adaab" (Sisters and brothers, at your service is Ameen Sayani, offering greetings). Likewise, he always closed with some variation of "Agle saptah phir milenge, tab tak ke liye apne dost Ameen Sayani ko ijaazat dijiye, namaskar, shubhratri, shabba khair" (We will meet next week; until then, allow your friend Ameen Sayani to bid you goodbye. Greetings and good night). With his intimate vocal style, Sayani presented himself as a knowledgeable friend, ever responsive to his audience's desires and requests.[83]

The listening formation described above suggests that the intimacy that radio famously fosters hooks into a much longer affective history in South Asia, one that has strong Islamicate resonances. In numerous literary, musical, and spiritual traditions on the subcontinent, we encounter the figure of a lover pleading for recognition by their beloved.[84] Drawing on this familiar affective trope, the *pharmaish* writer/listener cast himself/herself as a supplicant to the radio announcer.[85] Duggal cites one listener, Magadhiya, who borrowed directly from the *Mughal-e-Azam* qawwali "Teri Mehfil Mein" to say: "Mana ki farmaish bachpana barbad karti hai, Magar yeh kam hai ki duniya yaad karti hai" (Admittedly, requests ruin childhood, but is it not enough that we will be remembered by the world?).[86] Replacing *mohabbat* (love) with *pharmaish* in Anarkali's final couplet, the listener expressed a desire to be remembered for love—love of film song, but also perhaps love of radio, a particular radio show, an announcer's voice, one's name and place on radio, and so forth. No matter the object of affection, this is a love as intense and sublime as the court dancer Anarkali's for the crown prince Salim.

Tongue in cheek as this fan's declaration may seem, it clarifies the structure of feeling that permeates the classic qawwali as well as various overlapping listening formations of mid- to late twentieth-century India. Let's call this structure of feeling *ishq, mohabbat, pyaar* (love, in so many words).[87] Or "ishq ishq! ishq ishq!" as the qawwals in *Barsaat Ki Raat* intone, over and over—approximately 150 times, by Aarti Wani's reckoning—in the film's final qawwali.[88] Kumkum Sangari explains that love and its associated thematic *viraha* (pain in separation) fit the Nehruvian zeitgeist for several reasons. In the 1940s and 1950s, *viraha* "picked up and rephrased the pain of Partition, and came to be reinflected as a nationalist sign, because it gave a renewed agency to passion and suffering."[89] Friendship and romance also became symbols of the "national-secular," for they were each "elective affinit[ies] that insistently, even if briefly or casually lifted the barriers of caste, class, religion, region, and nation."[90] In a context in which relationships, families, and communities had been torn asunder, the episteme of love embodied the traumatic past as well as the aspirations of the newly formed nation-state.

Hindi film and film music occupied a somewhat contradictory position vis-à-vis this nationalist investment in romance. On the one hand, Bombay cinema's passionate love stories and songs, and the intermedial practices of listening to film music and/on the radio sustained the collective love affair with *ishq*. On the other, these films and songs were fraught signs of national culture. The substantial scholarship on nation in Hindi cinema has established how films of the postindependence period engaged with the Nehruvian project.[91] And yet, these films were routinely derided as mere flights of fancy or as hodgepodge artifacts that distracted from the serious work of nation-building. Hindi film songs famously met the opprobrium of B. V. Keskar, director of the Ministry of Information and Broadcasting, who banned musical genres deemed unworthy of a national audience. Keskar conceived of radio as a state apparatus responsible for turning the "masses" into good citizen-listeners: "AIR's primary task . . . was to train listeners to unlearn their bad [aural] habits and to ensure they knew how to properly appreciate India's

classical music traditions."[92] Keskar's lament about the decline in listeners'
tastes and classical music evinces a paternalistic and protectionist attitude
toward both. The communalism of his beliefs about the contours of "Indian"
music was in line with other Hindu majoritarian initiatives of the state. For
instance, Keskar's predecessor, Vallabhbhai Patel, eliminated broadcasting in
the hybrid idiom of Hindustani (the lingua franca of Bombay cinema of this
period) and replaced it with separate programs in Hindi and Urdu. Hindi
news bulletins became increasingly Sanskritized under Keskar. In tandem
with this "linguistic partitioning," Keskar's film-music ban attempted to "forge
a Hindu-oriented 'national' soundscape."[93] Listeners' response was to aban-
don AIR and tune in instead to Radio Ceylon for their favorite Hindi film
songs. With their unabashed focus on being in love, these songs "produced
the fantasy of modern individuality itself, one that was free to invent itself in
contradistinction from social norms and the ruling nationalist sentiment."[94]
In listening to Hindi film songs, thus, fans indulged affective investments and
soundwork not easily sanctioned by the state.

The *ishq* that classic qawwalis celebrate, then, is no simple matter. To sing
of *ishq* in the collective mode is to address the nation rather differently than
romantic duets do. What difference does it make that classic qawwalis use
the intersensorial poetics of romance to enunciate not just couplehood, but
a secular, syncretic listening public? First, the transgressions of the couple
make perfect sense when the public itself is cast as lover. What social resistance can there be to romance when those surrounding the love-struck couple are as invested in their desire? Second, the public-as-lover-who-listens
allows us to locate qawwalis as part of much broader interaural listening formations. We recognize the specific Islamicate functions the genre serves on
screen while also noting its embeddedness in, and links to, listening practices
that were far from exclusive to Muslim contexts. Third, given the ubiquity of
romance in discourses of nationalism around the world, the genre's romantic
poetics make its listening public readable as a *national* public.[95] That is, the
classic qawwali lays claim to the nation by imagining the nation *as audience*.[96]
It calls forth an appreciative and supportive community of listeners, bound
together in their shared appreciation of the affect, poetry, and musicality of
the qawwali performance. The interjections of the audience, vocal echoes
of the backup singers, percussive clapping, dialogic musical structure, syncretic history of the genre, and heterodoxic lyrics (particularly on matters
of romance and religion) together generate a polyphonic and utopian space.
Listening to qawwalis becomes a collective, secular, and national endeavor.

Thus, while classic qawwalis typically give voice to the pangs of separation, they simultaneously call into being an ideal aural community. This is a community aligned with the dominant episteme of the postindependence years (romance) as well as its reigning political philosophy (Nehruvian secularism).

Lest we slip into thinking that classic qawwalis simply shore up the nation—how odd, after all, for a Sufi genre to be aligned with the status quo—let us remember that the genre rarely portrays audiences as quiet or disengaged. Its listening public does not fit the postcolonial state's conception of listeners as docile citizens in need of musical education. In both Isabel Huacuja Alonso's and Vebhuti Duggal's scholarship, we encounter listeners acting in ways that upend the state's pedagogical project. For instance, in letters to film magazines, fans complained vociferously about the AIR ban and lauded Hindi film music as "the music of the 'common man,'" effectively turning Keskar's criticism of this "mass" genre on its head.[97] They also switched allegiance to Radio Ceylon for much of the 1950s (and beyond). The nonchalance with which listeners treated national boundaries is also apparent in the fact that AIR's Urdu service, originally conceived as a tool to counter Pakistani propaganda, drew legions of Pakistani listeners.[98] In similar vein, Duggal notes that even as the imaginary of *pharmaish* writers and radio listeners' clubs was enabled by the material infrastructure of the Indian state, it was "mediated by the local, the regional, and the transnational."[99] This delightful history of recalcitrant and boundless listening bolsters Aarti Wani's interpretation of "Na To Caravan" (from *Barsaat Ki Raat*) as being not just a "battle cry" for *ishq*, but a gleeful comment on the failure of the AIR ban on film songs, qawwalis, and other "nonclassical" genres. The state was forced to walk back its controversial position in 1957, just three years before *Barsaat Ki Raat* was released. The central place of the radio and AIR in the film's mise-en-scène and plot, and in "Na To Caravan" in particular, is thus easily read as a "willful teasing, nose-thumbing gesture at the gate keepers of 'national culture.'"[100] An exemplar of classic qawwalis, "Na To Caravan" shows that if on the one hand, the genre's interpellation of a secular listening public is coterminous with that of the Nehruvian state—demographically mixed and appreciative of the syncretic history and philosophical tenets of Sufism—on the other, it diverges sharply from the very same administration's conception of docile citizen-listeners and from the majoritarian "sound standards" AIR sought to enforce.[101] It offers a competing idea of listening and national belonging in the very form that Keskar despised, the Hindi film song. Fast-forward to the contemporary moment, and we find film qawwalis invoking a dramatically different listening public. And yet, as I argue below, millennial soundwork is also aligned with statist and majoritarian notions about culture and community.

## World Music and Postliberalization

While the qawwali did not entirely disappear from Bombay cinema in the 1980s, there were few hit film qawwalis in this decade and the next, making the "return" of the form in the early 2000s all the more dramatic. This comeback is typically linked to the rise of two artists: the renowned qawwal Nusrat Fateh Ali Khan and the music director A. R. Rahman. What is not often noted are the ways in which the Hindi film qawwali was shaped by the processes of technological, industrial, cultural, and ideological change we call "liberalization." The "re-sounding" of everyday life that has been underway since the 1980s and that reached its peak in the 1990s was not just the context and condition of possibility for the shifts in the cinematic qawwali.[102] The change in the form of the qawwali was *itself* part of that re-sounding, and that had important implications for Hindi cinema's conception of listening, collectivity, and the Islamicate. That the return of the qawwali is associated with two individuals is, in some ways, itself a mark of the times. The collective and collaborative ethos of the genre brushed up against the growing emphasis on the individual.

Also notable are the many different forms and directions the cinematic qawwali takes in the twenty-first century. It is as if the genre underwent a process of refraction, for it appears on screen today in the form of Sufipop, dargah qawwalis, and also item number–esque qawwalis. Each of these iterations of the genre differently inflects the configuration of love, listening, and community described in the previous section. The connections between those terms are sundered and reconfigured in substantial ways beginning in the 2000s. Sufipop expresses love and longing, without mooring romance in collectivity. The Islamicate imaginary of the qawwali—and, indeed, of Hindi cinema itself—morphs into more universal form. Dargah qawwalis visualize a masculine faith community but also emphasize individual moments of spiritual revelation. In sacralizing listening thus, dargah qawwalis move closer to more traditional shrine performances, but unlike classic qawwalis, they emphasize the "Islamic" over the Islamicate. Finally, in its most worldly form, the qawwali returns to the romance of classic qawwalis. The item number–

esque qawwali puts listening in the service of dancing, and the Islamicate in the service of the commodity spectacle, thereby rewriting the gender politics of the genre yet again.

In what follows, I describe how Nusrat Fateh Ali Khan's stardom and the sound of his voice came to shape the trajectory of the qawwali in South Asian public culture. I analyze two vastly different versions of his composition "Afreen Afreen," released twenty years apart, to elucidate how we get from the world music star's rhythmic innovations to contemporary Sufipop's individual and irrelational ethos. This section on postliberalization developments also departs from the emphasis on the (Indian) nation and cinema in the first part of this chapter. I demonstrate how the work of artists outside India and those initially on the edges of Hindi cinema made figurable the listening publics we encounter in the cinematic qawwali today.

## Nusrat Fateh Ali Khan's Innovations

The origins of the qawwali's postliberalization shifts lie in the late 1970s and 1980s, when the qawwali moved from shrines and concert halls in South Asia to the world stage. The Sabri Brothers, Ghulam Farid Sabri and Maqbool Ahmed Sabri, were among the first qawwals to receive not only national but international recognition, with their pioneering world tours and musical innovations in the 1970s. While other qawwals had released recordings in years prior, it was only with the circulation of qawwali performances on television that the Sabri Brothers, Aziz Mian, and Nusrat Fateh Ali Khan came to seen as "qawwali stars," with careers and roles independent of religious settings.[103] While all these artists had ardent fans on both sides of the India-Pakistan border, it was Nusrat Fateh Ali Khan's ascendancy on the world music stage in the late 1980s and 1990s that ignited the Sufi vogue still current in Indian media. His success did not just popularize the qawwali and other Sufiana genres; it opened doors for other Pakistani artists, including, most notably, his nephew and acolyte Rahat Fateh Ali Khan, now a leading playback singer in Hindi cinema.

Hailing from a hereditary qawwali family, Nusrat Fateh Ali Khan was well established in Pakistan before he became an international star. He was, and continues to be, widely recognized as having introduced important innovations while maintaining a traditional repertoire and a classically oriented style.[104] Speaking of his rendition of "Man Kunto Maula" (Whoever Accepts Me as Master), Sonia Gaind-Krishnan writes:

Nusrat's version is characterized by an extended introduction on the harmonium, followed by an exploratory alap, which establishes raag Bhupali one note at a time, and utilizes the text in much the way a more classical *khyal bandish* would: by breaking it down into parcels of conjoined phonemes and toying with them in ever more innovative ways. Through [his] vocal calisthenics, this sonic play then segues into the tarana section of the composition, a trance-inducing segment on "dar-a-dil-le"; this is meant to push the listener over the edge, through the disciplined bodily control of daily comportment, toward states of ecstasy.[105]

This description highlights the crucial importance of Hindustani classical music in Nusrat Fateh Ali Khan's style as well as his impressive improvisational skills. Given the "clarity of his tone, particularly in the upper registers," and the unparalleled agility of his voice, his singing centered the *sound* of the qawwali performance more so than the song's textual meanings.[106] This "sonic play" and rhythmic emphasis paved the way for Nusrat Fateh Ali Khan's genre-bending collaborative work with artists far afield from Sufi and South Asian circuits, as well as those in the diaspora.

In 1985, Nusrat Fateh Ali Khan participated in the WOMAD (World of Music, Arts and Dance) traveling world music festival organized by Peter Gabriel and was subsequently signed to the Real World Records label. Western film audiences were introduced to his virtuoso singing through his collaborations with Gabriel on his soundtrack (and 1989 album) for *The Last Temptation of Christ* (dir. Martin Scorsese, 1988), with Gabriel again in *Natural Born Killers* (dir. Oliver Stone, 1994), and with Eddie Vedder in *Dead Man Walking* (dir. Tim Robbins, 1995). Also pivotal was his work with Michael Brook on two experimental albums, *Mustt Mustt* (1990) and *Night Song* (1996), both released by Real World.[107] Nusrat Fateh Ali Khan's "rhythmic improvisational style" gave qawwali a place in "trendy, cosmopolitan, world music culture, whose audiences respond strongly, pulling the music away from its textual base."[108] Thus, even as musical prowess and "authenticity" are valued in the world music arena, the specifically spiritual dimensions of qawwali are eclipsed. The same might be said of *Magic Touch* (1991), an album of Bally Sagoo remixes that included the qawwali maestro singing such classics as "Kinna Sohna" (How Beautiful), "Jhoole Jhoole Lal," and "Mera Piya Ghar Aaya" (My Beloved Has Come Home). Music director A. R. Rahman also collaborated with Nusrat Fateh Ali Khan on the track "Gurus of Peace" on his patriotic album *Vande Mataram* (1997).[109] The popularity of these and subsequent musical experiments "moved [the qawwali] from being a genre characterized by a primarily textual mode of signification to a largely sonic one in diasporic spaces."[110] In India of the 1990s, and early 2000s too, the qawwali was embraced by lay audiences for its sonic—and specifically, rhythmic—qualities, which in turn initiated a host of other transformations in the genre.

### "Afreen Afreen"

Consider the song "Afreen Afreen," a collaboration between Nusrat Fateh Ali Khan and poet and lyricist Javed Akhtar (see video 2.2 https://doi.org/10.3998/mpub.11713921.comp.3). The nonfilm album of which it was a part, *Sangam* (1996), gained the star qawwal even more of a fan following than his prior work in Hindi cinema had. While "Afreen Afreen" may not technically be a qawwali (it is sometimes called a ghazal, sometimes a qawwali), it is closely associated with the latter genre because of Nusrat Fateh Ali Khan's voice.[111] The song has a percussive feel and foregrounds his distinctive style: harmonium, *matkas* (clay pots), and drums establish the catchy rhythm before Nusrat Fateh Ali Khan enters with his hallmark improvisation in *sargam* (solfège). A synthesizer keeps time and underscores his lines throughout the song, in effect taking the place of a qawwali troupe's clapping. The slick music video features a sultry Lisa Ray wandering a desert landscape, in a reprise of her appearances in advertisements for Bombay Dyeing textiles and Garden Vareli saris. A parallel thread shows a man driving around in a jeep, presumably looking for the ravishing young woman. He is thwarted in his search until the closing frames of the music video, when Lisa Ray's character appears as a *banjarin* who tends to him when he faints under the harsh desert sun. Interspersed with this romantic quest are close-ups of Nusrat Fateh Ali Khan singing and a few of Javed Akhtar smiling at the camera. Flashy editing complements the fusion and fashion-shoot aesthetic: extensive use of iris shots, wipes, and fades, as well as intercutting among the music video's various threads, makes it a technological mirage of sorts. This audible and visible use of technology gives the song a hip, cosmopolitan appeal, not unlike the rest of Nusrat Fateh Ali Khan's collaborations and Indipop music videos of the 1990s.

"Afreen Afreen" is also emblematic of the 1990s in its obsession with the body. Lisa Ray's deliberate gestures and seductive gaze into the camera as she poses in the sand and among ruins cast her as an elusive, sexualized object of desire. The lyrical focus of the song is the beauty of the beloved, understood more in earthly than in spiritual terms. Whereas the song's refrain praises the creator directly—"Afreen Afreen" (Praise to the creator/the most beautiful one)—most lines in the first verse begin with the word *jism* (body). The second verse in the music video replicates this structure with the word *aankhein* (eyes).[112] The longer version of the song, which is on the music album and which Nusrat Fateh Ali Khan typically sang in concerts, includes two other verses about the beloved's *chehra* (face) and *zulfein* (long tresses of hair). Although the similes and metaphors are drawn from a familiar repertoire of Islamicate tropes, Lisa Ray's performance in the music video makes it hard to read the song as a spiritual paean. The visuals amplify the carnal connotations of the lyrics.

The desert mise-en-scène and the figure of the *banjarin* also unsettle this song's association with Sufism, both as the spiritual, philosophical practice and as a cinematic marker of the Islamicate. As discussed in chapter 1, the 1990s saw the rise of the "ethnic" voice via the popularity of Ila Arun and her *banjarin* aesthetic. While "Afreen Afreen" refers to *banjaras* and their nomadic lifestyle, it does not include the *banjarin* voice (or any other woman's voice, for that matter). So, even as the visual iconography of the desert and Lisa Ray as *banjarin* add a sense of exotic otherness, their more important effect is to untether Nusrat Fateh Ali Khan's singing from prior representations of the qawwali in Indian public culture. The qawwal is pictured in the *banjaras'* campsite, seated beside a campfire and surrounded by tents, camels, and a few people; this is presumably the same caravan that traverses the arid landscape in other shots. In placing the star singer in the middle of the desert and in a nomadic group's camp, "Afreen Afreen" links his music to the borderlands of India and Pakistan. On the one hand, this geographic placement in the Thar Desert is apt for an album titled "Sangam" (lit. coming together), a cross-border collaboration between an Indian and a Pakistani artist. On the other, it casts the qawwali as more of a "border" genre than it seemed in its filmic manifestations. While classic qawwalis were often used to celebrate love across social boundaries, the genre itself was not represented as being *of* the borderlands. Not only does "Afreen Afreen" locate the qawwali in a new place, it also conjures a new kind of venue for the performance. The *banjaras'* camp is nothing like Sufi *dargahs* and other traditional *sama'* gatherings, or the indoor theaters and *mehfils* in which classic cinematic qawwalis and neighborhood *muqabilas* were set, or the concerts that gained Nusrat Fateh Ali Khan recognition abroad. Floating free of previous historical and spatial markers of the qawwali and the Islamicate, this music video gets attached to two stars: Nusrat Fateh Ali Khan and Lisa Ray.

The song's emphasis on its star artists, and on Nusrat Fateh Ali Khan in particular, pulls away from the collective ethos of the qawwali as a genre. The juxtaposition of Nusrat Fateh Ali Khan's singing with Ray's modeling forces a comparison of his artistry with the embodied beauty he sings of. His musical expertise and stardom (and, to a lesser extent, Javed Akhtar's) are front and center. Where Hindi cinema's classic qawwalis focused on romance and placed the couple in a community, this manifestation of the genre unravels those social bonds. Neither the "couple" wandering the desert nor the two collaborators on the album are anchored in a community. Nusrat Fateh Ali Khan's qawwali party is not pictured at all. Even more remarkably, the backup singers' aural presence is limited to singing the words "Afreen Afreen" a few different ways. Thus, the only community of artists to whom we might link Nusrat Fateh Ali Khan are the *banjaras* on screen. However, the shots of him in the *banjaras'* camp do not clarify whether the singer is a member of that group or whether he is simply performing for the travelers. There is, moreover, no listening public to speak of in this song—the audience at the campsite is not audible at all, nor very visible. The combined effect of these visual and musical strategies is an emphasis on the individual, particularly the star singer and his quest for (aesthetic if not spiritual) perfection.

If "Afreen Afreen" is remembered today as a Nusrat Fateh Ali Khan song, it is not just because of its musical qualities but because of the way it draws on iconography and discourses prominent in the postliberalization period. The song rewrites the representation of the qawwali in Indian public culture by linking the genre to one star singer, rather than a group, and diminishing the role of women. Lisa Ray embodies the aesthetic (and spiritual) perfection that Nusrat Fateh Ali Khan sings of, but her character does not get to sing herself. She briefly appears as a *banjarin* but is not granted an "ethnic" voice or any other vocal role. As I note in chapter 1, Sufi music became an important area of specialization for women singers in subsequent years (think, for instance, of the legendary Abida Parveen). However, in India of the mid-1990s, Sufi music was synonymous with the qawwali, which in turn was synonymous with Nusrat Fateh Ali Khan's name.

## "Afreen Afreen" Redux

Twenty years on, "Afreen Afreen" morphs into a romantic ballad in the 2016 *Coke Studio* remake of the song, rendered by Rahat Fateh Ali Khan and Momina Mustehsan. *Coke Studio* is a wildly popular music show that circulates via YouTube and various television channels. While it has inspired

numerous music shows since it first aired in 2008, including a less successful
iteration on MTV India, *Coke Studio* (Pakistan) remains unparalleled in its
production values and global digital reach. Each season, *Coke Studio* releases
thirty studio recordings that rework songs from various musical traditions;
many performances feature collaborations between artists whose work is
anchored in different performance contexts and genres.[113] As the show's tag-
line, "Sound of the Nation," suggests, the diversity *Coke Studio* showcases is
explicitly linked to its national aspirations. *Coke Studio* inspires a reimagining of Pakistani modernity, casting the populace and its culture as more
diverse than state-sanctioned narratives allow.[114] Its distinctive musical and
visual aesthetic is also in keeping with its corporate sponsor's economic
creed to transcend all boundaries. As befits a South Asian musical series
engaged in border crossings of various sorts, *Coke Studio* affords a special
place to Sufism.[115] Sufi artists, lyrics, and genres have been a constant on the
show over the years, notwithstanding changes in the production team and
approach. This emphasis is in line with the "quasi-national" status that qawwali as a genre has enjoyed in Pakistan from its earliest days as a nation-state
"search[ing] for a musically expressed identity apart from India."[116] Rahat
Fateh Ali Khan and qawwals Fareed Ayaz and Abu Muhammad are often
featured on *Coke Studio*, as are singers of Sufiana *kalaam* (poetic verses)
such as Abida Parveen and Sanam Marvi. Thus, the "unplugged" version
of "Afreen Afreen" (season 9, episode 2) is just one of *Coke Studio*'s many
Sufi experiments. Despite some mixed reviews, the recording quickly went
viral. It now tops the "Best of Coke Studio" list, having garnered a record 316
million views on the show's YouTube channel as of December 2020 (only a
fraction of those mine).[117]

Rahat Fateh Ali Khan and Momina Mustehsan's acoustic cover is virtually unrecognizable as a qawwali (see video 2.3 https://doi.org/10.3998/mpub
.11713921.comp.4). Whereas some of Rahat Fateh Ali Khan's other *Coke Studio* performances are more devotional in form, style, and spirit—think, for
instance, of "Rang" with the late Amjad Sabri (son of Ghulam Farid Sabri)
or "Chaap Tilak" with Abida Parveen—this version, arranged by singer and
producer Faakhir Mehmood, has a more pop feel. The song is slowed down to
showcase its "poetic and soothing sensibilities."[118] Rhythm is de-emphasized
in favor of developing the melodic line. In sharp contrast to the Nusrat Fateh
Ali Khan version, this "Afreen Afreen" opens with acoustic guitars and key-
board, and the improvisatory *sargam* is moved to the very end of the song.
Close-ups of the musicians and their instruments focus attention on the mel-

ody, which in turn encourages a far more romantic interpretation of the lyrics than the 1996 music video does. This version changes the lyrical structure as well. Rahat Fateh Ali Khan's first lines are drawn from the first *antara* (verse) of the original rather than its *mukhda* (opening refrain). His second verse, focusing on the beloved's *chehra* (face), comes from the longer version of the song, rather than the music video. The verses praising the beloved's *aankhein* (eyes) and *zulfein* (tresses) are omitted altogether. Instead, Momina Mustehsan sings an entirely new verse, penned by F. K. Khalish for this *Coke Studio* recording. The new lines help "transfor[m] the tone of the song, distancing it from a Sufi's allegorical exposition on the love of God, and making it more of a conversation between human lovers."[119]

The inclusion of a woman's voice in the *Coke Studio* version hearkens back to the romance of Hindi cinema's classic qawwalis. And yet, this song very much centers the star singer and celebrates *his* individual genius. This is Rahat Fateh Ali Khan's version through and through, just as the first "Afreen Afreen" was indelibly marked as his uncle's song. For much of the performance, the accompanists and backup singers provide what may best be described as a vocal and acoustic "wash," against which Rahat Fateh Ali Khan's voice stands out. As was the case with the older version, there is neither clapping nor a true polyphony of voices. The role of the three backup singers is limited to humming and soft melismatic vocalizing in between the star singer's verses. Thus, even as this "Afreen Afreen" is a romantic duet, it elevates the "maestro" over his "debutant" colleague.[120] Notably, Rahat Fateh Ali Khan only uses his *buland* (high, bright) qawwali voice on occasion, to emphasize particular words or lines. The song's soaring, minute-long finale has him improvising in the style of his uncle; he delivers most of his other lines in the soft, crooning style of (contemporary) Hindi film songs. Moving thus between two vastly different "vocal dispositions," Rahat Fateh Ali Khan showcases his moorings in the realm of traditional qawwali as well as his ability to cross over into Bollywood, where he reigns as a playback singer.[121] His vocal travels embody the "stylistic mediation" that is at work both in this performance and in Nusrat Fateh Ali Khan's version and that is also fundamental to *Coke Studio*'s aesthetic.[122] Meanwhile, Momina Mustehsan performs the supportive feminine role, with her "laid-back effortless velvety vocals" joining in toward the middle of the song. She also accompanies the backup singers in the chorus that follows her verse. That is to say, she is not set apart from the supporting vocal crew in the way that Rahat Fateh Ali Khan is. While her lyrical part is that of the beloved responding to her awestruck lover, the video

Figure 2.3. Momina Mustehsan looks on as Rahat Fateh Ali Khan sings in the *Coke Studio* version of "Afreen Afreen" (2016).

frames *her* as the awestruck one. The camera captures her looking over at her senior colleague, marveling at his voice just like everyone else in the room (see figure 2.3).

Juxtaposing the two "Afreen Afreens" drives home just how far the qawwali has traveled between 1996 and 2016. From world music to Indipop to Sufipop (the topic of the next section), the genre has been associated with, and influenced by, several developments in postliberalization South Asian soundwork. Its visual form has changed as much as its aural one, as the music industry has expanded to encompass different media. Its gendered composition and associations have also shifted in its travels from the *dargah* to the stage to screens of all kinds (television, film, and digital platforms). All these developments bear on the shape of the cinematic qawwali. Nusrat Fateh Ali Khan and Rahat Fateh Ali Khan had (and have) one foot in the traditional realm of the qawwali and another in the pop cultural one. Befittingly, in this chapter, their "Afreen Afreens" bridge different moments in the re-sounding of the qawwali. I contextualize below the popularity of the *Coke Studio* "Afreen Afreen" through a discussion of the growing interest in Sufism in the postliberalization period and the new genre of Sufipop. The latter's conception of listening and the Islamicate is a far cry from that of classic qawwalis, but it does connect with other manifestations of the qawwali in Hindi cinema today.

## De-Islamicization and Irrelationality in Sufipop

### Sufi Vogue

The popularity of "Afreen Afreen" and other *Coke Studio* performances is part of a broader "Sufi performing arts vogue" that has swept both India and Pakistan (and the South Asian diaspora) over the past two decades.[123] Nusrat Fateh Ali Khan's and the Sabri Brothers' international success spurred interest not only in the qawwali, but also in solo renditions of Sufiana poetry in various languages and in Sufi rock, a genre inaugurated in the 1990s by the band Junoon. A whole host of singers, with very different musical backgrounds and expertise, have been part of this boom in Sufi music, so much so that Shubha Mudgal (herself a part of this phenomenon) notes wryly, "The fad has become a way to legitimize a new kind of Hindi pop; pop singers just put 'Maula' [Lord] or 'Ali' in and call it Sufi music."[124] The longevity of this cultural phenomenon, however, suggests that it is more than a passing fad. Over the last twenty years, "Sufi" has developed the contours (however amorphous) of a genre, indexing a distinct vocal and visual aesthetic. Singing Sufipop is a more lucrative career choice than ever before, and, as I elaborate below, many a romantic Hindi film song is now imbued with a Sufi ethos.

   Following Peter Manuel, I read the flourishing of all things Sufi in India as being related to the growth of the middle and upper class in the postliberalization period, and to the concomitant rise of Hindutva (Hindu right-wing) politics. Nowhere was the changing economic situation of the nation in the 1990s more apparent than in the media landscape. The influx of private capital and growing consumer demand allowed the music industry to diversify its media offerings like never before. As I discuss in the section on dargah qawwalis below, A. R. Rahman's success as a music director and the Sufi musical markers he popularized are as important to this narrative of economic and musical transformation as Nusrat Fateh Ali Khan's stardom. The market for Sufism has grown substantially since these musicians first came into the public eye. It now includes products and opportunities that extend well beyond music, constituting a broad arena we might call pop Sufism.[125] "Sufi" appears draped in flowing designer outfits and markets itself to an upper-class, English-speaking clientele. Self-help books, voice-training classes, personal transformation workshops, and ritzy music festivals are all part of an ethical, self-fashioning project that aims to free itself of boundaries.[126] That *Coke Stu-*

*dio* has become *the* paradigmatic manifestation of, and platform for, Sufipop is itself a measure of the bourgeoisfication of Sufi musics. Not surprisingly, this boom has had little effect on the lives and livelihood of the qawwals who sing at *dargahs* or Indian Muslims more generally.[127]

A less cynical, but equally salient explanation for the heightened interest in Sufi genres is that it constitutes a liberal cosmopolitan response to the anti-Muslim politics of the Hindu right. As Manuel explains: since the 1990s, "liberal elements of the newly flourishing bourgeoisie have cultivated a fresh interest in and celebration of the syncretism and composite aspects of Indian culture and music; they have also promoted a renewed commitment to secularism (which in the Indian context implies tolerance and religious pluralism rather than opposition to religion)."[128] Following the December 1992 destruction of the Babri Masjid by a Hindutva mob and the ensuing riots, progressive nonprofit groups organized concerts celebrating communal harmony and rejecting sectarianism.[129] The promotion of qawwali and other Sufi genres was a crucial cultural-political strategy then, and it remains so today, given the mainstreaming of Hindutva politics and the growing Islamophobia of the past few decades. In Pakistan, too, Sufism has served a similar musical role: whether for Junoon or *Coke Studio*, to invoke Sufism in music is to announce one's commitment to cultural pluralism and tolerance. Across South Asia, pop cultural manifestations of Sufism exist on a continuum with the more traditional *dargah* scene. Together, these myriad Sufi forms articulate a critique of political extremism and religious orthodoxy in our contemporary moment, just as they did in decades and centuries past.[130]

Arguably, and perhaps ironically, one measure of the affective and discursive power of contemporary pop Sufism is its embrace by Hindutva forces. In recent years, the Narendra Modi government has been touting Sufism as an integral part of Indian culture and history, sponsoring Sufipop stage shows and including such performances in its political events.[131] Famously, Modi was the keynote speaker at the 2016 World Sufi Forum—the same year that Hindu nationalists called for a ban on Pakistani singers (many of whom specialized in Sufi genres) in Bollywood. A Texas-based qawwali troupe, Riyaaz Qawwali, was invited to sing at a function in honor of Modi's visit to the United States in 2019.[132] In "performing pluralism," the Bharatiya Janata Party and its allies seek not so much to lure Muslim voting blocs as to mollify Hindus turned off by more strident Hindutva rhetoric and violence.[133] As is the case with the cinematic dargah qawwalis I discuss later in this chapter, endorsements of Sufism by the Hindu right hail it as a "good," nonviolent sort of Islam.

The Hindu nationalist co-optation is made possible, in part, by the grad-

ual de-Islamicization of pop Sufism. Consider, for instance, the "Sufi" visual
and sartorial aesthetic, which now enjoys an allure not unlike that of the "ethnic" described in chapter 1. This is not an aesthetic grounded in a particular
religion or faith community. It instead signals an elite cosmopolitanism that
can afford to disregard borders. Indeed, Sufipop is increasingly disconnected
from the Islamicate altogether. Neither the Indian nor the Pakistani versions
of *Coke Studio* foreground Islamicate visual markers on set, opting instead for
a trendy, pared-down aesthetic emphasizing musicians, their instruments,
and Coke insignia. In the *Coke Studio* "Afreen Afreen," Rahat Fateh Ali Khan
sports a white suit and brown button-up shirt; none of the other musicians
wear traditional garments either (no *sherwanis*, no *dupattas*, no turbans).
The look of each *Coke Studio* (Pakistan) video tends to be tied to the genres in
play, which explains the broadly cosmopolitan but non-Islamicate treatment
of this pop version of "Afreen Afreen."

The de-Islamicization is also audible in Sufi soundwork, in film and otherwise. Matthew Rahaim explains the waning of aural Islamicate markers thus:

> Pop sufi is largely de-Islamicized by design, voicing a cosmopolitan subject
> rather than a devout Sufi, turned inward, toward a pristine individual self,
> rather than outward, in self-effacing devotion. Poetically, pop sufi sounds res-
> olutely Hindustani and folksy, shorn of the fancy *qofs* and *ghains* that mark
> the lofty Perso-Arabic loan words found in elite qawwali. The voices of pop
> sufi singers are often cultivated in much the same ways as qawwals, including
> both classical training in raga music and the studious adoption of sonorous
> and kinetic dispositions from classic recordings by Nusrat Fateh Ali Khan and
> the Sabri Brothers. However, unlike most shrine and khanqahi [Sufi lodge]
> qawwali, pop *sufi* often features gentle *filmi* crooning, interspersed artfully
> with high, bright *buland* voice.[134]

As Rahaim observes, even as Sufipop invokes some religious concepts and
names—"Maula" and "Ali" are favorites, in Mudgal's estimation—its tropes
and vocabulary are drawn from a more diffuse culture that registers as "Hindustani," rather than specifically Muslim or Islamicate. Knowledge of Urdu,
much less Persian or Arabic, is not required for pronouncing Sufipop lyrics.
The use of a familiar "filmi" vocal style further weakens the genre's link to
Islam in India.[135] This is a variation of Bollywood sonic aesthetics, punctuated
with gestures to Nusrat Fateh Ali Khan and other qawwals' *buland* voice.
Singers like Javed Ali, Javed Bashir, and Kailash Kher use this vocal style in
their cinematic qawwalis as well as more romantic numbers.

In apparent tension with the de-Islamicization of Sufipop is the fact that "Sufi" is sometimes construed as a metonymic of Pakistan. John Caldwell observes that the early 2000s was a time of "timbral turbulence" in men's playback singing in Bombay cinema, just as it was in women's playback.[136] As music directors (and audiences) sought new voices for the new sorts of film songs being composed at the time, Pakistani singers with qawwali and rock backgrounds found their footing in Bollywood. Rahat Fateh Ali Khan, Atif Aslam, Shafqat Amanat Ali Khan, and Adnan Sami came to dominate Hindi playback singing between 2005 and 2016, the year the Hindu right instigated a ban on Pakistani artists.[137] Notwithstanding substantial differences in musical background, timbre, and style, these men were grouped under the notion of a "Pakistani vocal sound."[138] This idea—coupled no doubt with the fabulous success of *Coke Studio* (Pakistan)—soon made "'Sufi' . . . a convenient metonym for Pakistan, even for voices that were decidedly not qawwali-inflected."[139]

Thus we have the de-Islamicization of pop Sufism on the one hand, and the association of Sufi music with Pakistan on the other. We might read these parallel developments against each other, as a tussle between India and Pakistan over a much-loved artistic and spiritual corpus. We might also read them in conjunction with each other, as a double-pronged pushback against the conflation of Sufism with religion (and Islam, in particular) and the heightened othering of Muslims and Pakistanis in recent years. No matter which line of argumentation we choose, what is certain is this: the Islamicate registers very differently in contemporary film soundwork, and in Sufipop more generally, than it did in previous eras. Whereas classic film qawwalis also voiced the transgressive and all-encompassing power of love, they did so by retaining their strong associations with the Islamicate. The genre sounded out the Islamicate heart of Hindi cinema, just as "Urdu, Awadh, and the Tawaif" did.[140] Love, listening, and (national) community were articulated in Islamicate terms. In the diffuse domain of pop Sufism and in contemporary Hindi cinema, these concepts are voiced, heard, and experienced rather differently.

## Singing Free

For one, pop Sufism places emphasis on the individual rather than the collective. For singers and listeners alike, Sufipop is an ontological promise embodied in sound. The self it represents and reaches for is "free, open, unhindered by boundaries."[141] Note that classic qawwalis such as *Barsaat Ki Raat*'s "Na To Caravan" also champion the dismantling of social boundaries. But, where those songs were fundamentally engaged with the social domain—the genre's staging of love was collective and public in nature—Sufipop turns inward. It is one of many "ways of voice [that] are founded in *irrelational* practices: turning away from, negating, or blocking normative forms of social relation."[142] While a Sufipop performance may be staged in front of an audience, the singer is not typically oriented toward the public. Those assembled are not the addressees. Instead, the artist sings for herself and, at times, to the divine. This "irrelational" disposition is visualized through a variety of performative and technological choices, including: "sensitive microphones and multitrack mixes that foreground the independent lead voice, staging and costuming that places the body of the artiste front and center, cameras and lighting that foreground their face (typically in an expressive attitude of searching or yearning), and eyes (typically closed in introspection or directed toward the distance, rather than attending to any particular listener)."[143] At first blush, this description of the Sufipop artist on screen is reminiscent of Lata Mangeshkar's stage performances in the 1970s and 1980s. Seeking to clear a space for herself within the existing social order, Mangeshkar projected a "contained," respectable femininity that refused the probing gaze of the public. By contrast, the Sufipop singer's disengagement with the audience is a rejection of the social. It enacts a radical individualism that, in theory, cares little for gender, sexuality, caste, or other social structures. It turns instead to "a radically different Listener."[144]

The (human) listener, too, understands that the performance is not an interactive relationship or a conversation in which she is involved. Instead, the fan listens to and "savors the artist's expressions of the artist's own feelings, the artist's own personal realization."[145] Unlike other performance contexts and genres, where singers and listeners are bound to each other in a "circuit" or feedback loop of sorts, the Sufipop singer is pointedly *not* attuned to the audience while singing.[146] Audience members may well be moved by her performance, but they are not a *part* of it. They are not bound to the singer in the way they were in Bombay cinema's classic qawwalis or as they are in a live *mahfil-e-sama*.[147] If there is a relationship that emerges over the course of the song, it is one that connects the music and the listener (including the singer herself). Eyes shut, immersed in the music and the affective intensity it inspires, the Sufipop artist "blur[s] the traditional relational dyad of a listener in *wajd* [ecstasy] and a qawwal."[148] On the one hand, this mode of singing and listening embodies a yearning for something beyond the self; on the other, it represents a doubling down on (or into) the self. Either way, the performance does not bring into being a collective or even a dyadic relationship between singer and listener, as Kate Lacey's notion of "listening out" suggests. It makes fans of listeners, but it does not foster communal feeling (in either sense of the word "communal," religious or collective).

Counterintuitive as it may seem, it is precisely this irrelationality of Sufi-pop that makes stars of individual singers. Recall the central position of Nus-rat Fateh Ali Khan and Rahat Fateh Ali Khan in their respective versions of "Afreen Afreen."[149] Recall the lack of emphasis on the qawwali troupe—the diminished sound of collective vocalizing and clapping—in both versions of the song. Even as Rahat Fateh Ali Khan is surrounded by an adoring crew of accompanists and singers, he is clearly the most important figure on the *Coke Studio* set. Recall, moreover, that neither "Afreen Afreen" features an engaged listening public of the sort found in classic qawwalis. It is as if these star sing-ers require no one but themselves, nothing but their talent to sing as well and as powerfully as they do. Their music is understood as springing from deep within themselves. While the two star qawwals' hereditary training, vocal prowess, and innovative musicking place them in a league of their own, other Sufipop artists are also construed in similar ways. Accomplishment in Sufi-pop comes not just from musical proficiency, but from the sense of authen-ticity, self-discovery, and uninhibited freedom conveyed in performance.

The conceit of individual brilliance and self-expression is one that Sufipop shares with a host of global popular musics that have found a home in South Asia, including rock, jazz, and, most recently, Indipop. Peter Kvetko argues that in 1990s India, the "ideology of Romantic self-expression" was mar-shaled by Indipop musicians and producers to distinguish the budding genre from the hegemonic Hindi film music, which was seen as overly commer-cial and formulaic.[150] Indipop videos and album covers featured the singer prominently—this was a sharp departure from the historical "invisibility" of playback singers. Tight close-ups, direct gazes into the camera, and a casual, intimate style created the impression that the artists' music was unique to them, and that they sought a genuine connection with their audiences.[151] While this personal relationship to the consumer is quite different from the irrelational disposition of Sufipop, both genres (like much else in Indian pub-lic culture today) are marked by a move away from a collective ethos.

The emphasis on the individual shaped not just the rhetoric and imagery of Indipop, but its sound as well. The very experience of listening to music was reconfigured as private: "sonic textures created in computer-based recording studios, often using acoustic guitars, crooning vocals, and a warm timbral mix, were evocative of an intimate and personal relationship between a consumer and his or her media."[152] Sound is understood here as evoking a particular sort of listening relationship. That is, it is not just that Indipop introduced new voices and textures into public culture. Nor it is simply that the genre was associated with new sorts of recording practices and spaces; more youthful, more middle- and upper-class Anglicized audiences; and more privatized technologies of consumption. Rather, the new sonic textures assumed, and elicited, a different sort of relationship between the listener and the music. They articulated anew audiences' embodied understanding and experience of themselves as citizen-consumers. This new "sonic sensibility" was nothing short of a reimagining of the individual's place in the world, a reframing of the relationship between self and other, between the individual and the collective.[153]

Building as it does on the musical and cultural shifts of the postliberalization years, Sufipop accentuates this focus on the individual. It makes listening even more private an experience than Indipop did, fostering a vocal disposition that puts distance between the singer and listener. Startling as it may seem, the irrelationality of Sufipop makes it a postliberalization (and millennial) genre par excellence. In fact, each of the overlapping genres I describe in the second half of this chapter—Indipop, Sufipop, dargah qawwalis, and item number–esque qawwalis—is shaped by the cultural politics of the 1990s, albeit to different degrees and in different ways. An interaural analytic clarifies the ground these musical forms share, how they cite and influence one another, and where they part ways. It demonstrates, furthermore, that these various forms of the qawwali not only brush against the genre's traditional emphasis on the collective but also put pressure on the utopian notions of community implicit in sound studies concepts such as "listening out" and "listening publics."

In its prior cinematic iterations, the qawwali articulated a sense of collectivity and belonging. Some of Hindi cinema's more recent qawwalis— composed by A. R. Rahman—do depict scenes of piety and communal prayer; however, their emphasis tends to be on an individual's spiritual journey and revelation. Here, as in Sufipop, listening binds one to god more than to other humans. Importantly, all the singing in these dargah qawwalis is done by men. This intersection of gender and religion inflects the representation of both listening and the Islamicate in troubling ways. In the following section, I describe key elements of A. R. Rahman's Sufi musical aesthetic and then analyze three of his famous dargah qawwalis—"Arziyan," "Kun Faya Kun," and "Khwaja Mere Khwaja"—to demonstrate how they construct their paradigmatic listener and his relationship to others.

## Pious Listening in Dargah Qawwalis

### A. R. Rahman's Sufi Soundwork

A. R. Rahman is the figure most responsible for the "return" of the qawwali to Hindi cinema in the first decade of this millennium. A Chennai-based music director who was not conversant in Hindi, Rahman was long considered an outsider to Bombay, the home of both the Hindi film and Indipop industries. That Rahman's breakthrough film was *Roja* (dir. Mani Ratnam, 1992), a Tamil film that was dubbed into Hindi and other languages, cemented his association with the "South." However, as Peter Kvetko observes, Rahman's "approach to composition and, more importantly, sonic design had much in common with his non-film peers at Magnasound in the 1990s."[154] Like his contemporaries in the Indipop realm, Rahman departed from the "old Bollywood" sound by cultivating a studio-based digital practice that allowed for more diverse vocal timbres, more textured instrumentation, and a much wider representation of the sound spectrum.[155] This is music crafted for a different listening experience than was previously possible: "audiences can now hear (and feel) the movement of the bass and low drums on the new sound systems that became available after economic liberalization."[156]

That Rahman's sonic aesthetic emerged from the same zeitgeist as Indipop is also evident in its individual and personal orientation. Whereas Indipop and Sufipop cast the singer as the creative agent, Rahman's pathbreaking work elevated the role of the music director (see chapter 1). From early in his career, he cultivated an "individual-centered" practice: eschewing huge orchestras and recording halls, he worked with a couple musicians at a time in his small home studio. His reliance on digital technologies "not only allowed sound to be manipulated one instrument at a time, but also one note at a time—a piecemeal approach that increased musical precision, intimacy, and nuance."[157] Rahman's songs bear his distinct stylistic imprint; some of them—his qawwalis and other Sufi-inflected compositions—are even understood to express his spiritual beliefs. When Rahman first catapulted to fame, his piety and the story of his family's conversion to Sufism were frequent topics of conversation in the media. That his religiosity would shape his music was, and is, taken as a given. I will return to the presumed connection between music and religion shortly. Here, I want to underscore the ways in which Rahman's oeuvre and approach are individual centered, for this characteristic sits in tension with the collective nature of the genre he is credited with reintroducing to Bombay cinema. Just as Nusrat Fateh Ali Khan was seen as a singularly brilliant qawwal, so too is A. R. Rahman regarded as a virtuoso who has single-handedly revitalized the cinematic qawwali. Such discourses of stardom help turn the genre into a less collective and more masculine form than it used to be in older Hindi films.

Sonic gestures to Sufism abound in Rahman's film compositions. Several of Rahman's early romantic hits have a palpable Sufi ethos. Think, for instance, of "Ishq Bina" (Without Love) from *Taal* (*Rhythm*, dir. Subhash Ghai, 1999), "Kehna Hi Kya" (What Can I Say) from *Bombay* (dir. Mani Ratnam, 1995), and "Chaiyya Chaiyya" (Shake It) from *Dil Se* (*From the Heart*, dir. Mani Ratnam, 1998).[158] In these and other songs, the qawwali is audible in the rhythmic clapping, chanting, and intermittent high-pitched passages in male voices reminiscent of Nusrat Fateh Ali Khan's style.[159] Typically, Rahman himself sings these passages—a choice that bolsters the notion that these songs are expressions of his personal faith. His lone voice expresses a sincerity and devotion that sound rooted in his personal relationship to Sufism. Once considered Rahman's musical signature, such plaintive vocalizing is now integral to all Sufipop:

> The characteristic vocal technique of pop sufi is not so much the sound of a qawwali party singing in unison, or in elaborate call-and-response, or the enunciation of esoteric poetry for elite listeners, but a single voice ringing out high and alone, free of any strophic or metrical boundaries. Nearly every blockbuster Bollywood film now has at least one moment of pop sufi spiritual revelation, featuring the high, lonesome sound of a single voice near the top of its range, shrouded in reverb, crying out wordlessly on a pure ā.[160]

Matthew Rahaim's description above underscores the irrelational vocal disposition that Sufipop demands. Even as this solo voice calls up the high-pitched and bright *buland* voice of expert qawwals (Nusrat Fateh Ali Khan, in particular), it eschews the collective thrust of the qawwali. It yearns for a love that is "free" of musical and social boundaries.

In Rahman's dargah qawwalis, this voice does not signal such an absolute

turn away from the social domain. Rather, it sounds out an affective orientation to the divine that is practiced in the company of other men. In qawwalis
such as "Piya Haji Ali" (Beloved Haji Ali) from *Fiza* (dir. Khalid Mohammed,
2000), "Al Maddath Maula" (Help Me, Lord) from *Mangal Pandey* (dir. Ketan
Mehta, 2005), "Khwaja Mere Khwaja" (My Lord) from *Jodhaa Akbar* (2008),
and "Kun Faya Kun" ([He Said] Be and It Is) from *Rockstar* (2011), Rahman's
distinctive vocal presence registers as the voice of a believer and, specifically,
as his voice. In some dargah qawwalis, this is true in a literal sense as well—
much of what we hear *is* A. R. Rahman's voice, even as the song is picturized
on multiple actors. Digital tools allow for the layering of vocal and instrumental tracks such that a single vocalist's work can produce the effect of a
chorus. "Khwaja Mere Khwaja," for instance, includes *just* A. R. Rahman's
voice (see video 2.4 https://doi.org/10.3998/mpub.11713921.comp.5). "Arziyan" (Requests) appears to be composed entirely of Javed Ali's and Kailash
Kher's voices. Whether they use a single voice or a few, dargah qawwalis do
not call up a secular community of listeners in the way that classic qawwalis
did, but they do not completely turn away from the collective in the manner
of Sufipop either.

## Sacred Settings

Whereas qawwalis of yesteryear were mainly secular romantic duets, more
recent films return the genre to its sacred setting—hence my term "dargah"
(shrine) qawwalis. These new qawwalis arise from very different song situations, and their ethos is different than that of their predecessors. They
are still used to articulate a syncretic ideal, featuring in films that are about
Hindu-Muslim unity (and/or Indian-Pakistani unity), such as *Veer-Zaara*
(dir. Yash Chopra, 2004), *Mangal Pandey* (2005), and *Bajrangi Bhaijaan*
(*Brother Bajrangi*, dir. Kabir Khan, 2015). But, where the emphasis in classic
qawwalis was on romance and Islamicate culture, now the emphasis is on
faith and Muslim devotional practices. The lyrics become more overtly religious, with references to Muslim and Sufi teachers, terms, and places, such
as Nizamuddin Auliya, Maula, Khwaja, and Haji Ali. Put simply, dargah
qawwalis value the "Islamic" over the "Islamicate"—religion over culture.
This admittedly reductionist formulation nonetheless captures a tangible
difference between the qawwalis of *Barsaat Ki Raat* (1960), *Amar Akbar
Anthony* (1977), and *The Burning Train* (1980) and those of *Fiza* (2000),
*Delhi-6* (2009), and *Rockstar* (2011). Cinematic qawwalis have long floated

free of the genre of the Muslim social—since at least the 1970s, these songs have not been limited to Islamicate milieus and genres. This makes the dargah qawwali's mooring in spaces of Muslim prayer particularly striking. The shift enacts a de-aestheticization and a resacralization of the Islamicate, a delinking of the genre from some performance contexts (theaters, *mehfils*) and a relinking to others (shrines, mosques).

The centrality of religious devotion is apparent not just in aural references—recall, in particular, the solo voice that reaches for the heavens—but also in the mise-en-scène and camerawork. In songs as diverse as "Aaya Tere Dar Par" (Arrived at Your Doorstep) from *Veer-Zaara* (2004), "Arziyan" (Requests) from *Delhi-6* (2009), and "Bhar Do Jholi" (Fill My Bag) from *Bajrangi Bhaijaan* (2015), we see that the performance space has shifted from the theater or *mehfil* (the site of classic qawwalis) to a more hallowed locale.[161] We typically get a roving camera that cranes high up to reveal the contours and scale of the *dargah* or mosque in which the song is set. This camerawork matches the soaring voice, as if reaching beyond earthly borders and diegetic spaces. It is a visual and spatial articulation of an "ethical soundscape" that ties believers to a transcendental presence, one that exceeds the bounds not only of the song sequence and the filmic narrative, but of worldly existence itself.[162] This is all very different than the flat, frontal aesthetic of the older, staged performances in Hindi films. Here, the monumentality of Islamicate architecture and the space of communal worship take precedence over the relationship between the qawwal and the diegetic audience.

Take, for example, "Arziyan," which is ostensibly set in Jama Masjid, an iconic mosque in Delhi. The song opens with a thirty-eight-second-long high-angle shot looking down at row on row of people performing *namaz*. It then cuts to a close-up of a devotee's face and hands as he prays. More shots of the grand exterior and unnamed men communing and praying alongside one another follow. Finally, a minute into the song, the camera lands on our hero, Roshan (Abhishek Bachchan), a diasporic Indian exploring his family's roots. A good tourist, Roshan watches respectfully as others engage in ritual practice. He listens to and records the qawwali troupe singing at the mosque. (The leaders sing in the voices of Javed Ali and Kailash Kher, artists known for their Sufiana timbre and style.) As is often the case with dargah qawwalis, "Arziyan" is a montage sequence, covering shifts in time and space, and drawing attention to the character's evolving consciousness. Images of Roshan's friends and family members, some of them engaged in Hindu rituals, flash across the scene as the singers intone the lines "More piya ghar aaya, Maula mere Maula" (My beloved has come home, O master). The structure of the sequence thus shifts attention away from the qawwali performance to the devotion of the protagonist and his family.

*Rockstar*'s "Kun Faya Kun" likewise uses the opening montage of the song to depict the struggles of the hero, JJ/Jordan (Ranbir Kapoor), up until the time he joins the community of the faithful at the Nizamuddin Dargah (see video 2.5 https://doi.org/10.3998/mpub.11713921.comp.6). His journey within the *dargah* is articulated in stages, as he goes from being unhomed and seeking refuge in the shrine, to being a curious observer of the rituals and qawwali performance, to being an engaged audience member, to participating as a musician and believer, and finally to experiencing *sama'* of sorts. The montage of Jordan gradually becoming an ideal listener enacts a key lesson of Sufi mystics, which is that approaching the act of listening with an open heart, the right moral disposition, moves one closer to god. In this framework, listening is an ethical, affective, and bodily performance.[163] The upward gestures and eye movements of the singers and audience in "Kun Faya Kun" indicate that this is a homosocial appeal to god. Tuning oneself to the divine entails, quite literally, *turning* oneself to the heavens. This performance is starkly different from the lateral exchange of glances (from the men's group to the women's group and back) in classic qawwalis. Halfway into the song, we witness a moment of spiritual enlightenment. The camera moves rapidly from a long shot of Jordan singing with the qawwali party to a low-angle medium shot that centers him, eyes closed, lost in the song.[164] As his voice (delivered by Mohit Chauhan) and movements get more intense, the camera moves back again and cranes up swiftly to give us a high-angle view, as if god were looking down on him. The shots that follow repeat this vertical structure, accentuating visually the relationship between the qawwal and his divine interlocutor (see figures 2.4 and 2.5). The camera dwells on his face to show his astonishment at the spiritual realization this music has brought him.

*Jodhaa Akbar*'s "Khwaja Mere Khwaja" does something similar. This qawwali is staged for the emperor Akbar and his wife, Jodhaa (Hrithik Roshan and Aishwarya Rai), and their respective retinues (see video 2.4 https://doi.org/10.3998/mpub.11713921.comp.5). While the song employs a frontal aesthetic that recalls classic qawwalis, it does so to draw attention to the whirling dervishes' religiosity. There are relatively few shots of the imperial audience. The singers' closed eyes as well as their upward gestures and glances indicate that they are addressing not their patron so much as god. A sequence of alternating low-angle and high-angle shots form the climax of the performance,

Figure 2.4. Jordan (Ranbir Kapoor) experiencing a spiritual moment during "Kun Faya Kun," *Rockstar* (dir. Imtiaz Ali, 2011).

Figure 2.5. God's-eye view of the dargah qawwali "Kun Faya Kun," *Rockstar* (dir. Imtiaz Ali, 2011).

indicating a connection between the men and god. As the dervishes rise and start rotating in place, Akbar closes his eyes and tilts his head up; a flash of light in the sky marks the heightened state he reaches in that moment. He then rises and joins the dervishes' whirling. The intensity of Akbar's spiritual experience is thus compared to Jodhaa's *bhakti*, her devotion to Krishna articulated elsewhere in the film.[165]

The songs discussed above evoke a cinematic experience of *sama'* while simultaneously narrowing the qawwali's listening public. They visualize the practice of listening to mystical songs in a sacred space and in fellow believers' company. In each case, the performance takes place in a public setting. However, the act of listening is rendered an intensely personal experience. While the hero experiences a spiritual awakening when among other men of faith, his connection to the divine is not a function of his interactions with them. These qawwalis dispense with the call-and-response structure of the genre; they do not enact a musical "dialogue" between two groups of singers. Instead, both singing and listening are oriented toward the divine. Thus, dargah qawwalis do away with the close link between listening and collectivity—in particular, the national community—that was an important feature of cinematic qawwalis but a few decades ago. There are fewer women present, and we tend not to hear vocal interjections from the diegetic audience. The listening public is clearly moved by the performance; we see people clapping and swaying with emotion. However, they don't interrupt with *wah wahs!* as the audience did in classic qawwalis. Listening is public, but not in the way it was in the time of classic qawwalis.

## Masculine Homosociality and the "Good Muslim"

As intimated above, dargah qawwalis rewrite the genre's gender and sexual politics in fundamental ways. Women fade from view, both as singers and as audience members. This erasure is startling given just how instrumental women were in classic qawwalis. In tandem with the diminishing role of the *tawaif* in Hindi cinema, the newly masculinized cinematic qawwalis silence the Muslim woman in song—more precisely, they enact such a silencing on the *cinematic* screen. On television and digital platforms, a number of women have created a name for themselves singing Sufiana music. The most famous of these artists are Abida Parveen and Sanam Marvi, but there are others, too, who make regular appearances on *Coke Studio*. In the world of Hindi playback as well are several vocalists who count Sufi genres among their specialties, including Rekha Bhardwaj, Harshdeep Kaur, Jaspinder Narula, Kavita Seth, and Richa Sharma. Thus, in extrafilmic soundwork, Sufism is powerfully audible in women's voices. It is only in Hindi films—and in qawwalis, in particular—that women are no longer accorded this vocal space. And so, in staging a return to the qawwali's sacred roots, A. R. Rahman's compositions extend the (re-)masculinization of the genre that began as the qawwali became synonymous with Nusrat Fateh Ali Khan in the 1990s.

Intriguingly, in most dargah qawwalis, the hero is not the primary qaw-wal. He is no longer presented as a singer-poet who composes inspired lyrics to woo his beloved. In fact, the addressee is more clearly a divine figure. The hero is part of the internal audience for the song—often because he arrives at the scene of the qawwali performance and stays because he is mesmerized. As the hero finds himself and a group that validates his existence and pain, he is cast as a pious figure. Romance gets elided, and, in the process, Muslim men are shut out of the "national romance" described earlier. What was once a playful, heterosexual romantic interaction becomes a serious, devotional experience that mostly occurs in the company of other men.

There are, of course, cinematic precedents for such prayerful qawwalis. "Sajde Mein Hai Sar" (My Head Is Bowed [in Prayer]) from *Mirza Ghalib* (dir. Sohrab Modi, 1954) and "Maula Saleem Chisthi" from *Garm Hava* (*Scorching Winds*, dir. M. S. Sathyu, 1973) come to mind here. Both qawwalis take a woman's experiences of love as their subject; the lyrics and the picturization focus on her sorrow. So, while these older qawwalis are also set in *dargahs*, they do not cast the genre in the masculine terms that contemporary dargah qawwalis do. "Piya Haji Ali," an A. R. Rahman composition from *Fiza* (dir. Khalid Mohammed, 2000), provides another instructive counterpoint. Set in Bombay's famous Haji Ali Dargah, the song uses the same freewheeling camerawork that other dargah qawwalis do to monumentalize its sacred location. The qawwali is rendered entirely by men: classical maestro Ustad Ghulam Mustafa Khan, his son Ghulam Murtaza Khan, A. R. Rahman, and Srinivas lend their voices for the qawwali party on screen.[166] Most of the song picturization, however, focuses not on the men gathered in the shrine, but on the hero's mother, Nishatbi (Jaya Bachchan); his love interest, Shehnaz (Shabana Raza/Neha Bajpayee); and their wistful memories of their beloved Amaan (Hrithik Roshan). Following Priya Kumar, we might read the physical absence of the hero in this peaceful, syncretic religious venue as part of the film's critique of the broader social context that associates Muslim masculinity with violence and terrorism. Where other dargah qawwalis create a space of masculine homosociality for Muslim men, this song laments the fact that the calmness a space like Haji Ali offers is no longer available to the male lead.[167]

Ira Bhaskar and Richard Allen see the rise of cinematic dargah qawwalis as a positive development, arguing that they undermine the association of Islam with terrorism in popular media, both in India and around the world. They mention the significance that the Haji Ali Dargah takes on in films like *Fiza, Salim Langde Pe Mat Ro* (*Don't Cry for Salim, the Disabled Man,*

dir. Saeed Akhtar Mirza, 1989), and *Mammo* (dir. Shyam Benegal, 1994)
through its "evocation of an Islam different from the one associated with
terrorism."[168] I am less sanguine about these contemporary dargah qawwalis, for their aural and visual rhetoric emphasize three worrying ideas. First,
in these examples, Sufism comes to represent Islam. This tight association
misses the diversity of Sufi traditions and their connections to the various *bhakti*, *sant*, and other artistic and religious movements dear to many
who do not call themselves Muslim. In tying Sufism to Islam (and nothing
besides), dargah qawwalis delink the genre from the vastness and hybridity
of Islamicate culture, which has shaped life in the subcontinent for centuries. This is, in a sense, the opposite of the de-Islamicization we witness
in pop Sufism in the Hindutva era. As my foregoing discussion of the two
"Afreen Afreen" versions demonstrates, nonfilm qawwalis have also been
shorn of their Islamicate associations in the postliberalization period; however, those pop cultural iterations of Sufism do not emphasize religion in
the way that dargah qawwalis do. In casting Sufism as Islam but simultaneously de-emphasizing other Islamicate artistic and literary precedents, dargah qawwalis cannot invoke the secular sense of community and belonging
that classic qawwalis did in the Nehruvian years. Listening in these qawwalis can bring one closer to god, but it cannot conjure a national listening
public in a Hindutva India.

Second, dargah qawwalis render Sufism the "good" kind of Islam: tolerant
and hip, sanctioned by Hindi cinema and by such venerated figures as Nusrat
Fateh Ali Khan and A. R. Rahman. By implication, all other ways of practicing
Islam are cast as "terror," threatening to the majoritarian status quo. My reading dovetails with Peter Manuel's insight that the elite in India has embraced
Sufi performances as a way to push back against the Hindutva-ization of the
public and political sphere. The problem is that such a "good Muslim, bad
Muslim" framing plays right into the hands of Modi and the rest of the Hin-
dutva brigade, as we see from the right's recent embrace of Sufism.[169]

Third, the fact that the qawwali becomes a masculine and homosocial
genre in films of the early 2000s has important implications for the representation of Muslimness and the Islamicate. Benign and tolerant as they appear,
dargah qawwalis animate cinematic representations of the "good" Muslim
man by drawing on entrenched notions of difference and impassioned religiosity associated with Islam the world over. Muslim identity, particularly that
of the hero, becomes about *religion* and not about culture, language, or lit-

erary and artistic sophistication. Muslim religiosity becomes an exceedingly gray and bearded affair. Indeed, listening to dargah qawwalis with a feminist ear makes apparent that Muslim men *and* women are written out of the romance of the nation in Hindi cinema, if in different ways. With a few exceptions such as "Piya Haji Ali," dargah qawwalis all but erase women, in both their picturization and their soundwork. As discussed above, women do specialize in a variety of Sufi genres today, but the qawwali remains out of reach. In parting ways with classic qawwalis and embracing the gendered musical norms of certain traditional contexts (*sama'* gatherings, for example), dargah qawwalis cast Islam itself as a conservative and segregated religion. Thus, a musical genre thought to project an open and secular conception of nation, in fact demonstrates the limits of discourses of national tolerance and religious syncretism in contemporary India.

## Spectacular Dancing in Item Number–esque Qawwalis

I have argued so far that the qawwali as a pop cultural genre undergoes a process of refraction in the postliberalization period. If Sufipop and dargah qawwalis have their roots in the transformations of the 1990s, then so too does the item number–esque qawwali. In this final section of my chapter, I trace the spectacularity, self-referentiality, and rhythmic emphasis of item number–esque qawwalis back to the remix and Indipop boom. The sexualization and commodification of dancing bodies in an Indipop number like "Q Funk" presage the cinematic qawwali's mutation into an even more marketable entity, as apparent in songs like "Kajra Re" and "Tumse Milke." My analysis of two recent send-ups of the classic qawwali—"Senti-wali Mental" from *Shaandaar* (*Grand*, dir. Vikas Bahl, 2015) and the comedy group All India Bakchod's "Creep Qawwali"—demonstrates, in a different way than dargah qawwalis did, that the form can no longer support the secular and syncretic listening public it did in the mid- to late twentieth century.

Sometimes called fusion or rock/pop/techno qawwalis, item number–esque qawwalis accentuate the "trance-dance associations and substitut[e] traditional instrumentation with synthesizers, hyped-up bass, and other sampled sounds."[170] Not surprisingly, these songs and their remixed versions become favorites in clubs. Some use Islamicate iconography and Urdu lyrics aplenty, but dispose of other musical features of the genre. Some are not picturized as item numbers per se, but are clearly crafted to be dance hits. For example: "Tumse Milke" (Having Met You) from *Main Hoon Na* (*I'm Here [Aren't I?]*, dir. Farah Khan, 2004) is an elaborate courtship fantasy, while "Ya Ali" from *Gangster* (dir. Anurag Basu, 2006) is a philosophical dargah sequence that is also the site of violence. "Kajra Re" (Kohl-Rimmed Eyes) from *Bunty Aur Babli* (*Bunty and Babli*, dir. Shaad Ali, 2005) and "Dil Mera Muft Ka" (My Free Heart) from *Agent Vinod* (dir. Sriram Raghavan, 2012) combine the qawwali with a seductive *mujra*. Each of these item number–esque qawwalis reinterprets the genre by merging song-dance conventions in ways that speak to the contemporary moment. What unites this category of qawwali is its foregrounding of rhythm and dancing.

This is, of course, not the first time that the qawwali has been closely associated with dance. As discussed earlier, Nusrat Fateh Ali Khan's world music stardom amplified the rhythmic nature of the genre. His arrival on the Indian music scene coincided with the popularity of Indipop and remix artists, and he capitalized on the "'beat,' 'pop,' and rhythm sensibility" of the 1990s by lending his voice to several experimental and remix albums.[171] Vebhuti Duggal links the heightened cultural interest in rhythm in the postliberalization years to the phenomenon of "jhankaar beats" in the 1980s and early 1990s. This popular practice, which entailed "layering singing voices with a rhythm and beat based track," was a precursor to the Hindi film song remixes that exploded a few years later.[172] The emphasis on rhythm in these genres— particularly, the "techno" sound introduced through the use of synthesizer samples—was taken to be the sign of the modern.[173]

This account of the rise of remix and dance music in the 1990s suggests that the popularity of the qawwali in those years also had to with rhythm. The qawwali's rhythmic and polyphonic thrust appealed to a youth culture tired of Bollywood fare and in search of new voices, styles, and, crucially, more danceable numbers. The layering and looping characteristic of Hindi film remixes were integral to qawwalis as well. Finally, the world music stardom of Nusrat Fateh Ali Khan heightened the appeal of the qawwali and served the Indian music industry well at a time when it was expanding its profile as a "global" Indian industry. In what follows, I analyze an Indipop number called "Q Funk," which gave the qawwali a makeover using rock, pop, and funk idioms. The song not only illustrates the sonic and musical shifts underway in the mid-1990s, it also foreshadows some of the changes to come in item number–esque qawwalis.

## *"Q Funk": The Qawwali Remixed*

"Q Funk" (short for "Qawwali Funk") was composed by brothers Philip and Gerard John (Phil and Jerry) for their Indipop/remix album *Oorja* (Magnasound, 1995). The music video featured a number of Indipop stars of the day—Shweta Shetty, Shaan, Sagarika, Style Bhai, and Babul Supriyo—singing snatches from four classic film qawwalis or qawwali-adjacent songs (see video 2.6 https://doi.org/10.3998/mpub.11713921.comp.7). "Q Funk" begins with the camera tracking upward, tracing the path of falling water, to the sound of synthesized droning and vocalizing. It pans left and around the liquid "screen" (*parda*) to reveal an empty dance floor abutted by a raised platform and three large screens. Dramatic opening chords and a deep, reverberating male voice name rhythm as the core element of the song—"Ladies and Gentlemen, the Rhythm"—and a dancer (an "item boy"?) and drummer appear on cue. In an instant, the space is filled with musicians and dancers, and the band launches into its refrain: "Q Funk is here to stay." The song's hybrid funk-pop-rock musical style, the rapid cutting, and the unsteady, mobile camerawork capture the raucous energy of a club.

That "Q Funk" aims to reimagine Hindi cinema's classic qawwali—and its gender and sexual politics, in particular—is evident from the start. A low-angle shot of a curtain with the words *Purdah hai* (There is a veil) projected onto it introduces Babul Supriyo's rendition of "Parda Hai Parda," the classic qawwali from *Amar Akbar Anthony* (1977, discussed earlier in this chapter). Supriyo looks directly at the camera as he sings the famous *mukhda* (opening refrain), but unlike Akbar, he is courting neither a lover nor a broader "loving" public. Indeed, he and the other Indipop leads in "Q Funk" do not even occupy the same space as the rest of the crowd. They appear on screens hoisted around the dance floor (as do sundry English lyrics). The next two stanzas are taken from the *mukhda* and first *antara* (verse) of "Kajra Mohabbatwala" (Kohl of Love) from *Kismat* (*Fate*, dir. Manmohan Desai, 1968). These verses, sung by Asha Bhosle and Shamshad Begum in the original, are rendered here by Shweta Shetty and Sagarika, respectively. The centrality of these women singers is crucial: it highlights the important presence of women in Indipop as well as in classic film qawwalis. In retrospect, the women's presence also sets into sharp relief the masculinization of the qawwali that was to come in dargah qawwalis. *Kismat*'s "Kajra Mohabbatwala" was sung by women but picturized with both actors, Biswajeet and Babita, in drag. In "Q

Funk," Shweta Shetty sings the *mukhda* of that song—including the man's and
the woman's parts—standing amid garlands of flowers (the strings of flowers
hang vertically, in the manner of Indian wedding decorations, forming a veil
of sorts). Sagarika sings the entire second verse (the man's part in *Kismat*)
but with one crucial change: *jhumka Bareilly-wala* (earring from Bareilly)
becomes *kurta jhaaliwala* (mesh tunic). This alteration makes the address of
"Q Funk" somewhat gender neutral, although the visuals suggest that the sexualized object of affection is the dancer wearing a mesh tunic. This revision
is perhaps also a subtle nod to Muslim masculinity, as working-class Muslim
men in Hindi films are often portrayed in mesh shirts with an undershirt. "Q
Funk" bears virtually no other trace of the Islamicate, reducing it to a handful
of gendered and generic markers.

The selective gestures to, and revision of, classic qawwalis continue in
the final two stanzas of "Q Funk." Sagarika is followed by her brother, Shaan,
singing part of the second verse of "Hum Kisise Kum Naheen" (We Are as
Good as the Best of Them) from the eponymous 1977 film. In Shaan's hands,
playback singer Mohammed Rafi's classic qawwali becomes a declaration of
youthful defiance, not love. Staring into the camera, Shaan paces behind a
wall of fire as he intones his lines, hard-rock style, before switching to an
Indian classical–influenced *alaap*. For the final stanza of "Q Funk," the four
lead singers come together to sing "Tayyab Ali, pyaar ka dushman, hai hai!"
(Tayyab Ali, enemy of love!). This fun song from *Amar Akbar Anthony* (1977)
has Akbar threatening to shame Salma's father if he doesn't approve of their
relationship. Famously, Akbar's backup qawwali party in this song is a group
of *hijras*.[174] Thus, we see how the Indipop qawwali cites classic qawwalis to
signal youth culture and masculinity, even as it pokes fun at the gendered
regime the genre represented in Hindi films of the late 1960s and 1970s.

"Q Funk" draws on the familiar repertoire of gestures, idioms, and song
lyrics of classic qawwalis. However, these fragmented citations do not call up
the listening public of yesteryear—or, arguably, *any* listening public. If there is
an internal audience or a qawwali troupe in "Q Funk," it is the mass of bodies
on the dance floor. The singers maintain a frontal orientation, but their song
is addressed not to a lover (or a loving audience) but to a group that wants
to groove to this new version of the qawwali. The song is also profoundly
de-Islamicized. The classic qawwalis quoted in this song no longer call up
the etiquette and cultured manners of a pre-Partition past or a shared subcontinental Hindustani culture. Instead, the qawwali is reimagined as a club-
friendly, international musical form.

If, at first, it seems that "Q Funk" strays far, far away from Sufism, a close analysis demonstrates that the song in fact *anticipates* some of the changes that were to come in item number–esque qawwalis. No matter their song situation or setting, this type of qawwali articulates a different relationship to gender and Islamicate culture than the other qawwali forms discussed in this chapter. Like classic qawwalis, these sequences are staged scenes of earthly (heterosexual) desire, but they are presented in far more spectacular fashion. More frenzied and elaborately choreographed, they amplify the historical functions of the genre in cinema while giving it the sexual energy of item numbers. The qawwali is no longer a seated affair. Dance and visual choreography come to the fore, even as these new qawwalis maintain the frontal, staged emphasis of classic qawwalis. The lyrics of item number–esque qawwalis may be as evocative as ever, but the subtle turn of phrase and poetry that was a mark of Islamicate genres is no longer key. These are qawwalis to be watched and danced to, not "just" listened to—they move us in other ways.

## Sexual Allures

A paradigmatic example of the item number–esque qawwali is "Kajra Re" (Kohl-Rimmed Eyes), the Shankar-Ehsaan-Loy composition hailed as marking the "reinvention of the qawwali."[175] One of the biggest hits of 2005, the song relied on the star power of Aishwarya Rai (in a cameo performance as a nightclub dancer), Amitabh Bachchan, and Abhishek Bachchan. The mise-en-scène is equally impressive. In a video about the making of the film, art director Sharmishta Roy describes the set she designed for "Kajra Re" as "kitschy . . . with an Old World charm . . . a combination between Indian architecture and a Broadway show."[176] The cinematography and choreography make it difficult to keep our eyes off Rai's character (see video 2.7 https://doi.org/10.3998/mpub.11713921.comp.8). Donning a long skirt and tight *choli* (blouse), she seduces Dashrath Singh (Amitabh Bachchan) with a performance that is part *mujra*, part qawwali. Her sensuous eyes, bare midriff, and *jhatkas* and *matkas* that rival Madhuri Dixit's "enfol[d] old and new configurations of the dancing woman as *tawaif*, Bollywood item girl, and bar dancer."[177] Traversing the length of her body at times, lingering on a specific part at others, the camera constructs her as a desiring and desirous body.[178] As Rai performs her signature dance moves (choreographed here by Vaibhavi Merchant), she and her backup dancers maintain a frontal aesthetic. But whereas classic cinematic qawwalis used frontality, intercutting, and tracking shots to establish the relationship among the dueling qawwals and between the singers and their appreciative audience, item numbers like "Kajra Re" use these very devices to keep us glued to the spectacle of danc- ing bodies. The relationship between the courtesan/bar dancer and her cli- ents in this song—mainly Dashrath Singh—is articulated through alternat- ing close-ups of the stars' eyes. The two Bachchans' characters constitute the second party in this qawwali. Other men remain on the sidelines, in the shadows, except when they serve as the backup qawwali party. That is, when the camera attends to them, it is to show them clapping and dancing behind the two male stars.

Even as "Kajra Re" turns the diegetic audience into a backup troupe of sorts, it diminishes the role of listening. This is an important divergence not just from the traditional qawwali form, but also from its cinematic counter- parts such as "Pal Do Pal" (the classic qawwali set on the train). As discussed above, classic qawwalis emphasized lyrical artistry and the relationship between qawwals and their listeners, be they on- or offstage. Dargah qawwa- lis emphasize the transformative experience of listening to qawwalis in (mas- culinized) spaces of Muslim religiosity. In its contemporary item-number garb, the Hindi film qawwali tends to highlight not listening or praying so much as desirous dancing. The camera no longer dwells on the appreciative diegetic audience. It is as if the spectacularity and star power of these "qawwa- lis on acid"—director and choreographer Farah Khan's term for her qawwali "Tumse Milke"—have made visual consumption and participatory dancing more important than listening.[179] This shift is crucial given the importance of sound in many strands of Islamicate philosophy and practice. Listening is no longer a means of communing with one's beloved, whether earthly or divine. The item number–esque qawwali draws instead on the logic of the commodity spectacle. This is not to say that listening is entirely disconnected from looking, dancing, or any other form of engagement. My point here is simply that the item number–esque qawwali involves the diegetic audience in a very different way than do other cinematic qawwalis. It models and elicits a different sort of attention from viewers and listeners.

Consider the aforementioned "qawwali on acid" from *Main Hoon Na* (2004), "Tumse Milke." The qawwali opens with a swift cut from a college scene of men ogling a woman to their singing a fantastical ode to her. It gives us two sets of dancing stars: Shah Rukh Khan and Sushmita Sen, and a younger couple played by Zayed Khan and Amrita Rao. There is no audi- ence within the song; *everybody* is a performer. In "Dil Mera Muft Ka," the

Kareena Kapoor item number in *Agent Vinod* (2012), the dancers do facilitate listening: they plant a microphone in the flowers they tie to the villain's wrist. This allows the cop (Saif Ali Khan) to listen in on the villains' conversation. The cop's ear is tuned not to the dancers and their *mujra*/qawwali, but to the criminals he is after. Violence and villainy are also center stage in "Ya Ali," where the qawwali is occasion for a gory internecine gangster battle. To be sure, there are precedents for spectacularity in qawwalis, and for the merging of *mujras* and qawwalis, particularly in 1970s masala films.[180] But the commodification of dancing bodies and the devaluing of listening that happens in its wake in item number–esque qawwalis are of a different order.

## Distorting Romance

I want to attend now to two more recent qawwalis that demonstrate that the classic film qawwali, and all it represented, is no longer tenable. The first, "Senti-wali Mental" from *Shaandaar* (2015), is a competition between the bride's and the groom's parties, as part of prewedding festivities. The song is set in a beautiful and grand theater, but this is a space that rings hollow; even the wedding planner JJ (Shahid Kapoor) is struck by the opulence and wastefulness of the rich. With just twenty people in a theater that could hold two thousand, this is a space emptied of the adoring crowds so crucial to the classic qawwali. The very first verse of the qawwali confirms that despite the familiar setting and Islamicate mise-en-scène—a group of men and women seated across from each other on a big stage, draped in colorful, sparkling outfits, scarves in hand—we cannot expect an endearing courtship ritual.

"Senti-wali Mental" is a mean-spirited battle of the sexes. Much to the surprise of the women on stage, the groom (Robin, played by Vikas Verma) and his party open with a verse that paints women as shallow, crazy, and self-absorbed. "Pyaar ho gaya, bhai" (It's love, brother), quips JJ upon hearing the men's opening gambit, but sisters Alia (Alia Bhatt) and Isha (Sanah Kapoor), the bride, recognize Robin's misogyny. They respond by deriding men for their blundering and stupid ways and their sex drive, which the women are careful to distinguish from romance. The barbs get sharper with each exchange, culminating with the fitness-obsessed Robin insulting women, and Isha in particular, for being fat. With the women completely demoralized, it is up to other men—JJ and the father of the bride, Bipin Arora (Pankaj Kapoor)—to save the day. This scene is oddly similar to the climax of the *Barsaat Ki Raat* qawwali discussed earlier, "Na To Caravan." In that song, the lovelorn Shama is unable to go on singing because her love is unrequited, and this compels Amaan to take over. In the *Shaandaar* qawwali, by contrast, it is the men's cruel put-down, rather than love, that silences the sisters and draws the patriarch into the fray. It is as if the more refined and respectful—not to mention artistic—exchange staged in the classic qawwali does not work in the contemporary moment. "Senti-wali Mental" thus marks an important shift in cinematic representations of gender, romance, and Islamicate culture. At the same time, through the oblique reference to *Barsaat Ki Raat*, it reveals (and rehearses) the gendered conventions of the classic cinematic qawwali. In both songs, men are cast as saviors; they are heroes deserving of women's undying love.

The comedy group All India Bakchod (AIB) takes this critique a step further in "Creep Qawwali" (2015), a viral video that is as much a send-up of the classic film qawwali as it is an ad for the dating app Truly Madly.[181] It shows two groups of women facing off in a musical contest to determine which of their stalkers is the creepier of the two (see video 2.8 https://doi.org/10.3998/mpub.11713921.comp.9). All the musical, visual, and gestural signs of the cinematic qawwali are put to work in this song. Two women, each with a group of backup singers, trade witty verses about gendered romantic norms—or, in this case, the violation thereof. Dressed in lavish, color-coordinated *angarakhas* (courtesan-style tunic), they perform synchronized gestures to the sounds of the tabla, harmonium, and rhythmic clapping. Static camerawork, intercutting between the two parties, and a frontal aesthetic emphasize the musical conversation and competition between the two seated groups. But, where classic qawwalis celebrated gendered conventions of romance, AIB's version satirizes those very conventions. The creep's infelicitous and grammatically incorrect language, his sleazy pickup lines ("I deliver your pizza / Will you deliver my baby?"), and his violation of the women's personal and online space make him the worst suitor possible. In fact, like the women in *Chaudhvin Ka Chand*'s "Sharmake Yeh Kyon Pardanashin," these singers know that the creep is watching them surreptitiously. In both songs, the camera reveals the voyeur, endorsing the women's critique of male aggression in the name of love. Thus, if love in the classic qawwali is a romantic quest that knows no boundaries, the AIB parody renders it as sexual harassment. And even as it turns out that the two women are singing about the same man (one Mr. Suresh Kumar) the problem extends far beyond this individual stalker. Both groups sing of how the internet and their neighborhood are full of such men. These women complain but do not need rescuing by other men; they rely on one another for support. Ending on a note of female solidarity, "Creep Qawwali" gestures to a cinematic precedent that has faded out of view in recent years, that of women singing qawwalis (among) themselves and presenting a distinctly gendered take on romance, modesty, and propriety.

In reading "Senti-wali mental" and "Creep Qawwali" as symptomatic of shifts in the genre in recent years, I posit that the gender politics of the genre are ever more visible today. Contemporary item number–esque qawwalis are more than just glamorous versions of the qawwalis of yesteryear. They depart from the homosocial, more pious overtones of the dargah qawwalis by returning women to the scene, primarily as objects of male attention. They also return rambunctious, romantic men to the genre. But, the transformation of performance practices and the relationship between qawwal and audience—the emphasis on dancing rather than listening for artistic or spiritual edification—suggests an altogether different configuration of gender, romance, listening, and the Islamicate. Like "Q Funk," the Indipop number with which I began this section, item number–esque qawwalis do not draw on or cite Sufism or Islamicate culture so much as the *cinematic qawwali* itself.[182] These film qawwalis gesture to other qawwalis in Hindi cinema's history. The itemization of aural and visual signs of Islamicate culture is of a piece with the waning of the figure of the *tawaif* and the ghazal. As qawwalis begin to look and sound like every other fast-paced, spectacular item number, they disrupt older lexicons of the genre. Where once the sensuousness and eroticism of the film qawwali were located in its lyrics, they are now articulated visually, as a commodity spectacle. No real community emerges in these songs, aural or otherwise. Listening inspires dancing, but it does not lead to a relationship with one's peers or with god. All in all, the qawwali as a cinematic genre can no longer sustain the romantic or political ideals of the past. Item number–esque qawwalis urge us to shed our nostalgia for the genre. But they also make that task immensely difficult. They move us, both literally and emotionally, in powerful ways, implicating us in both the sensuous pleasures and the complex gender, sexual, and cultural politics of the genre.

I have argued in this chapter that classic film qawwalis of the postindependence period envision a community aligned with Nehruvian ideals of secularism and syncretism. These songs enact a loving kind of listening, via recourse to cinematic conventions of heterosexual romance and desire. That an Islamicate genre is a crucial site for the valorization of listening in

Hindi cinema—listening as a means of aural belonging—is a critical intervention. It stands in direct opposition not just to the implicit communalism
of B. V. Keskar, who in his time as Minister for Information and Broadcasting sought to craft "sound standards" for the nation, but also to the more
explicit anti-Muslim rhetoric of contemporary right-wing forces.[183] As an
Islamicate genre in a Hindutva India, the qawwali today can only conjure a
broad, mixed listening public if it is sufficiently de-Islamicized, as is the case
with Sufipop and item number–esque qawwalis. The former generates little
sense of a public, and the latter deflects attention from listening to dancing.
Moreover, in its item number–esque form, the qawwali is thoroughly self-
referential: it appears to cite itself and its history in cinema, rather than
evoking syncretic cultural ideals of the past. By contrast, the Islamicate—or,
more accurately, Muslim religiosity—is front and center in the dargah qawwalis of the new millennium. These songs imagine a listening public composed of pious, nonthreatening, and peace-loving Muslim men. While this
representation seems admirable, it entrenches the good Muslim/bad Muslim binary. In tying the qawwali to Islam and spaces of worship, dargah
qawwalis also downplay the syncretic and artistic history of the form. Thus,
in articulating, disarticulating, and rearticulating the links between love,
listening, and the Islamicate, the cinematic qawwali unsettles the place of
Muslims in the "national romance" of India.

The qawwali's emphasis on the auditor attenuates the overwhelming
attention paid to voice in cinema and sound studies scholarship (to which, of
course, I contribute). It also challenges the notion that listening is a passive
activity. What is transformed as the qawwali travels from sacred venues to
the silver screen and, subsequently, to television and digital platforms is the
*kind* of aural community that listening materializes. Not all listening publics
are as utopian and egalitarian as some theorists of sound suggest. Listening to
cinematic qawwalis with a feminist ear draws attention not just to the shifting
gender politics of the genre, but to the ways gender, sexuality, and religion
intersect to uphold starkly different sonic conceptions of nation and community at different historical moments. The genealogy of listening publics that
I have crafted in this chapter points at once to the importance of the 1990s
in shaping how Indian audiences listen today (to the qawwali and much else)
and to the contingent and multifarious nature of contemporary soundwork.
Dwelling on listening—the different ways we listen, the different ways we did
listen and could have listened, to the Islamicate in Hindi cinema—prompts
a broader awareness of soundwork as object and method for cinema studies.

I take a different, more synchronic approach to unfolding the radical potential of listening with a feminist ear in the next chapter. Having already explored singing and listening, I turn up the volume on speaking. Attending to the materiality of accent and other cinematic sounds in the classic gangster film *Satya* (1998), I theorize language as sound and present a counterhegemonic reading of the politics of language and place.

Speaking

## CHAPTER 3

# Speaking of the Xenophone

*Language as Sound in* Satya

Most humanists today take as a truism that language names, describes, indexes, and even shapes reality. But there persists the notion that, in the final instance, language exists apart from the material realm. Such an "immaterial" conception of language misses the robust tradition in linguistic anthropology that shows that the media and formats in which we encounter language— the radio voice, the television screen, or the audiobook, say—are inextricable from what language "is" and how it operates. This makes language a fundamentally material entity. It has physical properties—audible, visible, even haptic qualities—and it is inextricable from social, cultural, political, and economic structures.[1] In the pages that follow, I home in on the materiality of speech by thinking about language *as sound*, as one of many sounds in cinema. In attending to the way language is voiced and heard in a key Bombay film, I am continuing the work I began in chapter 1. There, my project was to establish the singing voice as a bodily entity, as more than just a metaphor for presence. Here, my task is to theorize the material dimensions of the speaking voice—specifically, the materiality of language audible in films.

Recasting language as sound foregrounds the aural textures and rhythms of words spoken aloud. It turns dialogue and other oral performance into soundwork. Theorizing language as an aural artifact in this way does not diminish the importance of words. To the contrary, it amplifies the work that words perform. Spoken language sounds out hierarchies of gender, class, caste, religion, and region. That is, characters do not just speak Hindi or Marathi or Tamil on screen; they speak in specific accents and idioms. To audiences familiar with the language(s) and cinematic conventions at work, the sound of speech is a critical source of information. Characters' command of particular tongues, their ability to code-switch among different language varieties, the ease with which they quote poetry—these and other linguistic

skills signal spatial, class, and cultural distinctions. Speech thus places characters in precise ways.

I argue in this chapter that in addition to locating characters in particular
social realms, the sound of words can gesture to "unspoken" possibilities. It is
precisely the ability of language to call up speakers' (individual and collective)
itineraries and affiliations that makes possible—and *tangible*—alternative
conceptions of place and identity. My case study in this chapter is *Satya* (dir.
Ram Gopal Varma, 1998), a gangster film set in 1990s Bombay that quickly
came to be regarded as a classic of its ilk. Where other scholars have focused
on the film's visual and thematic innovations, I train my ear on three elements
of its soundwork: characters' accents, the relationship of speech to ambient
sounds of the city, and cinematic sound effects used in the score and song
lyrics. I pull together these aural elements using the "xenophone," Rey Chow's
term for foreign-sounding language practices. By making different aural iterations of Hindi part of the cinematic and urban sensorium, *Satya* revises the
way the city is imagined in public culture. The multiplicity of accents and
tongues in the film undermines the nativist narrative of Bombay that Hindu
right-wing groups routinely forward. Thus, in listening with a feminist ear,
one finds that, as grim a film as it is, *Satya* is utopian in its embrace of a multilingual, multiethnic conception of Bombay.

To begin thinking through the connections between speech, place, and
identity, let us pause over the scholarship on accent. In his ethnography of
call centers, *Neutral Accent*, A. Aneesh discusses how workplace training
programs attempt to reconfigure the sound of place in speech. He writes:
"Generally, accents have developed because speech tended to be place-
bound, acquiring a peculiar flavor through countless repetitions in face-to-
face interactions within a small radius of habitation. But, in itself, an accent is
not an accent at all. An accent becomes an accent when transportation allows
one to cross regions of speech; it is an accent only when juxtaposed with
others."[2] Setting aside for a moment the fact that accents can project other
identities and affiliations besides place (gender, caste, and class, for example),
I want to home in on the insight that comparatism defines accents. An accent
is only identifiable as such when it is compared, either implicitly or explicitly,
to other ways of mouthing a language. This much is apparent in the fact that
only some people—foreigners of one sort or another—are deemed as having an accent. Only *their* speech is heard as marked, as other. Shilpa Davé
makes a similar point in her discussion of brownface in US film and television: "accents appear only in comparison to 'normal' or standard speech."[3] To

be marked thus is to be audibly insufficient. Thus, the comparatism that gives rise to accents is no simple juxtaposition; it creates sonic hierarchies, aural rankings of difference.

Such hierarchization does not merely cast certain speakers as others, it also figures place in very specific ways. For example, Amanda Weidman's work on early twentieth-century sound recordings of *vikatam*, a Tamil genre of comedy sketches, demonstrates that mimics' juxtaposition of different ways of speaking mediated elite audiences' relationship to the rest of Madras. Set alongside other sounds of urban space (e.g., dogs' barking, music from courtesans' salons, the sound of trains), the parodic voices gained a sheen of authenticity, which in turn cast both gramophone and the *vikatam* artist as faithful reproducers of city life.[4] By contrast, the mimicry that contemporary call center agents are enjoined to perform is aimed at scrubbing speech of certain place-bound markers, conjuring instead a kind of "placelessness."[5]

These insights about the unstable relationship of spoken language to place—and the ability of accent to not reproduce so much as *produce* place—lead me to ask how the sound of speech configures the city in a Bombay-centric film like *Satya*. What does listening to the accents of particular characters do to our notions of the city, nation, and nationalism? Does the comparative frame that accents demand inevitably lead us to a hierarchy of tongues, or might there be another way of understanding the imprint of social and physical space on language? How might the sounds of language in turn shape our sense of the places we call our own?

A detour through Rey Chow's slim but luminous volume *Not like a Native Speaker* helps answer these questions. Like Aneesh and Davé, Chow dismantles the native/foreign speaker binary by noting the plurality and proximity of languages to one another: "A native speaker becomes audible or discernible only when there are nonnative speakers present, when more than one language is already in play, explicitly or implicitly, as a murmur and an interference."[6] For a language—and a "native speaker" of that language—to appear as a discrete and coherent entity, boundaries between different accents, idioms, and modes of speaking must be imagined and policed. The porosity of tongues must be denied. Histories of coercion and exchange, of travel and translation, that continually transform languages must be muted. To keep in play the multiplicity that is the very condition of language, Chow proposes the concept of the "xenophone." More than simply a "foreign-sounding speech/tone," the xenophone is a "creative domain of languaging . . . that draws its sustenance from mimicry and adaptation and bears in its accents the murmur, the passage, of diverse found speeches."[7] Chow's description calls up a speaker who may be from a different place, an elsewhere, an outside—but who is *not necessarily out of place*. She need not belong exclusively to one place. Her language and speech bear traces of multiple histories, some personal, some collective. She makes audible the fact that people are inevitably attached to many different places, pasts, and social stations. Thinking of her speech as an example of xenophonic languaging registers linguistic, ethnic, and other kinds of difference without positing a natural link between language, place, and identity.

But it does more than that, too. Note Chow's careful wording: she is referring not to a foreign speech or tone, but to a "foreign-*sounding*" one. Whether the speaker is a "foreigner" (itself a vexed category) is beside the point. It is *sound* that casts her as a foreigner. More precisely, it is a *way of making sense of sound*, of ascribing meaning to particular accents and intonations, that gives rise to the foreigner. The sounds the speaker makes are interpreted such that she is heard as being from a different place. Sound does not confirm her foreignness so much as *produce* it. It also produces its opposite, the figure of the native speaker, one who is so fluent as to not have an "accent"—a "(foreign) accent."[8]

What makes the xenophone so powerful a concept is that it uses sound not just to identify the hierarchical relationship between those deemed native speakers and those who are not (and can never be so), but to dismantle that structure. It teaches us to hear *all* accents as accents. To hear the discord in all our tongues. To hear in voice not one's ontological status (you are/are not a native) so much as histories of collective struggles over space, culture, and identity. The xenophone helps us listen for the copresence of other people, places, and pasts. For Mikhail Bakhtin, such polyphony and dialogism is built into language itself. Chow's term emphasizes how this multiplicity *sounds*.

Of course, it is not just accents and languages that sit, struggle, and converse in proximity to one another. So do other sounds. To put it another way, the sounds of speech are but sounds, and they exist alongside other sounds. To name a particular way of speaking an "accent" is to mark it as an unusual sound—but a *sound* nonetheless. It is to identify speech by its sonority, its materiality, rather than the exact meaning of the words. What I am doing here is extending the notion of the xenophone to include sounds that are apparently nonlinguistic—sounds that register as phonemes in some contexts but not others, words that register as a set of sounds (rather than linked morphemes), sounds that become words in the act of enunciation, sounds that allow other sounds to register as words. An aural concept at its core, the xenophone is capacious enough for such stretching.

It should be clear by now that the theoretical and methodological stretching I attempt in this chapter (and in the book as a whole) demands disciplinary and spatial roving. I draw not just on work in cinema studies, but also on scholarship in anthropology, literary studies, and sound studies. I invoke the politics and pleasures of orality (and aurality) in the various cinemas of India and in film-adjacent contexts. This move to aural worlds ostensibly outside film diegeses is critical, for it insists on and illustrates the "worldliness" of cinema.[9] As in the first two chapters, I am attentive here to the fact that cinema draws on, and responds to, a wide range of cultural forms and discursive conversations. My interaural analysis suggests that if Bombay film soundwork (re)configures imagined contours of belonging and prompts a "xenophonic" understanding of language and identity, that is because the boundaries of cinema are far more porous than we typically take them to be.

Further, my emphasis on materiality in this chapter closes the distance between speech and other sounds—between sense and non-sense, if you will—which in turn complicates notions of native and foreign tongues. In an attempt to pluralize both "language" and "sound" in this chapter, I ask: What languages do we hear in Bombay films? How does the "Hindi" of Hindi cinema hold in itself a multiplicity of tongues? What sounds count as language? Thinking of language as sound—and also the sounds of language(s)—helps get at the multiplicity that is routinely suppressed in both public and academic discourse in order for the category of "nation" to emerge. Thus, the line of inquiry I pursue here entails not just the transnationalization of film studies and sound studies (which typically theorize from Euro-American contexts), but also the provincializing and pluralizing of hegemonic "national" cinematic traditions such as Bollywood. While I do not approach *Satya* with a linguist's command of the prosodic and segmental features that distinguish one dialect or accent from another, I am concerned with the ways in which language, in its very materiality, carries claims about identity, experience, and affiliation. I demonstrate that linguistic multiplicity takes many forms in Bombay film soundwork and that this audible plurality matters deeply to the way we think about and study nation.

Given my focus on language, the city in *Satya* works not as an alternative framework to nation so much as a site in which to complicate the politics of nation. As work in linguistic anthropology and radio studies attests, the sound of language matters crucially to the way nation is imagined.[10] Listening to the way people (and texts) wield words can unearth the nuanced ways in which borders are conceived, maintained, and transformed. Also germane to my effort to theorize cinematic language as sound are two recent developments in South Asian studies: the turn to "region" and "network" as alternative theoretical frameworks in Indian cinema studies, and the burgeoning work on multilinguality by literary scholars and historians of the subcontinent.[11] These interventions caution against the "territorial fatalism" that such powerful concepts as nation can induce.[12] That is, they remind us that geopolitical borders have never determined nor exhausted the ways in which language, film, and other aspects of culture operate. A further complication is in the fact that "Indian cities have been the fulcrum of language movements, cultural and religious conflict . . . [and] the debate around linguistic and regional identities in India."[13] This makes a Bombay-centric film like *Satya* useful in thinking through the implications of the aurality of language.

My choice of *Satya* is also motivated by the fact that the film builds on a range of cinematic traditions that concern themselves, albeit in very different ways, with the politics of language. As I explain below, *Satya* extends the work that director Ram Gopal Varma began in films like *Siva* (1989) and *Rangeela* (1995), both of which treat language as important to urban tensions and identity. Francis Ford Coppola's *The Godfather* trilogy (1972–90) and Martin Scorsese's *Mean Streets* (1973) and *Goodfellas* (1990) were important reference points for the director and writers of *Satya*. These films are all classic examples of the Hollywood gangster genre, which "is virtually obsessed with the issue of talk."[14] Varma's film also draws on a disparate cluster of Hindi films featuring protagonists grappling with linguistic, regional, and communal divides, from Mani Ratnam's pivotal gangster film *Nayakan* (1987) to his terrorism trilogy. Last but not least, *Satya* makes the linguistic performance of the *tapori* (vagabond) in films such as *Rangeela* a key element of the Bombay gangworld. I argue that the accents of the *tapori*-turned-gangster's speech do not simply place Satya and his friends in Bombay; they reimagine Bombay itself.

The figure of the *tapori*, of course, is a masculine one, as is the gangster genre. The language the *tapori* speaks, Bambaiyya, is rooted in the "gully" and the footpath, urban spaces that are not always available to, or comfortable for, women.[15] Perforce, my analysis of language in this chapter has a distinctly gendered dimension. If the xenophonic soundwork of *Satya* renders Bombay a more welcoming and diverse space than some political groups would have it, then it is worth asking whether this alternative urban imaginary includes women on the same terms as men. The answer, it would seem, is "not quite." Instead of going down this path, however, I develop the concept of listening with a feminist ear in a different direction in this chapter. Having probed the aurality of gender and sexuality more directly in the preceding chapters, and with the understanding that these identity categories are inalienable from language politics, I explore how we might listen differently to the sounds of speech in *Satya* than we previously have. My hope is that the intersectional and interaural feminist method I model—one that is attuned not just to gender and sexuality, but also to class, nation, region, religion, and other ways of placing ourselves in the world—will enable others to pursue paths I do not take in this book. I aim to complicate our understanding of what we ought to listen to in cinema, and how, and to multiply and revise the questions we ask of cultural texts.

In focusing on the materiality and politics of language in cinema, I am returning to ground I traversed in a previous article, on *Ek Duuje Ke Liye* (*For Each Other*, dir. K. Balachander, 1981).[16] That film's protagonists move deftly between various languages and registers, staging the fluidity and multiplicity of language that has long characterized the cinemas of India at the level of production. While the various film industries in India are typically referenced by the primary language of the dialogues (e.g., *Hindi* film industry, *Tamil* film industry), the ongoing processes of remaking, adapting, and dubbing and the fact that film personnel on any given film come from all over the subcontinent suggest that linguistic and regional border-crossing happens all the time.[17] In that earlier article, I argued that although multilingualism is evident on film sets and although the question of language had been crucial to Indian filmmakers during the transition from silent films to the talkies, the hegemonic status of Hindi in the postcolonial period kept Bombay cinema from questioning the tongue it had chosen as its own. I proposed that it took until the early 1980s for linguistic conflict to become the primary driver of the plot.

Over the course of writing this book, I have learned to listen better. I have come to recognize that the politics of language dwell not just in film plots, but in the very fact that language is *audible*. While my analysis of *Ek Duuje Ke Liye* and my critique of the monolingual assumptions of the national-cinemas theoretical framework still ring true to me—indeed, I extend that aspect of my argument here—I want to revisit my suggestion that Hindi cinema has been largely "silent" on the question of language politics. Whether or not linguistic politics motivate narrative conflict, language is—and has always been—at issue in cinema. This is an insight that cinema studies as a discipline would also do well to embrace.

In the following section, I delineate the paucity of cinema studies' existing vocabulary for the study of cinematic speech. Not only is the terminology insufficient to understand the complexity of verbal performances on screen, it leaves unanswered questions about the cultural weight attached to particular ways of speaking. Taking a page out of the study of South Indian cinepolitics, I inquire into histories of public speech and linguistic nationalism in India that make cinematic language meaningful. Bombay cinema has always played a part in public cultural debates around language use, as evident in its marshaling of Hindustani, Hinglish, and Bambaiyya at different historical moments. Having sketched out the distinct utopian imaginaries of these Hindi film languages, I offer an analysis of dialogue in *Satya*, unfolding how the film multiplies the language(s) considered native to Bombay, and how its play with accents reimagines the city and the place of South Indians therein. Finally, in a move that broadens the work of listening with a feminist ear, I consider the treatment of language in *Satya* in relation to the so-called background score and sound effects. The aural materiality of language comes through powerfully in the sound of bullets (*dhichkiaoon!*) in the song "Goli Maar," with which the chapter closes.

## From Cinematic Language to Dialogue-*baazi*

Listening to speech is deemed so basic that cinema studies has been slow to develop tools for verbal analysis.[18] Work in radio and sound studies that theorizes and historicizes aural performance tends to get siloed in the name of medium specificity.[19] Worse, to speak of "cinematic language" in film studies is to concern oneself with images more than words. Filmmaking conventions around mise-en-scène, cinematography, and editing are said to compose a visual "grammar" of sorts. Other linguistic terms such as "accent," "idiom," and "syntax" likewise serve as metaphors for textual and visual elements, rather than sonic descriptors. Even among those who engage with questions of linguistic difference, foreign cinema, and translation, there remains a tendency to sidestep the aurality of language.[20]

This general disinterest in the *spokenness* of the spoken word may be a function of the discipline's historical ocularcentrism, its relentless championing of image over sound.[21] Even Michel Chion, who conceives of cinema as a voco- and verbocentric medium, frames speech largely in relation to the image.[22] His tripartite taxonomy—"theatrical speech" (dialogues), "textual speech" (voice-over narration), and "emanation speech" (unintelligible speech that is inessential to the narrative)—emphasizes the extent and kind of control audible language exerts over the mise-en-scène and narrative. For instance, he notes that actors' gestures and camera movements often draw attention to characters' dialogues, and voice-overs call up images and actions on screen. Despite the latter's power to set the temporal and spatial coordinates of the narrative, Chion holds that voice-overs are "abstract" and could never elicit the sensations that images do.[23] Such a polemic about the impoverishment of words is odd, not least because it implies that the more granular qualities of voice—its material aspects—can only be heard if there is a visible body synchronized with it (a position I undo in chapter 1). Chion's final category of audible language, emanation speech, suggests human presence, but it, too, is defined by its (lack of) importance in visual and narrative terms. Such speech may constitute the ambient sound of a space and the everyday conversation, the phatic talk, that tends to get dismissed as "verbal wallpaper."[24] Lying somewhere between theatrical and textual speech are a whole host of other aural forms, where the words we hear are not as tightly linked to the images of characters moving their lips—"interior monologues," "subjective sounds," "offscreen voices," and (epistolary) "writing voices," to name a few.[25]

What is striking about this array of cinema studies terms is that almost all of them concern the source of the sound and the relationship of sound to image. They ask: who is speaking, and do we see the person speaking? These are acousmatic questions, of the sort that Nina Sun Eidsheim powerfully dismantles in her book *The Race of Sound.*[26] The first question seeks to identify the source of the speaking voice; the second hopes to answer the first by locating an image in which to house the voice. What we hear gets defined in terms of what we see. Underlying both questions is an anxiety about origins, and an attempt to pin down the meaning of both sound and image. However, as I demonstrated in chapter 1, what and how a cinematic voice signifies is inordinately complex and malleable. Both singing and speaking voices resonate in ways that far exceed the boundaries of the cinematic frame and the diegesis. Accordingly, I propose that we open our ears to the aural materiality of speech in cinema, without constantly prioritizing its visual form or ascribing it narrative importance. In this chapter, I use the initial acousmatic question as a springboard for thinking about the interaural fields that make language so "deadly" a matter.[27] The question of who speaks cascades in this chapter into a series of other questions: Who speaks? How do they sound when they speak? What are the historical processes that allow that speech to register as it does? What else is audible in and alongside words? What are the implications of these sonic arrangements?

In listening to the sound of speaking voices, I take a page out of Sarah Kozloff's book (her second book, to be precise). In *Overhearing Film Dialogue*, Kozloff notes that speech in cinema has long been dismissed by critics as being too simple and transparent.[28] Pushing against such reductive characterizations, she foregrounds the crafted nature of dialogue:

> [Actors' lines are] scripted, written and rewritten, censored, polished, rehearsed, and performed. Even when lines are improvised on the set, they have been spoken by impersonators, judged, approved, and allowed to remain. Then all dialogue is recorded, edited, mixed, underscored, and played through stereophonic speakers with Dolby sound. The actual hesitations, repetitions, digressions, grunts, interruptions, and mutterings of everyday speech have either been pruned away, or, if not, deliberately included.[29]

These verb-filled sentences capture just how carefully planned and technologically mediated film dialogue is. Framing audible speech as performance, moreover, prompts us to listen not just to what is said, but to *how* it is said. Kozloff deepens our understanding of gendered genre conventions through her discussion of characters' verbal dexterity and style; their use of particular languages, dialects, and jargon; and the rhythms and repetition in their speech—what in Hindi film parlance is called "dialogue-*baazi*" (on which more anon). She also notes that voice-casting "assigns dialogue-as-written to a person, a body, a voice."[30] Rendered by a human body, dialogue is inherently material. Ian Garwood extends this materialist approach by drawing on the "sensuous" strand of cinema studies, scholarship attuned to the way film's tactile qualities shape the cinematic experience.[31] While this latter body of work distances itself from questions of narration so important to Kozloff (and, to a lesser extent, Chion), Garwood demonstrates that a film's appeal to the senses can serve its storytelling functions. While my own interest is not, first and foremost, on narration, I appreciate Garwood's exemplary attention to vocal textures, the way he listens for timbre, tone, cadence, pace, and so on. He makes a case for understanding voice-over narration not just in relation to images, but also in conjunction with diegetic sounds, music, other voice-overs, and even the sound of technology.[32]

Importantly, what gets left out of these and the few other studies of film dialogue there are—and what I underscore in this chapter—is a broader sense of how sounds come to mean what they do. Like so many scholars before me, I, too, find the sound-image relationship endlessly fascinating. My choice to open this book with a chapter on the shifts in Bombay cinema's audiovisual contract makes that much clear. But, as I demonstrate there with my discussion of bodily voices, the materiality of voice is not simply a function of the image attached to it or a quality inherent in a singer's vocal chords or the technologies used to manipulate and broadcast her voice. A number of historical factors, sociopolitical and industrial, cohere to suggest how certain sounds—certain voices—are to be heard and interpreted, both in relation to, and independent of, the visual domain of cinema. Focusing solely on the performance of an individual actor (or singer) or on the soundwork of a particular scene downplays the broader contexts and ideologies that render some sounds, and not others, meaningful. I carry this insight into the current chapter: even as my argument turns on a single film and a synchronic mode of analysis, I insist on the need to think about language as a material entity born of (and borne by) historically situated practices and encounters. Where others have built on Kozloff to explicate the "verbal style" of individual actors and filmmakers (or "verbal-visual style," in Jennifer O'Meara's formulation), I move from the material textures of cinematic soundwork to the interaural formations and the linguistic and cinematic histories that allow those sonic details to register as they do.[33]

To be clear: mine is no simple call for historicization or contextualization. What I am proposing is that we follow linguistic anthropologists in conceptualizing language itself as material, and recognize the social, political, and institutional histories that constitute its materiality. I call for us to listen with a feminist ear to how those histories bear on the spoken word in cinema—how they not only inspire certain ways of speaking, but also enable certain interpretations of those oral performances. Thus, here, as in the previous chapters, soundwork emerges as a question of *listening* as much as of voicing. If certain characters' accents are interpreted as foreign sounding, that is in no small measure because histories of linguistic nationalism have taught us to hear some people's speech as familiar and autochthonous, and others' as, well, "other." If certain words and sounds are understood to be emblematic of a place—the city of Bombay, say—that, too, arises from particular language ideologies and the imaginaries they inspire. Conceptualizing language as sound demands that we connect the aural materiality of speech in cinema to those broader discourses about language, and also listen for audible but "unspoken" gestures to alternative notions of linguistic belonging. Following

Alexandra T. Vazquez, we might conceive of this work as "listening in detail," for the cinematic and sociopolitical histories that *Satya*'s soundwork summons help me "assemble that inherited lived matter that is both foreign and somehow familiar into something new."[34]

## Language, Politics, and Cinema

While my methodological approach in this chapter may be novel, it builds from the simple observation that films have always been part of diverse and promiscuous aural fields. Such interaurality is readily apparent in the south of India, where onscreen oratory is a crucial element of "cine-politics."[35] The Tamil, Telugu, and Kannada film industries all boast (male) stars whose godlike status feeds their cinematic and politics careers. In the case of Tamil cinema, the years between 1949 and 1954 were crucial, for this was when "the emotive power of song shifted to rhetorically embellished speech."[36] Dialogue became more alliterative and allegorical, carrying in its rhythms and images the essence of Tamilness. This cinematic "elocutionary revolution" occurred in conjunction with the growth of Dravidian politics, which used a literary and archaic-sounding register of Tamil to embody an ancient and powerful civilization.[37] Writers and Dravidian movement leaders such as Bharatidasan, C. N. Annadurai, and M. Karunanidhi elaborated this linguistic and political paradigm not just in the film plots, but also in the song lyrics and their protagonists' extended, poetic monologues.[38] Their words gained especial power in the mouths of actors like M. G. Ramachandran (MGR) and Sivaji Ganesan, "endow[ing] the hero with the singularity required to overcome his enemies and transform society."[39] Needless to say, South Indian audiences' (and voters') embrace of the spoken word has been as fervent as cinema studies' dismissal of it.

The traffic between film, politics, and other domains of public culture in the subcontinent has a long history. Debashree Mukherjee identifies "impassioned speech" as an important trope in early Indian talkies, noting that it emerged in the context of heightened nationalist mobilization.[40] Cinema was but one "platform" among many expressive traditions, genres, and spaces in which stylized speech was performed and circulated on the subcontinent. Verbal soundwork was (re)produced in a media landscape that included newspapers, pamphlets, radio, gramophone, and films.[41] Colonial authorities had been concerned about "seditious eloquence" since at least the first decade of the twentieth century, when the Swadeshi movement began addressing broad publics in vernacular tongues.[42] What was said, how, by whom, to whom, in what language, and where—all of this was of deep concern to officials. What the talkies did, twenty years on, is locate impassioned speech in the figure of the woman barrister arguing a case in the courtroom, often in defense of a "fallen" woman. Thus, India's cinematic investment in speech is tied to the political struggles and gendered public culture of the early twentieth century.

Dwelling on "talk" in the "talkies" not only reminds us to think broadly about the politics of language in cinema, it also helps close the distance between Hindi, Tamil, Telugu, and other cinemas. No matter what filmic (or political) tradition South Asian audiences were part of and partial to, their love for soundwork grew out of contexts in which speaking and listening were not just enjoyable activities but highly public, high-stakes ones. I demonstrate in this chapter that this remains the case in contemporary Hindi cinema. Thus, even as I argue against the parochial politics of Hindu right-wing groups, I am proposing that we provincialize the way we study Hindi cinema.[43] Taking a cue from scholars of South Indian language- and cine-politics, we must tune in to the materiality of speech and the political implications those sounds hold for the study of cinema. Doing so will reveal the situatedness of Bombay cinema in interaural (and also interocular and intertextual) fields that sometimes allow it to speak for India, but just as often undermine the industry's and the nation's hegemonic claims.

At first blush, the link between cinematic speech and politics is not as strong in Bombay cinema as it is in the cinemas of South India. Stars are not taken to represent a whole linguistic or ethnonational community in the way that men like N. T. Rama Rao, MGR, and Rajkumar were (these men stood for the Telugu, Tamil, and Kannada nation, respectively). Even so, there has long been among Hindi film fans a deep investment in the spoken word. So recognizable a cultural entity is dialogue that certain turns of phrase and bombastic comments are routinely dismissed in casual conversation as being "filmi." The ability to quote dialogues and song lyrics is also a mark of cinephilia. In the case of some films, cassette tapes included not just songs but key dialogues as well.

Dialogue delivery can lift actors out of particular films or characters, and build their star image around the words they speak. Praseeda Gopinath identifies "dialogue-*baazi*, or dialogue game" as a key ingredient of masculine performance in Hindi cinema: it is "a special form of dialogue delivery that requires the right amount of over-confidence and playfulness, a deliberate theatricality that reflects the epic archetype of the hero/anti-hero, or villain."[44] Skillful dialogue-*baazi* can make a character's signature lines circulate far beyond the bounds of the film, much like songs do. While Gopinath's essay focuses on a contemporary star, Ranveer Singh, her analysis clarifies that dialogue-*baazi* has been a critical element of Hindi cinema since at least the 1970s, when the omnibus masala form gained prominence. It is an important locus of style not just for heroes, but also for comedic sidekicks and villains. Consider the words by which Ajit is still remembered: "Lily, don't be silly," "Mona darling," and "Saara shahar mujhe 'Loyan' ke naam se jaantha hain" (The entire city knows me by the name "Loyan" [lion]).[45] Uttered in the 1970s, these snatches of dialogue are quite autonomous of the films and scenes in which they were spoken. More recent villains known for their "verbal star turns" include Manoj Bajpayee's Bhiku Mhatre in *Satya*, Amrish Puri's Mogambo in *Mr. India* (dir. Shekhar Kapur, 1987), and Amjad Khan's Gabbar Singh in *Sholay* (*Flames*, dir. Ramesh Sippy, 1975).[46] A "Loyan" in his own right, Gabbar comments on his aural stardom when he boasts, "Yahan se paanch paanch kos door, gaon mein jab bachcha raat ko rota hai, tho maa kehthi hain 'Beta soja, soja nahin tho Gabbar Singh aa jayega'" (In a village far far away, when a child cries at night, the mother says "Sleep, my dear, sleep or else Gabbar Singh will come"). Gabbar's aural specter haunts Hindi film history, just as it does a little boy in a faraway village.[47]

As we take note of the materiality of spoken language in Bombay cinema, we realize that what characters like Gabbar offer is more than the occasional rhetorical flourish, a set of memorable lines that fans can recite endlessly. In amplifying the aural pleasures of speech, they teach us to listen beyond the connotative or denotative meanings of words. Ajit's *loyan*, for example, works not simply because it casts the villain as a ferocious animal and "king of the jungle," but also because it is a notable aural shift. Only *this* word is in English; the rest of his monologue is in Hindi. The actor's (mis)pronunciation also distinguishes his character from others. *Loyan* thus raises the twin questions of language and accents, of how speech holds aural clues to social and geographic location.

The relationship between speech and place is often framed in terms of origins—one's language, and accent, in particular, is said to "betray" where one comes from. While this may be true to some extent, the way one speaks may also be an audible "biography of migration," a hodgepodge collection of various modes of expression one has picked up over the years.[48] Speech may also be aspirational, signaling not necessarily who one is but who one wishes to become or be perceived as. For instance, Hindi film fans' dialogue-*baazi* is itself a citational oral practice that announces a cinephilic and audio-philic identity. The "neutral" accents of call center agents likewise present the speakers and their workplace as simultaneously "global" and "placeless." In short, whether in cinema or in everyday life, the sounds of one's tongue(s) are no mere ontological markers. They bear a complicated relationship to his-tory and personal experience, and to the discourses and contexts that ascribe meaning to words spoken aloud.[49] Assumptions about embodiment and enunciation come undone when we listen to Hindi cinema (and all else) with a feminist ear. In naming the social dynamics inscribed in how we speak—and in how we listen to, and make sense of, speech—we may yet land on other ways of calibrating our relationships to place and to one another.

I argue below that the aural materiality of language in Hindi cinema turns on very particular conceptions of place and belonging. The next section dis-cusses three ways of speaking Hindi that Bombay cinema has historically employed: Bambaiyya, Hindustani, and Hinglish. The first of these is the hybrid tongue *Satya* plays with and multiplies. Listening to the languages and accents in *Satya* in relation to the rest of the soundwork, as well as to the histories of linguistic struggle and movement (both on- and offscreen), clarifies the intimate ties between location and locution. Listening with Rey Chow's "xenophone" in mind, moreover, reworks those ties. It helps revise our conception of both Bombay city and its cinema.

## Hindi Film Languages

One place to hear the xenophone in Bombay cinema is *tapori* films. In the early to mid-1990s, there emerged a clutch of Hindi films that used the fig-ure of the *tapori* (vagabond) to reclaim urban space for the subaltern (male) subject. Recall Ranjani Mazumdar's insightful reading of Aamir Khan's *tapori* roles in *Rangeela* (*Colorful*, dir. Ram Gopal Varma, 1995) and *Ghu-lam* (*Slave*, dir. Mahesh Bhatt, 1997).[50] A cinematic invention with roots in Bombay street culture, the *tapori* "stands at the intersection of morality and evil, between the legal and the illegal, between the world of work and those without work."[51] From this liminal location, he offers a spirited cri-tique of the lives of the wealthy and the powerful, even as he yearns for a less precarious life for himself. His loquacious performance reworks the figure of the angry young man popularized by Amitabh Bachchan in the 1970s.[52] Aamir Khan's Munna (in *Rangeela*) is not driven by past traumas in the way that Bachchan's Vijay was. He is concerned with the here and now, and little besides. And while the Bachchan character also gave us some of Hindi cinema's most memorable and poetic lines (thanks to the scriptwriting duo Salim-Javed), the *tapori*'s speech is of a different order.[53] His performance is distinguished by wit and colloquial turns of phrase. His humor is not contained in a handful of scenes; sharp and funny one-liners tumble out of his mouth incessantly. Mazumdar argues that the *tapori*'s agency lies in his stylized banter and carefree style. The Bambaiyya language he uses is a mishmash of tongues arising from the many groups who have settled in the city and shaped its culture over generations. Together, the energies of Gujarati, Marathi, Hindi, and other languages spoken in Bombay sustain Bambaiyya. As such, this working-class figure's language allows for the transcending of regional identity through cinematic performance.[54]

The sound of multiplicity and mixing in Bambaiyya returns us to the xenophone. What Chow's theoretical construct brings alive on the page, the *tapori*'s speech evidences on screen. The rough-and-tumble language of the streets of Bombay is but one lively example of how histories of conflict and coexistence make their mark on our tongues. Borders between languages being porous and dynamic, they generate innumerable instances of linguistic hybridity around the world. The history of the Bombay film industry gives us at least two other examples: Hindustani and Hinglish.

Hindustani is the name for the overlap between Hindi and Urdu, languages that developed discrete communal identities in the late nineteenth and early twentieth centuries as the British colonial government worked to drive a wedge between Hindus and Muslims. Theorizing Hindustani as a shared idiom (rather than a language), Madhumita Lahiri writes: "The historical articulation of Hindi and Urdu as distinct languages is inextricable from the violent politics of Hindu and Muslim differentiation, and the existence of a common colloquial register of Hindi-and-Urdu has then been mobilized, under the name of Hindustani, as evidence of a syncretic subcontinental civilization."[55] Noting that Hindustani is mainly invoked in terms of its colloquial use across North India, Lahiri underscores the idealism of the leftist intellectuals who championed it.[56] Hindustani found a home in the Bombay film industry in the postindependence years because of the efforts of scriptwriters and lyricists seeking to undermine the Hindi-Urdu—and, by extension, Hindu-Muslim—split. These linguistic efforts were linked to the idealized representations of the qawwali and its listening public (and the Islamicate, more generally) in the Nehruvian era, which I discuss in chapter 2. Of salience, as well, is the way caste and region figured into Hindi cinema's utopian aesthetic project.[57] The urban writers and poets who were part of the Bombay film industry were partial to Urdu; by contrast, proto-elite "Hindi-wallahs" of the nineteenth century tended to be upper-caste Hindus from rural backgrounds.[58] For these and other reasons, Bombay cinema tended to speak and sing for many decades in a widely understood, yet also poetic and cultivated, tongue. Even now, despite the ongoing Sanskritization of Hindi in the public sphere and the industry's eager embrace of English and Hinglish in recent years, the sonic and linguistic idiom of Hindustani is still audible in Hindi films. Were it not for the xenophonic history of Hindustani in Bombay cinema, the metaphors and vocabulary of musical genres such as the qawwali and the ghazal would be more foreign sounding than they are today.

Hinglish is of more recent provenance, a product of the postliberalization era. As its hybrid name suggests, it is the casual mixture of Hindi and English used to great effect in commercial media to represent, and court, contemporary Indian youth.[59] Moving between English and Hindi with careful nonchalance, Hinglish showcases the constant border-crossing and translational practices of multilingual speakers in India, especially those of the urban middle and upper classes. The ease with which these speakers switch in and out of English signals a cosmopolitanism particular to the late twentieth and early twenty-first century. In its sounds, one hears a newfound confidence about India's place in the world. That English is one of the languages in the mix is important, for that colonial and global tongue remains the language of upward social and economic mobility in India.[60] The social valence of English, Francesca Orsini observes, makes Hinglish "*both* the informal language of the globalized Indian middle class *and* the aspirational language of the upwardly mobile vernacular lower-middle, middle, and working classes who are 'asking for more,' but clearly have very different linguistic repertoires and grasp of" Hindi and English.[61] The social, political, and economic aspirations that undergird Hinglish—the linguistic reaching for a place in the nation and the world at large—are thus quite different from those that suffuse Hindustani. Moreover, unlike the latter, Hinglish is characterized by a self-conscious citationality: "The intense re-mixing, re-use and re-accenting of Hinglish catchphrases such as '*Dil Maange* More' (this heart asks for/longs for more) or 'Emotional *atyachaar*' (emotional torture) show how much Hinglish is a consciously citational code (with invisible inverted commas) constructed and circulated through the commercial systems of advertising, TV, media, films and radio, which in turn pick up innovative phrases from speakers."[62] Thus, as colloquial as it is, Hinglish is a thoroughly mediated, intertextual mode of speaking. Orsini's use of words such as "re-mixing" and "re-accenting" captures just how much of the potency of Hinglish lies in the aural, even when it is used in textual and visual advertisements.[63]

What distinguishes the *tapori*'s Bambaiyya from these other hybrid languages spoken by Hindi cinema is its specificity of location and its class politics. Both Hindustani and Hinglish are pan-Indian in aspiration, addressing people across the lines of gender, class, religion, and so forth. Bambaiyya does not reflect such all-encompassing desires. It, like the rest of the *tapori*'s performance, is clearly of Bombay. Even as it absorbs other languages into its fold and makes them its own, it does not pretend to be the lingua franca of a nation. It does not call up gendered metaphors of kinship and divinity that fuse notions of land, nation, language, and identity (e.g., "mother tongue"). It does, however, center a particular form of subaltern masculinity associated with the city of Bombay. Bambaiyya is resolutely a language of the streets. It is urban, but not urbane in the way that Hindustani was. Like Hinglish, Bambaiyya is casual and performative—but it is very clearly *not* the language of upward social mobility. It projects an edgy, rebellious kind of cool that makes it the perfect resource for men of the streets like Bhiku in *Satya*. While the xenophone in its initial formulation was about the sound of place in speech, casting Bambaiyya and the *tapori*'s performance as examples of the xenophone foregrounds the intersection of gender, class, and place to articulate a complex critique of language politics.

I have argued so far that speech in cinema is more than a stylish means to stardom or a vehicle for plot progression. The sound of language is both dramatically and politically salient. Conceptualizing language as a material entity can deepen our understanding of how the spoken word matters, in Bombay cinema but also in relation to broader political debates about language and nation in India. In the rest of this chapter, I offer an analysis of *Satya* that demonstrates how the film imbues the sound of language with utopian potential. Listening to the xenophonic soundwork with a feminist ear conjures unexpected temporal, spatial, and affiliative possibilities. The sound of words renders present and viable an alternative understanding of language, nation, city, and cinema.

## Accenting Bambaiyya

*Satya* (dir. Ram Gopal Varma, 1998) opens with its eponymous hero (J. D. Chakravarthy) arriving in the city from some unstated place. A series of unexpected run-ins with a local don lands him in prison, where he meets the famed gangster Bhiku Mhatre (Manoj Bajpayee), who takes him under his wing. A quick study in the life of crime, Satya helps make key decisions in the internecine war unfolding between Bhiku's gang and a former associate's faction. In the midst of the escalating tensions, Satya falls in love with his neighbor Vidya (Urmila Matondkar), prompting ethical questions about the violence in which he routinely engages. True to the genre, brotherly love interrupts heterosexual romance, and the film ends in spectacular gore.

Framed in this way, *Satya* seems like an unremarkable genre film. But in fact, it is remembered as the most important and vibrant example of its kind. Even as it paid homage to Indian and American film history, *Satya* was instrumental in shifting Bombay cinema's representation of the gangster. Drawing on the dystopian energies of a city in turmoil and extending the work begun in films like *Parinda* (*Bird*, dir. Vidhu Vinod Chopra, 1989) and *Raakh* (*Ashes*, dir. Aditya Bhattacharya, 1989), Varma's film made "Bombay noir" a mainstream genre.[64] It also established the director as an auteur in the Bombay film industry. The film swept the Filmfare Awards that season, along with Mani Ratnam's *Dil Se* (*From the Heart*) and Karan Johar's *Kuch Kuch Hota Hai* (*Something Is Happening*). The biggest coup was that *Satya* won all three Filmfare Critics' Awards—Best Film, Best Actor (Manoj Bajpayee), and Best Actress (Shefali Chhaya)—in addition to Best Sound (H. Sridhar), Best Background Score (Sandeep Chowta), and Best Editing (Apurva Asrani and Bhanodaya), and garnered several other nominations.[65] Manoj Bajpayee won the prestigious National Award for Best Supporting Actor, and the Star Screen Award for Best Screenplay went to writers Anurag Kashyap and Saurabh Shukla. This resounding critical and commercial success was a surprise, for *Satya* was a low-budget venture with few stars among its cast and crew.

While popular and scholarly critics alike offer unflinching praise for *Satya*'s visual aesthetic, few comment on the politics of sound and language in this film. I find this remarkable for a number of reasons. First, the historical moment in which *Satya* locates itself is a period when the Hindu right-wing party Shiv Sena had amassed significant political power with its virulent brand of nativism. The heightened gang warfare and communalism Bombay witnessed in the mid-1990s is inseparable from the linguistic and regional chauvinism that led to the renaming of the city as Mumbai. Since language featured prominently in debates around the identity of the city at this time, it behooves us to consider whether films that take Bombay as their subject address this matter.

Second, the careers of many who were involved in the making of *Satya* reveal their interest in aural matters. S. V. Srinivas notes that geographic and linguistic sensitivity is something that director Ram Gopal Varma carries over from his early Telugu films. For instance, in Varma's directorial debut, *Siva* (1989), local Hyderabadi gangsters are defeated by men who are clearly from the coastal Andhra region. The Hyderabadis speak in the regional Telangana dialect, and this distinguishes them from the hero and his compadres, who use a more "standard" dialect of Telugu. Thus, *Siva* speaks to ongoing struggles over regional, cultural, and linguistic identity, and maps those onto the city.[66] Varma's first two Hindi films, *Rangeela* (1995) and *Satya*, are both unabashedly Bombay films. Like *Siva*, they are inseparable from their urban location, and they mobilize language to comment on the history of the city.

Several others on the team are also known to have a keen ear. Vishal Bhardwaj, the music director on *Satya*, went on to establish his reputation as producer-director with his Shakespearean tragedies *Maqbool* (2003), *Omkara* (2006), and *Haider* (2014). All of the films in this trilogy, and *Omkara* in particular, play with language in interesting ways. So do the black comedies he cowrote and coproduced, *Ishqiya* (*Passionate*, dir. Abhishek Chaubey, 2010) and its sequel *Dedh Ishqiya* (*Passionate One and Half [Times Over]*, 2014). Another filmmaker who rose to prominence after *Satya* was Anurag Kashyap, who served as cowriter on the film along with Saurabh Shukla. Stylized language is now recognized as a trademark of Kashyap's oeuvre, as is evident in the two-part *Gangs of Wasseypur* (2012). It should thus come as no surprise, in retrospect at least, that *Satya* too concerns itself with language.

My interest in this chapter, however, is not simply with language but with the notion of language *as sound*. That is, I want to think about the ways in which the sonic materiality of words shape conceptions of place and identity in Bombay cinema. Listening to this film with a broad conception of the xenophone in mind—one that makes room for familiar and unusual sounds— leaves no doubt that the relationship between language, identity, and place is in fact much more flexible and historically contingent than it would seem from the essentialist claims of linguistic nationalist movements. Thus, even as it is set at a time when language politics were at their most fervent in Bombay, *Satya* undermines the nativist logic that turned Bombay into Mumbai in 1995, just a few years before its release. Where others mainly see in *Satya* transformations of genre and visuality, I hear in it a refutation of the Shiv Sena's violent efforts to make Bombay a Marathi city, the exclusive home of Marathi speakers.[67] Whereas Ram Gopal Varma's prior Hindi film, *Rangeela*, sidesteps the "traditional Hindi-Urdu conflict" by adopting an idiom as mixed as the streets of Bombay, *Satya* adds yet another level of complexity via the accents that the *tapori*-turned-gangsters use.[68] The range of accents audible in the film also attunes us to the connections between Hindi cinema and the film industries of South India. It unsettles the (presumed) monolingualism that has kept in place the hegemony of "Bollywood" for so long. Listening to the xenophonic accents of the Bombay underworld in *Satya* affirms the proximity of the many languages and the many cinemas of India.

## Hyderabadi Politics

*Satya* gives us three different South Indian characters who speak very different dialects and accents—Jagga, Kallu mama, and Satya—all marked, none of them mocked. Let us begin with Jagga (Jeeva), the minor gang leader we meet in an early scene. He arrives at the beer bar in which Satya works to shake down the owner. His opening gambit is this: "Salaam Shanti sheth! Kya [hona], bhai? Counter ke peechche baita bahut notaan gin raha hein?" (Greetings, Shanti seth! What's going on? You're counting a lot of notes sitting behind the counter, are you?). Jagga's use of the plural *notaan* for "notes" is the most obvious marker of his Hyderabadi moorings. In his fawning response, the bar owner (Shanti seth) uses the more common suffix for pluralizing Hindi words, *-ein*. Jagga's *notaan* becomes *notein*. The bar owner thus effectively translates Jagga's Hyderabadi phrasing, thereby highlighting Jagga's linguistic choices. In case we haven't been able to place his accent and dialect, the singsong cadence audible even in his angry outbursts, Bhiku explicitly names Jagga as a "Hyderabadi" just a few short scenes later.

That Jagga is from Hyderabad is a subtle sign that language politics are in play. The postindependence linguistic organization of states in India grew out of the agitation in Telugu-speaking areas. The creation of Andhra Pradesh in 1956 did not settle questions of linguistic and cultural identity in the three distinct regions the state spanned. Hyderabad, the erstwhile capital of Andhra Pradesh (and, since 2014, of Telangana), occupies a complex position in relation to linguistic nationalism and cinema. Given the city's geopolitical history—it is located in Telangana, which was under indirect rule by the British, governed by the Nizam—its lingua franca in the mid-1950s was Urdu, not Telugu. The city did not figure prominently in the Telugu literary and cinematic imagination.[69] It was an important distribution center for Hindi and English films, more so than Telugu ones. Until the 1990s, most Telugu films were produced in Madras (now Chennai), an important hub for South Indian film production since the 1930s. Between the 1960s and 1980s, however, filmmakers and other cultural brokers worked hard to make Hyderabad a *Telugu* film city by developing the city's infrastructure for film production and consumption.[70] Agitations for Telangana statehood continued alongside such efforts to consolidate the status of Hyderabad as the cultural center of Andhra Pradesh, culminating in 2014 with the establishment of Telangana and Andhra Pradesh as distinct states (with Hyderabad and Amaravati as their respective capitals). By casting Jagga as a Hyderabadi and making audible his ties to that city through the Hindi he speaks, *Satya* offers the attentive listener a critique of the political struggles that turned Bombay into Mumbai in the 1990s.

It is true that Jagga is cast as a villain in the film; it is by murdering him that Satya enters the community of gangsters. But, the film does not vilify Jagga for being an outsider to Bombay. After all, the hero of the film, Satya, is also an outsider. The bar scene in which the two first encounter each other begins with four women dancing to "Tum To Thehre Pardesi" (You Are But a Foreigner), singer Altaf Raja's 1997 hit. The chorus announces the film's and the gangster genre's interest in loyalty and place: "Tum to thehre pardesi / Saath kya nibhaoge" (You are but a foreigner / you won't stand by me). If at first these words seem to apply to Satya, who has just arrived in Bombay, it quickly becomes apparent that the city is filled with people with attachments to other places.

Jagga enters the bar and begins a conversation with Shanti seth in the middle of this song. The chorus continues throughout his chat with the bar owner, pausing only when Jagga yells and lunges at Satya for not mixing his drink properly. As violence takes center stage, the pop musical commentary stops. Melodramatic sound effects and music drown out not just the song but also Jagga's furious words. Instead, we hear what sound like human voices going "Boom. Boom. Aaaa! Boom. Boom." Heavy reverb and a dramatic melody on strings heighten the impact of this moment. These sounds mark other instances of violence in the film as well, and I return to them later in this chapter. Here I want to note how this use of sound frames Jagga's accent. Like his Dubai-based boss, Guru Narayan—and like Satya, who has just arrived in town—Jagga is perhaps a *pardesi*, a "foreigner" to Bombay. His accent is the most stereotypical of the film's three South Indians. But generic and stylistic elements, particularly the booming vocal sounds, keep mockery at bay. There is a price to be paid for disrespecting Jagga, for laughing at him. *Satya* helps us avoid that mistake by *not* marking encounters with him as comic interludes (as is Hindi cinema's wont) and by instead moving to violence very quickly.[71]

Also note that Jagga's is one among a slew of Hindi accents in *Satya*. This suggests that *everyone's* speech patterns are tied to some place or another. All accents are oral performances, intentional or otherwise, of people's travels, histories, and identities. Hearing an accent like Jagga's in the context of a range of other Hindi accents turns his voice into something other than a stereotype. Writing about Vishal Bhardwaj's brilliant rendering of *Macbeth* as a Bombay crime story, Moinak Biswas notes that in *Maqbool* (2003) the stereotype of the Muslim mafia is "neutralized" and transformed into something else: "The density of details—extending from accents, vocal inflections, gestures to clothes, architecture, food and ritual—lends an almost moving solidity to [that] mode of community living."[72] Something similar is going on here. Jagga, being a minor character in *Satya*, remains a cardboard figure. He is not painted with the kind of precision that Jahangir/Duncan (Pankaj Kapoor) is in *Maqbool*. And yet, the plethora of xenophonic accents in the film, including Jagga's, draws attention to the aurality of language and attunes us to the social landscape of the city and its underworld.

## Xenophonic Natives

In the sound of Kallu mama or Mamu's (Saurabh Shukla) language, we have a quite different representation of a South Indian. A high-ranking figure in Bhiku's gang, Kallu mama is marked as South Indian by his dress: he always wears a white *veshti* with a thin border and a white *baniyan* (undershirt). He uses a thin cotton towel of the kind used in Tamilnadu and Kerala. The reference to darkness in his name (*kallu* or *kaalu* is an insult meaning "black" or "dark") and the honorific title for uncle (*mama*) might also be derogatory references that have stuck over time. But despite these and other hints in the dialogue to Kallu mama's southern roots, he is far from an outsider. In the opening sequence, just as the narrator says the words "Mumbai underworld," the film cuts to a close-up of Kallu mama pointing a gun at the camera—*he* is the definitive Mumbai gangster. As the film unfolds, it becomes clear that he is a veteran criminal, regarded as the most intelligent of his motley crew.

His command of Bambaiyya, the hybrid tongue of Bombay, indicates that he has been raised in the streets of the city. He confirms his rootedness in a throwaway phrase during an extortion encounter. "Kya lagta hain tereko, log idhar Alibag se aaya hain?" (What do you think, people here have come from Alibag?) he roars at a builder, using a turn of phrase that distances him from naive out-of-towners. Thus, Kallu mama claims implicitly what Bhiku declares explicitly: "Main Mumbai ka hain" (I am of Mumbai).

Then again, Kallu mama's claim to the city is not the same as Bhiku's, for Bhiku marks himself as Maharashtrian. Bhiku's most famous line in the film is a question he shouts to the sea: "Mumbai ka king kaun? Bhiku Mhatre!" (Who is the king of Mumbai? Bhiku Mhatre!) (see figure 3.1). In this and other scenes, he uses the Marathi word for the city, rather than the Hindi or English one (Mumbai, rather than Bambai or Bombay). In so doing, he announces himself as primarily a Marathi speaker.[73] Chander (Snehal Dabi) does the same. Like others in their gang, they speak Bambaiyya; however, they use more Marathi words and pronunciations than their peers do. For example, Chander frequently adds and stresses vowel sounds: *mast* becomes *mast-uh*, and *aurat* becomes *ow-rath*. This "breakthrough of native language phonology" is what linguists call an L2 accent.[74] Conversations in Bhiku's family move fluidly between Hindi and Marathi. The first shot of Bhiku also shows him to be Maharashtrian: he is seated at home reading *Loksatta*, a popular Marathi newspaper. He and his wife, Pyaari (Shefali Chhaya), struggle with English and tease one another about their discomfort with the language. While out to dinner with Satya and Vidya, Bhiku describes *Jurassic Park* (dir. Steven Spielberg, 1993) as the "chipkali-wali picture" (lizard film). His use of the Hindi word *chipkali* tells us that he and Pyaari have watched the film in its dubbed Hindi version, rather than in English.[75] Even as he shares a funny anecdote about their experience of watching the film, Bhiku is clearly unaware that *chipkali* is an unfortunate, if necessary, translation of "dinosaur." He also confuses the title of the film with a famous green space in Bombay, Jijamata Park, which he pronounces "Jijamata *Par-uk*," revealing yet again the sounds of Marathi in his speech patterns. As Pyaari tries to correct him, she falters: "Jusar... Jucas...." Neither of them knows the meaning of the word in scientific discourse. At this point, our heroine, Vidya, guesses the title. Living a life of big money and violence, Bhiku and Pyaari are worldly subjects, but Vidya, with her ease in English, is the more cosmopolitan one. The couple is well aware of this, and so it is a point of pride that their children are fluent in English. When the family visits him in jail, Bhiku laughs in delight as his

Figure 3.1. "Mumbai ka king kaun?" asks Bhiku Mhatre (Manoj Bajpayee) in *Satya* (dir. Ram Gopal Varma, 1998).

daughter recites the nursery rhyme "Twinkle twinkle, little star." Implicit in his laughter is the knowledge that the colonial tongue is a mark of sophistication. Bhiku's fluency in Marathi and Hindi—and Bambaiyya—demonstrates his rootedness in Bombay, but it also threatens to mark him and his family as too provincial.

Satya, by contrast, seems to come from nowhere. He rebuffs Bhiku's questions about his hometown or his family, hinting only at some trauma in his past: "Kya farak padtha hai? . . . Jaantha nahi. . . . Shayad mar gaye honge" (What difference does it make [where I come from]? . . . I don't know . . . [My relatives] may have all died). The narrative voice-over at the beginning of the film also gives us no clue as to where he comes from or why he arrives in Bombay. All we are told is that he arrives from "somewhere" at a particularly charged historical moment, when gang warfare and police violence are at an all-time high.[76] Satya is fluent in Hindi, but like many in his line of work he, too, is rendered a xenophonic speaker of Hindi in Bombay. The fact that he does not use Bambaiyya, as the other gang members do, confirms that he is a recent migrant to Bombay. Satya is a man of few words, so his accent can be hard to hear except in the handful of scenes when he is moved to speak at some length. When he makes his case to Bhiku and Kallu mama that they ought to kill the police commissioner, Satya's pronunciations evidence the fact that he comes from a South Indian place or family, where Hindi is not the language of daily transactions.[77] For instance, he does not aspirate certain syllables (he says *kushi* instead of aspirating the first syllable: *khushi*). That his South Indian accent is more audible in moments of crisis is telling. It is in these moments that his performance of masculine mastery, including his linguistic command of Hindi, breaks down.

It might be easy to dismiss such moments as reflecting actors' insufficient vocal skills. That is, we might say that J. D. Chakravarthy's and Jeeva's accents say little about their characters (Satya and Jagga, respectively); their accents simply announce the fact that the actors are Telugu speakers. Similarly, we might argue that Kallu mama's lack of a South Indian accent reflects actor (and cowriter) Saurabh Shukla's inability to modulate his accent to fit his character. This lack of linguistic fidelity is not a problem for Bombay cinema, whose conventions have not historically required pristine accents. Moreover, as Uday Bhatia notes in his book about the making of the film, "the idea of imposing standards of excellence on a mongrel tongue [Bambaiyya, in particular] seems to miss the point."[78] Like me, he adores the multiplicity of audible speech in *Satya*:

> One of the smaller pleasures of Satya is the melding and clashing of accents and tones. There's Shukla's no-nonsense rasp; Snehal Dabi's tapori patter; Chakravarthy's look-before-you-step negotiation of the Hindi language. Bajpayee's lilting voice contrasting with Shefali Shah's [Chhaya] middle-class Maharashtrian accent adds an extra bit of frisson to their combustive pairing. ("Bheeku doesn't sound like a Maharashtrian, Pyaari does," [Anurag] Kashyap told me. "But when they use Bambaiyya, people don't question it because it's a mix of all immigrant languages.")[79]

Thus, the cinephilic pleasures of dialogue-*baazi* in *Satya* come not from its realism, but from the sense of plurality this verbal soundwork generates. The actors' performances are true to a certain idea of Bombay and Bambaiyya, one that thrives on multiplicity and difference.

The soundwork of *Satya* amplifies the argument against linguistic purity and exceptionalism implicit in Bambaiyya and, more generally, in the *tapori*'s performance. What I hear in this film is not simply Bambaiyya, but the association of certain characters with Bombay (Kallu mama, Bhiku Mhatre, Chander) and others with Hyderabad (Jagga) or South India more generally (Satya). The Bombay-based characters are themselves differentiated by their familial and/or regional backgrounds. Thus, where films like *Rangeela* present us with a Bambaiyya-speaking *tapori* as an alternative to the generic North

Indian hero, *Satya* gives us many different iterations of Bambaiyya. In other words, this gangster film does not privilege particular Hindi or Bambaiyya accents over others. Instead, it multiplies the accents we hear in the criminal heart of the city. In the process, Bombay is rendered even more clearly as a motley space, filled with people with multiple attachments and histories. In casting everyone—from Satya to Bhiku to Jagga—as xenophonic speakers of Hindi, *Satya* argues that many different groups can lay equal claim to the city and its language(s).

## Language, Violence, and Marginality

*Satya* also extends the sonic and linguistic performance of the *tapori* by giving it a violent edge. Satya's silence and stoicism, not to mention his proclivity for violence, make him more Bachchan-esque than *tapori*. It is Bhiku and his associates who are more *tapori*-esque. Bhiku, Kallu mama, the lawyer Mule (Makarand Deshpande), and others in the gang use language that is even more in your face, more thrilling than the *tapori* idiom. They up the ante by giving us language that is as violent and crude as it is funny. In one sense, *Satya* is true to form. Speaking of Hollywood gangster films, many of which inspired *Satya*, Sarah Kozloff writes: "just as the gangster is unrestrained in his approach to violence, so is he promiscuous in his approach to words."[80] One finds many a garrulous and acerbic mafioso in the genre. In another sense, though, *Satya* is exceptional, for it represents a sharp departure from Bombay film conventions. As Amitava Kumar explains: "In a film like *Satya*, more than the guns exploding on the screen, it is abuse that erupts over and over again. This is the spectacular eruption of language from the street. Fresh, energetic, highly gregarious, utterly welcome—the film's dominant idiom constitutes a full assault on the ears previously attuned to hearing only syrupy declarations of platonic love."[81] Indeed, *Satya* revises more than just Hindi cinema's romantic idiom. It reconfigures representations of the city and the place of language in the life of Bombay. In Kumar's description, language has a kind of tactility and volition. If, as Ranjani Mazumdar observes, language is the *tapori*'s "weapon," this is especially the case in *Satya*.[82] Language "erupts" from the streets; it "assaults" the ears. It is as violent as the gun battles on the streets of Bombay. Emerging from the same spaces, it is as much a part of the cinematic and urban sensorium as the bullets are. This is what happens when the vagabond, the *tapori*, turns violent.

In depicting the city's underworld as a multiethnic, polyglot space, *Satya* follows its cinematic predecessor *Nayakan* (*Leader*, dir. Mani Ratnam, 1987). Mani Ratnam's take on *The Godfather* was produced in Tamil and dubbed into Telugu (and, a decade later, into Hindi as well).[83] It quickly came to be regarded as a classic of Indian cinema, winning the National Awards for Best Actor, Best Art Direction, and Best Cinematography. *Nayakan* tells the story of Varadarajan Mudaliar, or Varda *bhai* (brother/boss), a Tamilian migrant to Bombay who rose from being a petty smuggler working on the Bombay docks to become the don of Dharavi and adjacent suburbs. The gangster in the film, Velu, is addressed as Velu *nayakar* or just *nayakar*. This respectful Tamil title underscores his popularity—the film casts him in the mold of Robin Hood— and the fact that many residents of his stronghold are Tamilian. His non-Tamilian associates refer to him as Velu *bhai*. As he attempts to wrest power from politicians, businessmen, and fellow gang leaders, Velu repeatedly confronts the place of language in gang-world machinations and his own unease with Hindi. When he arrives at a summit of the city's dons, for instance, the convener, Lalaji, introduces him to the Reddy brothers, Chandrakant Kohli, and Mustafa *bhai*. While the negotiations take place in Hindi, the introductions and asides confirm what we can guess from the men's names: they are all primarily speakers of other languages—of Gujarati, Telugu, Marathi, and Urdu, respectively. While Velu follows much of the conversation and manages to broker a risky deal by the end, he must rely on the translational skills of his right-hand man.

A lot changed in Bombay, particularly in the city's underworld, in the ten years that separate *Nayakan* and *Satya*. For one, Bombay became Mumbai. The change was a linguistic shift, in that the name commonly used in English was replaced by the one used in Marathi. (The city has long been called "Bambai" in Hindi.) The official renaming of Bombay was ostensibly a move away from the colonial past. The city was owned by the Portuguese before it came into the hands of the British, who used an Anglicized form of the Portuguese *Bom bahia* (good bay). The shift to the more indigenous-sounding Mumbai in 1995 was the culmination of a concerted campaign by the Shiv Sena to claim space, jobs, and other resources for native Maharashtrians.[84] The communalization of the public sphere that had been underway for several decades worsened in the 1990s, and Bombay felt the brunt of it. The riots that followed the demolition of the Babri Masjid by Hindutva forces in December 1992, and the bomb blasts that rocked the city a few months later, apparently orchestrated by the Dubai-based crime boss Dawood Ibrahim to avenge anti-Muslim violence, created a rift in Bombay's criminal networks. The financial and production circuits of the Hindi film industry were such that it was deeply imbricated with crime syndicates. Films of this era underscored this porous relationship between cinema and crime.[85]

Even as it acknowledges the heightened communalization of the Bombay underworld, *Satya* insists on the multiethnic composition of the city and its criminal underbelly. The film announces its indebtedness to *Nayakan* in its opening credits: small, shabby boats on the Bombay shoreline, one of them steered by two boys, form the backdrop to the name of the director and the film. Following the credits is a sequence of unglamorous shots highlighting the violence that pervades the city. For its part, *Nayakan* begins with a young boy, Velu, running away to Bombay from Thoothukudi (in Tamilnadu) after killing a police officer who had used him to locate and murder his father. Lost and alone at first, Velu finds succor in Bombay when another Tamilian boy, son of a fisherman and petty smuggler, invites him into his family. *Satya* follows *Nayakan* in focusing on everyday life and the most marginalized inhabitants of Bombay. Both films begin with violence and poverty, and with those who escape to the metropolis in search of a better life.

That said, unlike Mani Ratnam's film, *Satya* does not foreground South Indians' marginal status in the city. Here we have a figure who knows Hindi well and does not need to rely on translators for any of his social or business transactions. From the moment he arrives at the city's iconic Victoria Terminus, he is at home in the city.[86] As he walks past the station, he does not look lost; he does not stop to ask for directions, and, in the very next shot, he arrives at the dairy stable where he rents a corner. If he is a stranger to Bombay, he does not act like it. *Satya*'s consistent refusal to name where he comes from means that he is associated with no place but Bombay. In this regard, *Satya* recalls Vidhu Vinod Chopra's *Parinda* (1989), that other classic gangster film that features a Tamil overlord whose past is a bit of a mystery. In that film, Nana Patekar plays the gangster known only as Anna (the Tamil word for "older brother"). He does not speak in a stereotypical South Indian accent, indicating that he, like Kallu mama in *Satya*, has lived in Bombay for decades. A flashback of an adolescent Anna bullying other street kids confirms his long association with the city. What is key for our purposes is that *Satya* is among a cluster of Bombay crime films that feature Tamil protagonists. While these films broach the matter of the gangsters' past quite differently, they do clear a space in the city for their South Indian antiheroes.[87]

Linguistic and regional divides also feature prominently in Mani Ratnam's

terrorism trilogy—*Roja* (1992), *Bombay* (1995), and *Dil Se* (1998)—particularly
in the Tamil version of *Roja* and in *Dil Se*. As S. Shankar has pointed out, the
dubbed Hindi version of *Roja* does not capture the linguistic dislocations that
make its heroine's struggle in Kashmir so poignant.[88] Her battle is not just
with the militants who have taken her husband hostage, but with the military
and political authorities who fail to understand or care. Given the linguistic
incomprehension of the state, she must rely on a fellow Tamilian she encounters, a translator figure, who helps her navigate the bureaucracy and daily life
in a new place.[89] *Bombay*, the second film in the trilogy, focuses on the riots
that tore its titular city asunder in the 1990s. Disowned by their respective
families in Tamilnadu, an interreligious (Hindu-Muslim) couple elopes to
Bombay, only to have communal animus rear its head in their adoptive home
a few years later. The links between linguistic, religious, and regional otherness come to a head in a different manner in the final film, *Dil Se*. The hero
Amar's hegemonic position is clear in his naive reporting on the populace's
opinions on the fiftieth anniversary of Indian independence. Here, as in the
rest of the trilogy, it is women who represent the ambivalence and alienation
that various marginalized groups feel toward the nation-state.[90] As I argue
elsewhere with regard to *Ek Duuje Ke Liye* (1981), *Dil Se* uses romance to stage
for the Hindi film viewer the life-or-death stakes of linguistic and other kinds
of difference.

I mention this coterie of films dealing with South Indians' relationship
to the conceptual and physical terrain that Hindi cinema takes as given (i.e.,
the notion of India and the city of Bombay) because what *Satya* does with
that terrain is different—and arguably, more radical. Rather than asserting
the hegemony of the Hindi-speaking subject and casting South Indians as
subalterns, as most of the aforementioned films do, *Satya* makes xenophonic
speakers of Hindi a powerful and quintessential part of the city. Embedded in
the city's organized crime network, they are at the heart of the crises that beset
Bombay in the 1990s. Their accents make Bombay a very particular kind of
city, one that is as diverse as it is dark. It gives them such solidity of presence
that it forces us to acknowledge that they have long been a part of Bombay,
and cannot be driven back to "where they came from." The whispers of else-
wheres in their speech affirm that one can be attached to multiple places at
once. Much more than an assertion of Tamil presence, the audibility of South
Indians in *Satya*'s diegesis (some who are fluent in Hindi and Bambaiyya,
others who are less so) is a reminder that *all* people speak with an accent, and
that hybrid linguistic practices are an everyday occurrence in a multilingual

space like Bombay. By giving us a multitude of xenophonic voices, by making both Maharashtrians and South Indians xenophonic speakers of Hindi, *Satya* offers a counterhistory of the city to the one proposed by nativist groups. In other words, even as Satya attempts to silence his own traumatic past, the sound of his and his associates' speech articulates the collective past and present of the city as polyphonic and violent. The film thus extends the characterization of Tamil subalternity in Bombay that was begun in *Nayakan* and that continues even in more recent films like *Kaala* (dir. Pa. Ranjith, 2018).

## *Dhichkiaoon!* and Other Cinematic Sounds

*Satya*'s distinctive sound design and score help root the diverse accents in the space of the city. Satya and his accomplices' voices are so much a part of the space that they cannot be distinguished from the other sounds that constitute Bombay. For instance, when Satya is beaten up on a rooftop patio, his screams and the taunts of his attackers meld with the sounds of the traffic below. The horn of a passing train gets louder as Jagga walks up to the camera overseeing the torture. In this moment, the iconic sound of the city train *becomes* Jagga's voice. Even in scenes that call for a less intense ambience, sounds of traffic function as the aural signature of Bombay. For example, we hear the rain and rickshaws over Chander's boastful chitchat as he escorts Satya to his new residence. Unlike Bhiku, who is able to quiet his children when their noisy play intrudes on his phone conversation, Chander cannot shut down the din of urban public space. Sounds of the city routinely overwhelm his and other characters' words. The noisiness of the beer bar discussed above is also a case in point. The song to which the bar dancers perform, "Tum To Thehre Pardesi," persists throughout Jagga's conversation with the bar owner. When Satya fatally shoots Jagga in a later scene, the film song playing in the bar, "Hanh Mujhe Pyaar Hua Allah Miya" (Yes, Dear Allah, I fell in Love) (from Judaai [Separation, dir. Raj Kanwar, 1997]), does not even bother pausing. In the famous chase sequence that ends with Guru Narayan's death on a railway bridge, the tense music that leads up to the murder is as loud as Bhiku's rant about his collaborator-turned-nemesis. Thus, it is not just ambient sounds but also the score that "talks over" the characters.[91]

In all these scenes, language is treated *as sound*—and as part of the film's soundwork. In chapter 1, I discussed how voice comes to be construed as a musical instrument that playback singers can deploy in different ways. The widespread use of digital technology in Bollywood today also allows music

directors to manipulate the vocal parts they record. The singer's voice has
become one of many sonic fragments out of which music directors piece
together a song. In *Satya*, the sounds produced by actors—that is, their
*speaking* voices, not just singing voices—are treated in much the same way.
Attempting to evoke the terror of living in Bombay in the late 1990s, the film
uses an aural style that is at once highly naturalistic and highly stylized and
melodramatic. It evinces great fidelity to the spaces in which the action takes
place, while also emphasizing the dangers and conflicts Satya encounters.
Language is an important element of both these aspects of the soundwork.
But words are not prioritized over other sounds in the mix. Both diegetic
and nondiegetic sounds frequently fuse with, and sometimes overpower, dialogues. Words sometimes take the place of other sounds. That is, the film
sometimes uses words where one would otherwise expect music or sound
effects. Thus, it is not just the intelligibility of words but their *sonority*, the
way they sound, and their relationship to other sounds that matters.

A story from the making of the film underscores this point. In an early
scene, a local gangster, Pakya (Sushant Singh), threatens Satya with a knife as
he demands money to set up a neighborhood "orchestra." Satya's response to
this extortion attempt is to slash the man's face. During the shoot, Sushant
Singh improvised a bloodcurdling scream that clarified for the director the
"tone" and "metre" of the film.[92] *Satya* became a film that made audible
and visible the visceral terror of violence. On screen, the scene begins with
the startlingly realistic sounds of a working dairy stable—buffaloes grunt-
ing, men sweeping water out of animal sheds—but ends on a highly stylized note. Deep, percussive male voices define the standoff between Pakya
and Satya. "Boom. Boom. Aaaa! Boom. Boom" intone the anonymous voices
as the former is revealed to be Jagga's henchman. Comical as these sounds
look in print, they make for a rather scary scene. The tension between Jagga
and Satya is held in these voices. They mark the first encounter between the
two men in the beer bar scene described earlier. They follow Pakya when he
retreats to his boss's hotel room to show him his wounds. They also carry
over into the next scene, when Jagga exacts revenge. In the face-off at the
stable, the aural suspense is broken the moment Satya turns on his harasser.
Loud, melodramatic strings accompany Pakya's scream. He issues a torrent of
abuse and a counterthreat: "Maar dala, re! . . . Jagga bhai! Tabela jala dalega!"
([He's] killed me! . . . Jagga bhai! [I will] burn down the dairy stable). Pakya's
precise words in this moment are hard to discern, loaded as they are with
agony and anger. They are also indistinguishable from the orchestral sounds

that accent Satya's first act of violence in the film. As "dramatic speech" turns into "emanation speech" in this scene, the distinctions between Chion's three categories of spoken language in cinema seem unnecessary. The words Pakya screams functions like, and alongside, the dramatic sounds that punctuate the film. Words operate *as sound*. They are part of the film's "sonic weave," its soundwork, and the aural sensorium of the city.[93]

Sandeep Chowta's award-winning score for *Satya* contains a mix of vocal and nonvocal elements. There are the familiar plaintive *alaaps* and melodies that convey pathos.[94] But there are also machine-generated and machine-modified voices that rise up during crisis points. These sounds are audible not only during Satya's confrontations with Jagga, but also in the scenes where Bhiku's gang threatens a music director and attacks a rival gang. The prison fight between Bhiku and Satya uses similarly foreboding vocal sounds: the soundtrack's growls seem to be voicing what Bhiku recognizes as Satya's Bachchan-esque anger. Likewise, when Bhau Thackeray arrives at Bhiku's gang headquarters, a clipped chant that sounds like a Hindu prayer (also in a male voice) leads him into the space. A similarly eerie, if somewhat clearer, chant marks the scene of his murder at the seaside Ganesh Chathurthi festivities. In all these examples, the power of words—and sounds that *sound or act* like phonemes—lies less in their precise meaning, or even in their rhetorical flourish, than in their aurality.

By conceiving of language as sound, *Satya* pushes us to do more than listen for the denotations and connotations of words. We must make sense of the sound of words in other ways as well. The injunction to listen carefully is implicit in the film's use of an opening voice-over. It takes a while for the character who issues this opening pronouncement to appear on screen as Khandilkar (Aditya Srivastava), the rising star of the city's police force and the person who eventually kills Satya. The very first dialogues we hear come from an offscreen dairy worker, Bhure, whom we never see or meet. Satya's landlord (Manoj Pawa) chitchats with him before leading Satya to the corner he rents out to him. Joking about what a wonderful spot it is, he notes the sound of the buffaloes on his property: "There is no need for an alarm clock. [You start your day when] the buffalo says, 'Get up! Bheinnn!'" The film thus tells us from the very beginning to open our ears to words issuing from unseen, unexpected sources, even when those sounds do not seem meaningful at first. Another reference to acousmatic voices lies in the fact that Satya's beloved, Vidya, is an aspiring playback singer. She, too, introduces herself vocally before she appears on screen (she lights a match to reveal her face in the darkness of a power cut). These various moments rely on the audience's acceptance of the sound/image split, and the particular forms it takes in Hindi films. We must listen even when the source(s) of sound remain somewhat unclear. Words may be spoken, sung, or screamed—or mooed, for that matter. In each case, sound amplifies, extends, supplements, and augments the sense that the words are meant to convey.

Some of the words that come at us in *Satya* are cinematic sounds, particularly those used to denote violence on screen. If words function as sound in the scream that inspired the film's tone, the reverse occurs in the raucous Kallu mama song. A cinematic sound (effect) functions as a word. "Goli Maar Bheje Mein" (Shoot a Bullet through the Brain) is the song sequence that marks the gang's drunken celebration of Bhiku's release from jail (see video 3.1 https://doi.org/10.3998/mpub.11713921.comp.10).[95] A highly ironic, self-conscious number, "Goli Maar" mobilizes two aural conventions of mainstream Bombay cinema: the lip-synched song-dance sequence and the sound effect that accompanies gunshots, *dhichkiaoon*. It acknowledges how out of place such "melodramatic" conventions are in a film like *Satya*, and yet it manages to use them to great effect. This is one of many sequences in which the film "reminds us of all the *dhishoom-dhishoom* fights we have witnessed in 1970s movies like *Deewar*."[96] "Goli Maar" heightens the force of those action sequences by multiplying the gunshot in the opening stanza (and hook).

> *Goli maar bheje mein—dhichkiaoon!*
> *Bheja shor karta hain*
> Shoot a bullet through the brain—*dhichkiaoon!*
> For the brain makes a lot of noise.

To say that violence echoes through this song is an understatement. We get not one or two, but *four* instantiations of the gunshot. The injunction to shoot a bullet ("Goli maar bheje mein") is followed by the onomatopoeic word that signifies cinematic bullets (*dhichkiaoon*) and the actual sound of a gunshot. Later on, we see Kallu mama pick up a gun and fire it (see figure 3.2). Like *dhishoom-dhishoom*, the sound of heroes and villains throwing punches, *dhichkiaoon* is a sound effect that has entered the vocabulary of Bombay, and of Hindi film fans in particular. Such sounds-turned-words call up the gloriously over-the-top aural and visual aesthetic of action sequences in Hindi cinema. By making sound part of both the lyrics and the music—that is, by repeating the word for a sound over and over, while also incorporating the sound effect itself into the music—"Goli Maar" keeps both sound and sense in play.

Figure 3.2. *Dhichkiaoon!* "Goli Maar Bheje Mein," *Satya* (dir. Ram Gopal Varma, 1998).

Earlier in this chapter, I argued that *Satya* mobilizes xenophonic accents that might otherwise seem out of place in Bombay. Notice how the film makes the same point, if in more abstract and playful fashion, with cinematic sounds not usually heard as language. *Dhichkiaoon* is a sound that is musical—pronouncing this sound effect demands familiarity with its musicality, the ebbs and flows of this arrangement of phonemes.[97] This sound/word/sound effect erases the line between music, speech, and sound. It is, in so many ways, the perfect "aural *punctum*."[98] It demonstrates that even words that sound nonsensical (to some) can make sense and speak to our senses. This is particularly true in the cinematic city of Bombay, which *Satya* takes as its subject. The film reminds us to attend to sounds of all kinds, whether or not they are words voiced by the hero, and whether or not those words are pronounced "correctly." "Goli Maar" ends with a loud crash. We have no option but to listen.

Even as they sound out violence, words like *boom* and *dhichkiaoon* are tongue-in-cheek references to filmic action sequences. These are cinephilic words. They call on our love of Hindi cinema. They inscribe our knowledge of film into the language we speak. To use these words, as writer Amitava Kumar does in the quotation above, is to announce one's awareness of Bombay film history, a knowledge of how it has represented violence on screen for several decades. Cinephilia is thus harnessed to the project of xenophonic languaging. The audible materiality of the gunshot in *dhichkiaoon* is as violent, as piercing, as it is loving. But remember that *Satya* urges us not to limit our love of cinema to Bombay. In its accents, but also in its visuals and narrative logic, the film gestures to South Indian (cinematic) worlds. As several commenters have observed, *Satya* blurs the boundaries between cinema and everyday life, between spaces of violence and domesticity. My analysis demonstrates that it also dispenses with the boundaries between languages and between various filmic traditions. These are all shown to be as proximate as speech is to other sounds.

In this chapter, I have examined how the sound of speech gets at the complexities of place, language, and identity in Bombay cinema. I have argued that *Satya*'s sonic choices, particularly the *tapori*-turned-gangsters' accents, attune us to the promise of xenophonic languaging, both as a theoretical construct and as a way of inhabiting a polyglot, multiethnic, and cinephilic city like Bombay. I have treated the film's soundwork as a whole, listening to the materiality of words in the dialogues, opening voice-over, songs, "background" score, and sound design. The very fact that the lines between speech and other sounds are imprecise in *Satya* is part of the film's argument against a narrow, ethnocentric conception of identity. Thus, even though *Satya* takes the city as its focus, its critique applies to the nation at large. This is a film about not just gang violence and police violence, but also the violence of linguistic nationalism.

Beyond arguing that *Satya* offers a radical take on Bombay and language politics, I have sought in this chapter to unpack how speech signifies in cinema. Foregrounding the oral and aural materiality of language remains an important intervention in the staunchly image-centric realm of cinema studies. It alerts us to the ways in which filmmakers "relativize" speech, the way they "inscribe [it] in a visual, rhythmic, gestural, and sensory totality."[99] Language materiality encompasses the media form of a text (e.g., oral or written, televised or tweeted); its "sensuous" or embodied textures (e.g., grain of voice, pitch, tone); the registers, accents, dialects, and languages deployed; the historical processes and contexts that allow sounds to resonate as they do; and the accretion and circulation of meanings through the interplay of different semiotic domains, within and across texts. It may well be impossible to study every one of these dimensions at once. Still, keeping as many of them in play as possible can not only deepen our understanding of soundwork in a particular film, but also situate that textured analysis of speech in broader political debates about linguistic identity and regional and national belonging.

Homing in on sounds that are "unspoken" even as they are spoken aloud—and that offer discrete but audible affirmations of plurality—I have demonstrated the need to conceptualize cinematic speech not just as stylish verbal performance but as a material site of politics, one that demands multilingual, interaural, and interocular modes of analysis. Such analysis allows us to see and hear some of the connections between Hindi, Tamil, and Telugu cinema, which in turn lays the groundwork for writing new and different histories of cinema in India. That is, listening with a feminist ear makes possible film historiography that is attentive to geography and language, but not bound by these constructs. All in all, conceiving of language as sound—and as one among many sounds—furthers the project of dismantling hierarchical relationships among various languages, accents, and cinematic traditions.

Coda

# Listening, Loving, Longing

A man sits in his cramped quarters sipping whiskey and listening to Lata Mangeshkar. The camera dwells lovingly on his feet and visage. He sways to the beat and sings along, tearing up every now and then: "Aapki nazaron ne samjha pyaar ke kaabil mujhe" (Your gaze found me worthy of love). This touching scene comes midway through *Aligarh* (2015), Hansal Mehta's acclaimed biopic about Ramchandra Siras. A linguist and professor of Marathi literature at Aligarh Muslim University, Siras was suspended from his job upon being exposed as "homosexual." The story garnered national attention in 2010 when Siras took the university to court and won the case, only to be found dead days before he was to resume his post. *Aligarh* focuses on Siras (Manoj Bajpayee) in the last few months of his life, when a journalist, Deepu Sebastian (Rajkummar Rao), befriends him and follows his case as it wends its way through the court system.

*Aligarh* is a "songless" film, realist in style and devoid of spectacular musical numbers. It is, in fact, a fairly quiet film, in keeping with its protagonist's introspective and pensive personality. Yet, one of the most talked-about moments in this film is a "song sequence" (a "song-dance sequence," in fact). While the film quotes older Hindi film songs on several occasions, it is the whiskey-and-music scene described above—a reprisal of a 1962 song, "Aapki Nazaron ne Samjha"—that tends to be singled out for comment. A four-minute song such as this is remarkable in an offbeat film, given that Hindi filmmakers have eschewed lip-synched song sequences for the past several years. Sangita Gopal notes that for decades, the romantic duet was a primary means by which Bombay cinema constituted the couple as a sovereign unit. With New Bollywood taking the postnuptial couple as its starting point, the song-dance number becomes "an asynchronous object, whose time has already passed or is yet to come."[1] Given this recent use of musical numbers, it is tempting to read Siras as both a nostalgic figure—one whose

179

most cherished object is the tape deck on which he plays classic Hindi film songs from the 1960s and 1970s—and someone whose mode of loving is too transgressive for his times. *Aligarh* certainly supports such a reading of Siras as being out of step with the times. However, I want to suggest that the film's soundwork casts Siras's relationship to pleasure and temporality in more complicated fashion.

Attending to the specific way in which *Aligarh* incorporates film songs facilitates a conceptual shift from "soundtrack" to "soundwork." The latter, I have argued, covers much broader intellectual terrain and inspires questions about voicing and listening; sound, speech, and song; language politics; and much more. Listening to *Aligarh*'s soundwork with a feminist ear, we grasp not just its critique of homophobia but also the way it clears a space for those habits of being and belonging, those ways of finding connection and cama-raderie, those experiences and imaginaries that are sidelined or disregarded in the narrative. In other words, the "critical utopianism" of the film becomes more legible when we center soundwork in our analysis and listen with a feminist ear. This is not to say that *Aligarh* is a hopeful or uplifting film. Nor is it to excuse the film's missteps, its "constitutive forgettings"—how it fig-ures Irfan, Siras's lover, as an all-but-silent subaltern or how it makes Siras's casteist beliefs around food seem endearing.[2] Rather, to listen for alternative configurations of desire and temporality in *Aligarh*'s soundwork is to render it more complex. It is to keep in play the film's caste, class, and sexual politics in its auditory realm as much as in its visual one. It is to value the sonic frag-ment such that it staves off the crushing weight of the narrative, and takes us out of our habitual ways of interpreting cinema, if for just a moment, one long moment.[3]

## Textual and Aural Pleasures

*Aligarh* is a film about a man (and his partner) not granted sovereignty or pri-vacy. The film begins at the scene of violation, Siras's apartment, on the fateful night when he and Irfan are ambushed while in bed. The intrusion sets in motion a crisis that forces Siras to keep rehearsing the incident in his mind's eye. The scene appears multiple times, in fragmented form, in a slightly differ-ent way and from a slightly different perspective each time.[4] Another pressing frame in *Aligarh* is the legal battle against Section 377, that part of the Indian penal code (and the colonial British one) that deems certain sexual activities as being "against the order of nature," and thus criminal. Soon after the opening credits comes a statement indicating that the 2009 Delhi High Court decision "declared Section 377 as unconstitutional, effectively decriminalizing homosexuality." The film closes by noting the reversal of that decision in 2013.[5] The events of *Aligarh* are thus firmly located in the period between these two momentous legal decisions. The film's court scenes also underscore the rhetorical importance of privacy in Siras's case and in the Section 377 legal proceedings more generally. So, if *Aligarh* calls up classic Hindi film songs, it is because its protagonist does not have what "the space of a song" used to allow.[6] Tellingly, the film's two "song sequences" cannot constitute the couple form as Hindi film songs of yore did, as they are not typical romantic duets.[7] What they *can* do is render music, and Hindi film music in particular, as Siras's refuge—a refuge that is increasingly made unavailable to him. They stage the intrusion of the outside world into his interior spaces, both physical and affective, and thus map his spatial dislocation through sound.

Siras's crisis is readily apparent when we consider the whiskey-and-music scenes in his various abodes. The first places him in his university flat, listening to "Aapki Nazaron ne Samjha" (Your Gaze Found [Me Worthy of Love]), a song starring Mala Sinha and Dharmendra in *Anpadh* (*Illiterate*, dir. Mohan Kumar, 1962). It is a scene of emotional retreat, for it comes on the heels of him reluctantly signing a letter that expresses shame at having been caught in a compromising position. Both aurally and visually, the sequence constructs a self-enclosed world. Siras is in his apartment by himself. The only sounds apart from Mangeshkar's voice are those of him pouring whiskey and water into a glass and then singing and humming along. The only movements besides his are those enacted by the camera, as it shifts from long shots of the street and the exterior of the building, to a close-up of his tape deck, to medium shots of Siras's seated profile in a mirror, and finally to close-ups of him immersed in the music (see figure 4.1). We stay at this scene of pleasure and pathos for several minutes before a loud crash interrupts the reverie. Siras whips around to the window behind him; the music ends abruptly, and he tiptoes to the door, brandishing a walking stick as weapon. We hear the sound of a motorcycle driving away. Described thus, *Aligarh*'s "Aapki Nazaron" is a metaphorical restaging of the violation Siras has already endured. It demonstrates that Siras's nightly ritual cannot stave off the homophobic depredations directed at him.

*Aligarh*'s second "song sequence" depicts Siras listening (or trying to listen) to another Hindi film song, "Betaab Dil ki Tamanna Yahi Hai" (This Is

Figure 4.1. Ramchandra Siras (Manoj Bajpayee) enjoying whiskey and music in "Aapki Nazaron," *Aligarh* (dir. Hansal Mehta, 2015).

[My] Restless Heart's Only Desire), which first appeared in *Hanste Zakhm* (*Laughing Wounds*, dir. Chetan Anand, 1973). Like the previous song, this one is a Mangeshkar solo that is picturized on a couple (played by Navin Nischol and Priya Rajvansh) in its original filmic iteration. In *Aligarh*, this song marks Siras's forced move from university-owned premises to a small rented room. Surrounded by piles of belongings, Siras attempts to re-create the sanctuary he once enjoyed. The attempt is doomed to fail, for he lacks even running water for his drink here. His listening session is interrupted by mosquitoes buzzing around him and his attempts to squash them. Thus, what we get in this "Betaab Dil" is not so much a song, but the annoying aurality of daily life. In contrast to *Satya* (dir. Ram Gopal Varma, 1998), where such sounds ground the xenophone gangsters in the space of the city (chapter 3), the soundwork here is unsettling. This whiskey-and-music scene ends quickly—it lasts no more than a minute—cutting to the space outside the flat, where we see trucks drive by on the adjacent flyover. Music wafts out of Siras's flat, but neither that space nor Mangeshkar's voice provides him with the refuge he seeks.

By the time Siras lands in his third apartment, there is no music whatsoever. He barricades himself in the room and makes no attempt to lose himself in aural or gustatory delights. We hear street sounds and neighbors' voices, but not Lata Mangeshkar. The next time Siras appears on screen, he is in his flat sleeping with the television on. He is roused from his slumber by the ringtone on his cell phone. It is a call from Deepu. Siras speaks of leaving for the United States after retirement: "I hear people like me can live there with dignity." Thus, *Aligarh's* two "song sequences," in conjunction with the "missing" one (in his third apartment), mark Siras as a man out of place, a man being *pushed* out of place.

In an excellent and important essay, "Queer Intimacy during Seditious Times," Nishant Shahani reminds us of the moral weight of Mangeshkar's voice and the implications of linking it to a figure such as Siras:

> [If] Mangeshkar serves to index the "heart of India" [as music director Naushad once claimed] then the centrality of Siras's attachment functions to suture the gay body to national citizenship so that the potential threat of queerness (historically marked as western and "anti-Indian") gets circumvented. Instead, the legibility of queerness as refracted via Mangeshkar must depend on its proximity to national belonging so that it can be justified as deserving of protection from the law.[8]

In other words, Mangeshkar's voice does more than just lend pathos to the first whiskey-and-music scene. Her voice has accrued such ideological power over the decades that it cathects him to the nation, and cordons him off "from the stigmas of public sexuality" and the racialized politics of caste and communalism.[9] Shahani's argument dovetails with the story I tell above, of how *Aligarh's* soundwork illustrates the destruction of Siras's personal, private refuge. It is not just that Siras cannot enjoy the usual comforts of his home and music. The songs are his claim to a space within the nation—they emplace him in the national imaginary—and that tenuous claim, too, is being threatened. Shahani argues that the film's "homonationalism" (Jasbir K. Puar) rests on the erasure of the lower-class Muslim man who is Siras's lover: Irfan is the "silent subaltern who has no place in the film's present tense."[10] This is a crucial point. Irfan is mainly present as an absence in *Aligarh*, for Siras cannot bear to speak of him or their relationship for much of the film. In his place, Siras has Lata Mangeshkar and Deepu Sebastian. The film also disavows the violence of caste by turning Siras's brahmanical rejection of food that Deepu has touched into a benign, even winsome, character-study moment. I want to build on Shahani's insights about the seditious intimacy of caste and queerness, by listening for moments in which they perhaps "touch" and where the soundwork challenges homonationalist longings.[11]

Aligarh's "Aapki Nazaron" and "Betaab Dil" sidestep conventions that have historically been crucial to the representation of desire in Hindi cinema. No interplay of looks between lovers, no scenic destinations in which to romp around. Siras is alone in his flat when he listens, sings, and sways (dances?) to these songs. Later in the film, at a party celebrating his imminent victory in court, two gay men dance to "Namak Ishq Ka" (The Salt of Love), an item number for Omkara (dir. Vishal Bhardwaj, 2006). While the men do not mimic Bipasha Basu's moves, it is clear that they are staging a seductive number for each other and for their friends in the audience. Brief as it is, this is an alternative picturization, a "re-animation" of "Namak Ishq Ka" in queer mode.[12] The scenes of Siras listening to music similarly give us alternative picturizations of the songs from Anpadh (1962) and Hanste Zakhm (1973). At one point, when asked why his wife left him, Siras insists to Deepu that it was not because of his "sexual preference." He says: "Main apni kitabon, Lata Mangeshkar mein hi uljha rehta tha. Merese bor hokar woh chali gayi" (I used to be engrossed in my books, Lata Mangeshkar [songs]. She got bored of me and left). In other words, Siras attributes his failed marriage to his textual and aural pleasures. It is these very pleasures that are the focus of the whiskey-and-music scenes. Aligarh's "song sequences" articulate different kinds of sensory pleasures, not just the pain of a romance that was and cannot be.

The romantic lyrics of "Aapki Nazaron" notwithstanding, the pleasures the sequence offers in Aligarh are not visual so much as aural and gustatory in nature. Siras listens to music and sips his nightcap. While we hear the hegemonic voice of Mangeshkar, the visual tropes that typically accompany her voice in Hindi cinema are absent. Instead, we are drawn into a scene of listening. Bajpayee's performance, the choreography and editing, and the sheer length of the sequence draw attention to the "sensual aspects of listening."[13] Close-ups of Siras's face render him a "sensate listening body," one that responds to the affective charge of the music and the poetry.[14] The close-up of his crossed legs as he sways his feet to the melody is especially notable. This ten-second-long high-angle shot of his feet lasts the length of the musical interlude between stanzas. The next cut takes us to a close-up of Siras's face that lasts over a minute and a half. Clearly, this is an alternative performance of song and dance, one that does not simply render Siras nostalgic or stuck in the past. The sequence elongates time and draws attention to the intensity of the moment (one long moment). It centers the bodily pleasure of listening, reframing the Hindi film song's codes of pleasure, passion, desire, and the body. Eyes closed, Siras sings along, a bit behind, a bit out of tune, a bit out of time at times. He pauses as he misses a lyric and interrupts his singing to express appreciation (*Wah!*). Throughout, he listens intently, overwrought with emotion. His crumpled face expresses his feelings about not just the past (his memories of lovers in whose eyes he felt himself beloved) but also the present (the pain of not being recognized as one worthy of love in the eyes of society)—and the distance between the past and the present. Thus, we are witness to a double temporality. In Sangita Gopal's argument, song sequences of older Hindi films "visualized and made audible desires, intensities, affects, aspirations, and most importantly *futures* that were in excess of the narrative and its parameters of enunciation."[15] This is also what happens in "Aapki Nazaron." Where other New Bollywood films cast the lip-synched song sequence as a vestige of the past, *Aligarh* uses it to dwell at once in the present and future.

## Translation and Temporality

To fully grasp the critical import of *Aligarh*'s temporal disruptions, I want to turn to a later scene that mobilizes both a Hindi film song and Siras's Marathi poetry. Following a pleasant afternoon together (they eat lunch, go on a boat ride, and chat), Siras hands Deepu his book of poems, *Payakhali Hirwal* (Grass under My Feet). Early in the film, he had sent Deepu home with the book as an autographed souvenir. This copy is more special, for it includes Siras's handwritten English translations, scribbled in court when he was bored with the legal proceedings.[16] As Siras presents the gift, another Lata Mangeshkar (and Kishore Kumar) song begins playing quietly: "Kora Kaagaz Tha Yeh Dil Mera" (My Heart Was a Blank Page), featuring Sharmila Tagore and Rajesh Khanna in *Aradhana* (*Worship*, dir. Shakti Samanta, 1969). This romantic duet acknowledges the friendship that has blossomed between the two men. Deepu is *quite* straight. The film is at pains to assure us of his masculinity and heterosexuality (note the hookup scene with his boss, Namita). Even so, the film renders Deepu's relationship with Siras queer time and again. Siras's gift to Deepu (a book of poems he has translated specifically for him), the duet that plays softly in the distance, and the affectionate tone of the exchange render their relationship in homoerotic terms.[17] Siras, we understand, has filled the blank page (of his heart) with love poems for Deepu.

As Deepu reads from the book on his bus ride back, the voice-over presents Siras's poem in his own voice:

O beloved moon, fear not the dawn that separates us,
For we will meet again when the world goes to sleep
In the light of day, I am unseen. It is in your light, my heart awakens.
We will dance as shadows dance, to the songs of nightingales.
We will touch as shadows touch, becoming one in the midnight sun.
O beloved moon, fear not the dawn that separates us
For we will meet again when the world goes to sleep.

The visuals in this sequence take us from the bus (present) to Siras's memory of the night with Irfan (past). This is the most romantic rendition of their time together. It is as if the joyous play of light and darkness, day and night, in "O Beloved Moon" rewrites the metaphorical darkness of the night Siras and Irfan were attacked. This revision happens, in part, through the use of future tense and the indicative mood. In the lines above, the speaker states as factual what *is* (I am unseen, my heart awakens) and what *will happen* (we will meet again, we will dance, we will touch). The poem also keeps returning to the imperative form in the words "fear not." And yet, the poem as a whole functions as an expression of desire and, as such, is closer to the subjunctive in its feel. The certitude of the indicative and imperative moods notwithstanding, the future that the poem reaches for is uncertain. The beloved fears it; the speaker of the poem looks forward to it. This affective disjuncture—a disorientation toward the future—is important because it captures the uncertainty of what lies ahead. The pleasure of this poem rests in the tension between the present and the future, between the speaker's and the lover's affective states. What the soundwork offers is not a clear goal—a queer progress narrative such as the struggle to repeal Section 377—but a dwelling in feeling, a tarrying that cuts across temporal and affective registers. In this, the poem is not unlike the first whiskey-and-music scene, which compels us to listen. In the elongated time of "Aapki Nazaron," we listen not just to Lata Mangeshkar, the ideal and heteronormative voice of Indian femininity, but also to, and with, Siras. While the scenes of listening I explore here do not conjure publics in the way that the qawwalis I analyze in chapter 2 do, they do similarly rework the connections between listening, loving, and (national) belonging.

"O beloved moon, fear not the dawn that separates us."

Figure 4.2. Deepu Sebastian (Rajkummar Rao) reads Siras's poem "O Beloved Moon" in *Aligarh* (dir. Hansal Mehta, 2015).

Listening and voicing are intimately related in "O Beloved Moon" (see figure 4.2). Recall that Siras's translation of the poem reaches our ears in his own voice, his "writing voice." The term is Rey Chow's, and it names the convention of using voice-overs to make audible words written on a page (typically, letters).[18] The writer is not physically present at the scene of reading, and the text on the page may not be visible to the audience. And yet, the audible words are understood to be the writer's, for the voice is recognizably his. Rendered aloud in an apparently different time and place than the moment of composition, the writing voice is a powerful and special example of Michel Chion's acousmêtre. This acousmatic voice is not just a metaphor for and metonym of presence, or an audible sign of an invisible presence (say a ghost or an omniscient narrator).[19] It is an entity that can travel and materialize in different forms. It can jump off the page and manifest in thin air, as it were. It can translate itself. It also turns a scene of reading into one of listening. It condenses writing, speaking (reciting), reading, listening, and imagining, cutting across as it does the temporal and spatial location of each of these actions. (These boundaries are also breached in the song "Kora Kaagaz," which uses writing as one of several metaphors for loving.) Thus, in more ways than one, Siras's poem materializes movement across time, space, and language. These are generative and pleasurable dislocations, unlike those set in motion by Siras's colleagues' homophobia.

Siras's investment in the capacious politics of language lies at the heart of the argument I am developing here.[20] It *matters* that we hear "O Beloved Moon" not in Marathi, but in English translation. Siras tells Deepu that he fears that "[his] English is not as good as you people's English," hinting at the class, caste, and regional differences between them. Yet we know from prior conversations that Siras is more than proficient in English. He has long been unhappy with the English translation of his book that is in circulation and has considered producing a better translation himself.[21] The crossing of linguistic borders is not just a professional pursuit for Siras, but an aspect of his daily life, his very being:

> *Dekho, mein yahaan bahar ka aadmi samjha jaata hoon.* An outsider. *Urdu bolnewaale shahar mein Marathi sikhata hoon. Shaadishuda logon ke beech akela rahta hoon.*

> Look, I am considered a man from elsewhere. An outsider. I teach Marathi in an Urdu-speaking city. I live alone in the midst of married folks.

Here, Siras makes explicit reference to his outsider status, drawing a connection between linguistic and sexual otherness. In a previous scene, at a gay party, he recites Marathi poetry and translates it into Hindi for his doting audience. I am by no means arguing that queer people have a special affinity for language(s). Rather, I am arguing that the literary pleasures of reading, writing, translating, and listening to poetry are rendered romantic and utopian in *Aligarh*. They inspire border-crossings and forge bonds of various sorts.

Earlier in the film, when Deepu confesses that he does not understand poetry, Siras chides him, saying that poetry resides not in words but in the spaces in between. ("Poetry *shabdon mein kahaan hoti hi, baba? Kavita shabdon ke antaraal mein milti hain.* Silences *mein,* pauses *mein.*") He also critiques the rush to label things, and implores Deepu to instead embrace ambiguity, complexity, and multiplicity. In short, his is a xenophonic orientation to the world. Aptly, actor Manoj Bajpayee's vocal performance casts the poet as a xenophonic speaker, one of many such in the film.[22] My claim is based not just on the L2 accent Bajpayee deploys in the voice-over, but also on "the murmur, the passage, of diverse found speeches" in Siras's poem.[23] As I discuss in chapter 3, Chow's notion of the "xenophone" bolsters the expansive interpretive practice I call listening with a feminist ear. There, I argue that the multiplicity of tongues in *Satya* conjures an alternative present and future for Bombay city, one that is not riven by the chauvinism of linguistic nationalism; here, I link *Aligarh*'s eschewal of linguistic and other boundaries to its caste and queer politics.

## Seditious Touching in Soundwork

I hear in "O Beloved Moon" at least two sets of references: one that calls up Mangeshkar and, by extension, the homonationalist desires that Shahani identifies in *Aligarh*, and another that suggests a more transgressive imaginary. Bajpayee's vocal style, the way he stresses certain words ("dance" and "touch," in particular) and pauses at crucial junctures, makes this rendition quite different in tone from the previous instance in which the poem is invoked (by a lawyer at the gay party). Siras's love of classic Hindi film songs, and Mangeshkar's voice in particular, is apparent in the line about lovers frolicking: "We will dance as shadows dance, to the songs of nightingales." Mangeshkar is often lauded as the "Nightingale of India." Famously, Gandhi bestowed the same title to fellow nationalist and poet Sarojini Naidu. Thus, both the filmic and nonfilmic connotations of the phrase imbue the poem with the romance of nation. We might also hear in the "shadows" of Siras's poem a gesture to the third stanza of "Aapki Nazaron," which begins: "Pad gayi dil par mere aapki parchaaiyan" (Your shadow fell over my heart)." Love liberates the speaker in that song from fear, just as it does in the poem.

The lovers' and shadows' "touch" in "O Beloved Moon" also recalls casteist and homophobic injunctions against touch, which Siras upholds and ignores in turns. For the most conservative, the mere shadow of a lower-caste person, especially one who is Dalit, is considered polluting.[24] Siras does not express this particular casteist superstition in *Aligarh*, and yet, as Shahani suggests, caste casts a long and mostly silent shadow in this film. Brief as it is, the reference to shadows and touching, and "shadows [that] touch," is an instance in which Siras reaches beyond the boundaries of caste that he himself erects when he refuses to eat food that the "nonvegetarian" Deepu has inadvertently touched. On the page and out loud (and, evidently, in bed), he explores the thrilling affective potential of touch in a way that he will not over a shared meal. The queer touch that "O Beloved Moon" imagines and vocalizes is thus also a breaking of caste taboos.[25]

To grasp the proximity of caste and queerness in *Aligarh*—the "seditious touching" of these categories and all the transgressions they imply—we must tune in to the soundwork's "haptic temporalities." Tina M. Campt writes: "The haptic is not merely a question of touch. It is the link between touching and feeling, as well as the multiple mediations we construct to allow or prevent our access to those affective relations. These haptic relations transpire in multiple temporalities, and the hands are only one conduit of their touches."[26] Playing on the double meaning of "touching," Campt argues that the quiet "lower frequencies" of images may be apprehended in multiple modalities. Whereas her focus is on visual archives of the Black diaspora, I want to think about "haptic temporalities" by juxtaposing various moments of "sonic contact" in *Aligarh*.[27] Sound touches and moves us, just as it does Siras. Sound touches in unexpected moments and surprising ways. Theorized aurally, the temporality of touch is not limited to the moment when, or the scene (or an image) in which, bodies touch. The "touch" that materializes in "O Beloved Moon" extends beyond that poem and that scene of reading/ listening, to other moments where Siras is touched by, and touches, other bodies, including those he would otherwise perceive as "lower caste." Listening across diverse moments and forms in *Aligarh*'s soundwork, we realize that the temporalities of listening, loving, and longing are not singular or teleological. Thus, even as the film betrays a homonationalist logic, there is a way in which it simultaneously challenges the grand, and profoundly uninclusive, narratives of nation through its soundwork. At minimum, valuing soundwork over the visuals is a way to continue Siras's refusal of that narrow conception of identity and visibility encapsulated in the notion of "coming out" (and that I explore in relation to voice, in chapter 1) and the violence of surveillance to which he and Irfan are subject.

Over the course of this book, I have made a case for reconceptualizing the aural domain of cinema as soundwork. *Listening with a Feminist Ear* asks that we think beyond and across the bounds of sound, speech, and song; stretch the sound-image relationship as far as possible; engage in willful acts of translation, juxtaposition, and connection; eschew linguistic, sonic, and disciplinary boundaries; and listen to it all, together, at once. The book begins by tracing sonic representations of gender and community across seven decades of Hindi film history. In chapter 1, I lay out the audiovisual logic that makes meaningful the shifting texture of women's singing voices from the 1950s through the present. I follow this analysis of vocality with an exploration, in chapter 2, of representations of the Islamicate and listening in the qawwali during the same time period. Both chapters listen for the history of gendered sounds and audiovisual tropes that shore up the romance of the cinematic nation. Together, these genealogical studies of *singing* and *listening* link aural shifts in gender and sexuality to the cultural politics of the postliberalization period. Changes in other domains of public culture—television and music, in particular—in the 1990s allowed new voices and genres to emerge and revitalized Bombay cinema. I argue that the sound of womanhood and that of the Islamicate were both reworked in this moment of cultural change, with wide-ranging implications for aural notions of selfhood and belonging on screen.

The third chapter takes us from listening back to the question of voicing—to *speaking*, in particular. Whereas chapters 1 and 2 delineate a history of key audiovisual conventions, chapter 3 takes a different approach to defamiliarizing and questioning the normative imaginary reified by those stubborn habits of the ear and eye. In asking which sounds and tongues Bombay (cinema) calls its own, chapter 3 continues the project of bringing a feminist ear to Hindi cinema. As I analyze *Satya*, I do not just listen for difference; I listen to the film differently than other scholars have. Placing spoken accents in relation to other cinematic sounds and cinephilic song lyrics, the history of linguistic nationalism and Hindutva politics, and other filmic traditions besides Bombay cinema, I theorize language as sound and as a material site of politics in cinema. Thus in chapter 3, as in this coda, I take seriously the radical potential of listening and model a critical orientation to the aural that can engender new imaginaries, while still being attuned to questions of difference, power, and privilege. Along the way, I mobilize and revise a number of theoretical concepts and frameworks influential in cinema and media studies and sound studies, including Chion's audiovisual contract, Lacey's listening publics, and Chow's xenophone. My analysis of *Aligarh* in this concluding essay approaches questions about materiality and the body; interaurality; the sound-image relationship; and gender, sexuality, and romance that I explore elsewhere in the book from a different perspective. In so doing, I demonstrate that listening to cinema with a feminist ear may take many forms.

Listening with a feminist ear is, or tries to be, what Eve Sedgwick calls a "reparative critical practice."[28] Perhaps more accurately, we might say that listening with a feminist ear is at once paranoid and reparative, embracing the task of exposing troublesome concepts that take form in sound as well as that of offering alternative formulations that revel in aural and oral pleasures. Such critical listening can produce concepts, genealogies, and futures that challenge those prescribed by nationalist imaginaries, be they heteronormative or homonationalist ones. The point is not to recuperate *Aligarh*, *Satya*, or any other film, or Bombay cinema in general. It is to amplify sonic details such that they foster a critical and utopian interpretive practice that can do what filmic narratives and our ocularcentric and siloed disciplinary formations often struggle to accomplish. Listening with a feminist ear is necessarily a tentative and provisional practice, wary of fixity and ever open to retuning and revision. It is an invitation to listen—and to listen again and to listen anew.

# NOTES

## Introduction

1. Gopinath, "Don't Hold Back Jack," 50.
2. Deo and Duggal, "Radios, Ringtones, and Memory Cards."
3. Punathambekar and Mohan, "Sound Clouds."
4. See, for instance, Jay and Ramaswamy, *Empires of Vision*. While I do not delve in this book into the intersection of technologies of visuality and those of empire, I do challenge the hegemony of the image in scholarly discourse. To assert the intertwining of empire and vision is not to propose that sound (or music) is somehow neutral or inherently liberatory. Michael Denning encapsulates a whole body of scholarship on colonialism, nationalism, and music when he notes: "colonial music practice instituted new disciplines of the body— new ways of singing, of dancing, of marching, of playing instruments. To speak of the colonization of the 'ear' is thus a metonymy: for the reshaping of the musical subject is not only a reshaping of an individual's muscles—the articulated flesh and bones that make up the singing voice, the instrument-playing hands and lips, the dancing feet and hips. It is also the reshaping of the order of the group—the creation of marching bands and church choirs: a colonization not only of the body, but of articulated bodies." Denning, "Decolonizing the Ear," 36.
5. As I discuss in chapter 3, Bombay was renamed Mumbai in 1995. With a few exceptions that pertain to the time period and film in question, I refer to the city as Bombay throughout this book.
6. Gopal and Moorti, *Global Bollywood*; Booth, *Behind the Curtain*.
7. Arnold, "Hindi Filmī Gīt"; Manuel, *Cassette Culture*.
8. See Ranade, *Hindi Film Song*; Morcom, *Hindi Film Songs and the Cinema*; Beaster-Jones, *Bollywood Sounds*; Weidman, *Brought to Life by the Voice*.
9. Notable touchstones in this category are Gopalan, *Cinema of Interruptions*; Majumdar, *Wanted Cultured Ladies Only!*; Mehta, *Censorship and Sexuality in Bombay Cinema*; Gopal, *Conjugations*.
10. Growing scholarly interest in South Asian sound studies was evident in symposia at the University of Michigan and Northwestern University in 2016–17; a series of essays gathered in the special forum "Gendered Soundscapes of India," edited by Monika Mehta and Praseeda Gopinath on the sound studies blog *Sounding Out!* in 2017; and Brueck, Smith, and Verma's 2020 edited volume *Indian Sound Cultures, Indian Sound Citizenship*.
11. Majumdar, "Beyond the Song Sequence."

12. Weheliye, *Phonographies.*

13. Desai-Stephens, "Tensions of Musical Re-Animation"; Weidman, "Voices of Meenakumari."

14. Neepa Majumdar models such an approach as she explores how the distinction between "live" and recorded sound was represented (and experienced/understood) in the early years of sound cinema. The term "interruptions" comes from Lalitha Gopalan's insightful discussion of the structural functions of film songs in Hindi cinema. Monika Mehta teaches us to think about how the material and industrial forms that the Hindi film song takes (in DVD compilations and award shows, for instance) shape audio- and cine-philia, and the very idea of what a "song" is. Majumdar, "Beyond the Song Sequence"; Gopalan, *Cinema of Interruptions*; Mehta, "DVD Compilations of Hindi Film Songs"; Mehta, "Authorizing Gesture."

15. One of the few scholars writing about these sonic elements is Budhaditya Chattopadhyay. See his articles "The Auditory Spectacle," "The Cinematic Soundscape," and "Sound Memories."

16. Sterne, "Sonic Imaginations," 3.

17. Smith, "Futures of Hearing Pasts," 13–14.

18. Kheshti, *Modernity's Ear*, xx.

19. Sterne, "Sonic Imaginations," 3–4.

20. Lipari, in particular, frames listening as an ethical orientation to the world. However, the notion of listening as an ethical activity runs through several key texts in sound studies. See Eidsheim, *The Race of Sound*; Kheshti, *Modernity's Ear*; Lacey, *Listening Publics*; Lipari, *Listening, Thinking, Being*; Stoever, *Sonic Color Line*; Hirschkind, *The Ethical Soundscape*. For a useful summary of the many different ways in which "listening" is conceptualized in sound studies, see Rice, "Listening." Other useful theorizations of listening by scholars of music and sound include Bonenfant, "Queer Listening to Queer Vocal Timbres"; Furlonge, *Race Sounds*; Jarman-Ivens, *Queer Voices*; Ochoa Gautier, *Aurality*; Vazquez, *Listening in Detail*; Zuberi, "Listening while Muslim."

21. Sterne, *The Audible Past*, 19. Roland Barthes makes a similar distinction, casting hearing as a "physical phenomenon" and listening as a "psychological act" that allows auditors to "decipher" sounds. Barthes, "Listening," 245.

22. Sterne, *The Audible Past*, 13. Sterne notes that he is building on Marcel Mauss's theorization of "body techniques" (and that Mauss influenced Michel Foucault's thinking on the subject as well).

23. Huacuja Alonso, "Radio, Citizenship, and the 'Sound Standards,'" 139. For a discussion of the "art of listening" in relation to radio and other sound technologies, music education, and Carnatic music, see Weidman, *Singing the Classical, Voicing the Modern*, 245–85.

24. For a recent discussion of a range of "ways of listening" on the subcontinent, see Rahaim, *Ways of Voice*, 96–144.

25. Sterne, *The Audible Past*, 92; Lipari, *Listening, Thinking, Being*, 52–58; Becker, *Deep Listeners*, 69–86.

26. Ahmed, *Living a Feminist Life*, 203.

27. Ahmed, *Complaint!*, 8.

28. Some influential texts include Barkin and Hamessley, *Audible Traces*; Brett, Wood,

and Thomas, *Queering the Pitch*; McClary, *Feminine Endings*; Radano and Bohlman, *Music and the Racial Imagination*.

29. Stoever, *Sonic Color Line*, 232 (original emphasis).

30. Kheshti, *Modernity's Ear*, xix. For yet another inspiring rumination on the sonic as a counterintuitive and radical modality of perception, see Campt, *Listening to Images*.

31. Eidsheim, *The Race of Sound*, 27–28. While my work falls more squarely in the symbolic analysis camp that Eidsheim critiques, I do share her interest in unsettling the givenness of voice, identity, and listening.

32. I borrow the generative phrase "other times, other places" from a prior essay of mine: Sundar, "Of Radio, Remix, and *Rang De Basanti*." See also Denning, "Decolonizing the Ear"; Kun, *Audiotopia*.

33. Gorbman, *Unheard Melodies*. Elsewhere, I use the phrase "listening with an accent" to inspire a relationship to language that playfully and carefully delinks the static associations between bodies, identities, and place thought to inhere in the way we speak. Listening with a feminist ear is similarly attentive to power and politics, and similarly utopian in its aspirations. It is, arguably, more expansive a concept in that it is not limited to sounds we hear as "speech." See my essay "Listening with an Accent—or How to Loeribari" in Rangan et al., *Thinking with an Accent*.

34. Hilmes, "On a Screen Near You," 177.

35. Hilmes, "The New Materiality of Radio," 60n2.

36. Thompson, *The Soundscape of Modernity*, 1. Also see Samuels et al., "Soundscapes," for an invaluable discussion of the travails of "soundscape" (and affiliated terms) in the context of their call for a sounded anthropology.

37. Ian Garwood astutely argues that even though fewer songs are now incorporated as discrete musical numbers, the prior functions of the song-dance sequence have been taken over by other cinematic elements in "songless" films. Meanwhile, Sangita Gopal avers that the discrete film song (of the kind Bombay cinema has long been known for) is today a queer, asynchronous entity. A nostalgic sign of an older cinema, it is now attached to the bodies of non-heteronormative couples. She also links the "retreat" of the song sequence and simultaneous rise of the item number to the conjugal possibilities of new Bollywood. While I find both of these arguments enormously convincing and generative, I shy away from descriptors that suggest linear temporality or lack, reminiscent as they are of colonial frameworks that place the colonized "behind" or "outside" time. I offer in this book a few other, complementary ways of making sense of the aural in (contemporary) Hindi cinema. Garwood, "The Songless Bollywood Film"; Gopal, *Conjugations*, 23–59.

38. Beaster-Jones, "A.R. Rahman and the Aesthetic Transformation of Indian Film Scores"; Sundar, "Making-of Videos."

39. Both Sangita Gopal and Gregory D. Booth use the term "new Bollywood," if in slightly different ways. Gopal, *Conjugations*; Booth, *Behind the Curtain*.

40. Hilmes, "On a Screen Near You," 177.

41. See, for example, André, *Voicing Gender*; Fleeger, *Mismatched Women*; Stoever, *Sonic Color Line*.

42. See, for example, Punathambekar, *From Bombay to Bollywood*.

43. Rajadhyaksha, "The 'Bollywoodization' of the Indian Cinema"; Jenkins, *Convergence Culture*.

44. Iyer, *Dancing Women*.

45. See, for, instance, Duggal, "The Community of Listeners"; Duggal, "The Hindi Film Song Remix"; Duggal, "Imagining Sound through the *Pharmaish*"; Huacuja Alonso, *Radio for the Millions*; Kunreuther, *Voicing Subjects*; Weidman, *Singing the Classical, Voicing the Modern*; Weidman, "Sound and the City"; Weidman, *Brought to Life by the Voice*.

46. Here, I am riffing on Arjun Appadurai and Carol Appadurai Breckenridge's formulation of "interocularity" in their foundational work on museums and South Asian public culture more generally. (Their term alludes to Mikhail Bakhtin's notion of intertextuality.) Woodman Taylor notes the intersection of the visual, the aural, and the tactile in the representation of desire in film songs. Appadurai and Breckenridge, "Museums Are Good to Think"; Taylor, "Penetrating Gazes."

47. Hilmes, *Radio Voices*; Douglas, *Listening In*; Casillas, *Sounds of Belonging*.

48. Lacey, *Feminine Frequencies*; Murphy, *Behind the Wireless*.

49. Ehrick, *Radio and the Gendered Soundscape*; Kunreuther, *Voicing Subjects*.

50. The articulation of gender, sexuality, and nation on screen has been critical to film studies scholarship on India. Foundational texts on this topic include: Virdi, *The Cinematic ImagiNation*; Chakravarty, *National Identity in Indian Popular Cinema, 1947–1987*.

51. Radhakrishnan, "Region/Regional Cinema"; Srinivas, "Regional Cinemas of India"; Vasudevan, "Geographies of the Cinematic Public"; Wani, "Region"; Mazumdar, *Bombay Cinema*.

52. Thoraval, *The Cinemas of India*; Dechamma C. C. and Elavarthi, *Cinemas of South India*.

53. Virdi, "A National Cinema's Transnational Aspirations?," 2.

54. Neepa Majumdar's chapter "The Embodied Voice" remains an invaluable piece of scholarship on the topic.

55. See Chion, *Audio-Vision*.

56. Hodgson, *The Venture of Islam*, 59.

57. Manuel, "North Indian Sufi Popular Music." Henceforth, I italicize the word *dargah* only when using it as a stand-alone word. I do not italicize it when using it as part of the term "dargah qawwali" or the name of a famous location, such as Haji Ali Dargah. (I follow a similar strategy with the word *masjid* [mosque], as in Babri Masjid).

58. My postcolonial studies training is evident in the phrase "listen back," which riffs on the notion of "writing back" to the empire. Ashcroft, Griffiths, and Tiffin, *The Empire Writes Back*.

59. Lacey, *Listening Publics*.

## Chapter 1

1. "Neeti Mohan, Neha Bhasin, Aditi Singh Sharma, Jonita Gandhi | Female Singers' Adda."

2. The conceptual dominance of the virgin/vamp binary leaves little room to understand the appeal of someone like Geeta Dutt, a contemporary of Mangeshkar and Bhosle and a star in her own right. In fact, by itself, this framework does little to explain the complicated position of even the singer who was the "lesser" term in that binary formation, Asha Bhosle, who was as famous for her sexy cabaret numbers as for her romantic *ghazals*.

Both Dutt and Bhosle regularly sounded coyer and more brazen than Mangeshkar ever did, but neither occupied the position of the "bad girl" in any straightforward way. The binary also says little about men's singing voices. This is not a problem in and of itself, except that our focus on Mangeshkar's voice has kept us from examining how the cultural, historical, industrial, and political contexts of postindependence India configured men's playback. Another unfortunate effect of this focus is that it has flattened the history of Hindi playback singing to such an extent that singer-actors and playback artists of the 1930s and 1940s are rendered silent in popular and critical memory. They merely serve as the backdrop to Mangeshkar's rise, and then too they get no more than passing mention. While my chapter does not focus on that cohort, I want to signal the pressing need for research on their voices and on other aspects of playback singing.

3. See Chion, *Audio-Vision*.

4. Gorbman, "The Master's Voice," 8. Gorbman names Sarah Kozloff's *Overhearing Film Dialogue* as one of the few texts, apart from Chion's corpus, that acknowledges that the vocality of film dialogue, the way it is rendered by the actor, is distinct from the words scripted on the page. I discuss the materiality of spoken language in chapter 3 of this book. Here, I take as my object the materiality of the singing voice.

5. Gorbman, 8; Barthes, "The Grain of the Voice." I use the "grain of the voice" as a central concept in my essay "*Meri Awaaz Suno*: Women, Vocality, and Nation in Hindi Cinema."

6. Sjogren, *Into the Vortex*, 25, 219n80.

7. The few exceptions come from feminist musicology. For a wonderful example from this body of work, see Cusick, "On Musical Performances of Gender and Sex."

8. Garwood, *The Sense of Film Narration*, 104.

9. Spivak, "Can the Subaltern Speak?"

10. Amanda Weidman makes a similar point in much of her writing on voice. See, for instance, Weidman, "Neoliberal Logics of Voice."

11. On the institution of playback singing, see Booth, *Behind the Curtain*; Indraganti, "Of 'Ghosts' and Singers"; Majumdar, "The Embodied Voice"; Majumdar, "Beyond the Song Sequence"; Jhingan, "Lata Mangeshkar's Voice in the Age of Cassette Reproduction"; Srivastava, "The Voice of the Nation"; Weidman, "Neoliberal Logics of Voice."

12. Chion, *Audio-Vision*, xxvi.

13. These moments of apparent mismatch—as in the case of Usha Uthup and Falguni Pathak, singers I discuss elsewhere, whose voices belie their appearance—illuminate the audiovisual contract. They alert us to both the fact of its existence and the fact that it may be in the process of being revised. Sundar, "Usha Uthup and Her Husky, Heavy Voice"; Sundar, "The Queer Sound of the Dandiya Queen, Falguni Pathak."

14. Chion, *Audio-Vision*, 63 (original emphasis).

15. While not all Hindi film songs are lip-synched, most of them have been produced using this system. It is only recently that the non-lip-synched song has gained prominence in Bollywood. I explore the implications of this shift in the final section of this chapter.

16. The most Chion says about cultural specificity is the following: synchresis, he notes, is "also a function of meaning, and is organized according to gestaltist laws and contextual determinations." This gesture to context is what I seek to elaborate here. Chion, *Audio-*

*Vision*, 63. For a different, but compatible, use of Chion in analyzing playback singing in India, see Weidman, *Brought to Life by the Voice*, 8.

17. Chion asks whether it is "an unseen actor [who] molds her diction to moving lips [so that] her voice is hitched to the image," or whether it is the visible actor's "body that molds itself to voice, [so that it is] the image that is constructed to match the sound." Chion, *The Voice in Cinema*, 154.

18. The dubbing of dialogues is standard practice in India: it is used for *all* films, not just those dubbed into other languages. All actors dub their dialogues after their scenes have been shot. Gregory D. Booth dates this practice to the late 1970s and early 1980s; several "dubbing theaters" were constructed during this time, and some of these spaces doubled as music recording studios. This is why the use of sync sound in *Lagaan* (*Land Tax*, dir. Ashutosh Gowariker, 2001) was hailed as an innovation. Booth, *Behind the Curtain*, 80. Tejaswini Ganti has written extensively on the practice of dubbing Hollywood films into Hindi. See, for instance, Ganti, "Creating That 'Local Connect.'"

19. For years, the person to emulate was Lata Mangeshkar. Such famous playback singers as Kavita Krishnamurthy, Anuradha Paudwal, and Alka Yagnik—who sings for the heroine in "Choli Ke Peeche," a song I analyze later in this chapter—began their careers in this manner. Jhingan, "Lata Mangeshkar's Voice in the Age of Cassette Reproduction."

20. Altman, "The Evolution of Sound Technology"; Booth, *Behind the Curtain*, 39.

21. Mukul Bose, sound recordist for the Calcutta studio New Theatres, used playback singers in the Bengali film *Bhagya Chakra* (*Wheel of Fate*, dir. Nitin Bose, 1935); the film was remade in Hindi later that year as *Dhoop Chhaon* (*Sun and Shade*).

22. Indraganti, "Of 'Ghosts' and Singers."

23. On the emergence of "songless" films and the revised function of songs in new Bollywood cinema, see Garwood, "The Songless Bollywood Film"; Gopal, *Conjugations*.

24. While my focus in this chapter is on the audiovisual contract in Hindi cinema, many of these clauses operate in other Indian cinemas as well.

25. Fleeger, *Mismatched Women*.

26. The notion that a singer's voice is "mismatched" emerges most strongly when she sings. Thus, in many a case, the artist's speaking voice preserves the "illusion" (of meekness or weakness, for example) that her voice unravels in the act of singing.

27. Majumdar, "The Embodied Voice," 167.

28. This sound/image disjuncture is crucial in the case of the non-Tamil-speaking heroines of contemporary Tamil cinema. Nakassis, "A Tamil-Speaking Heroine."

29. Smith, "Black Faces, White Voices," 37.

30. Sundar, "*Meri Awaaz Suno*," 149. Note the caste connotations of the word "cleansing."

31. Majumdar, "Beyond the Song Sequence," 304. Walter Murch uses similar wording ("stretching") to describe the "fruitful tension between what is on the screen and what is kindled in the mind of the audience" in his foreword to Chion's *Audio-Vision*. Murch, foreword, xix.

32. As noted above, Chion's neologism "synchresis" is a combination of the words "synchronism" and "synthesis." Chion, *Audio-Vision*, 63.

33. Majumdar, "The Embodied Voice," 175.

34. Rosie Thomas makes this point powerfully in her early article on *Mother India* (dir.

Mehboob Khan, 1957). Other scholars have done much to explicate how the dynamics of stardom shape film reception and interpretation. Consider, for instance, Vijay Mishra's work on actor Amitabh Bachchan as a parallel text, and Neepa Majumdar's book on stardom and early cinema culture in India. In the Hong Kong context, Brian Hu writes about the ways in which K-pop music cultures shape audiences' engagement with music (and artists) in films. Thomas, "Sanctity and Scandal"; Mishra, *Bollywood Cinema*; Majumdar, *Wanted Cultured Ladies Only!*; Hu, "The KTV Aesthetic."

35. Genette, *Paratexts*; Gray, *Show Sold Separately*.

36. Gray, *Show Sold Separately*, 7. Monika Mehta's work on the many paratexts of Hindi cinema is extremely valuable; see her essays "DVD Compilations of Hindi Film Songs," "Fan and Its Paratexts," "Authorizing Gesture," and "Analyzing Credit Sequences."

37. I mean "extra" in both senses of the word: external and additional. My implicit critique here is of Chion, who uses the term "added value" even as he challenges the notion that "sound is unnecessary, that sound merely duplicates a meaning which in reality it brings about, either all on its own or by discrepancies between it and the image." Chion, *Audio-Vision*, 5–6.

38. Majumdar, "The Embodied Voice," 175.

39. Chatterjee argues that the "women's question" that had consumed social reformers in India in the mid- to late nineteenth century—the question, that is, of women's position in a modern society—was resolved (or, more precisely, ignored) by twentieth-century nationalists, who conflated womanhood, spirituality, and tradition, relegating these matters to an inviolable "inner domain." This discursive sleight hinged on imagining India in stark opposition to—and as morally, culturally, and spiritually superior to—the West. While I'm using Chatterjee's framework to explain Hindi film's gendered anxieties, it should be apparent that similar politics operate in other contexts. Scholars of early sound cinema in the United States have also discussed the gendered, ethnic, and racial politics of song dubbing. Chatterjee, "The Nationalist Resolution of the Women's Question"; Smith, "Black Faces, White Voices"; Taylor, "Speaking Shadows."

40. See, in particular, Srivastava, "The Voice of the Nation," 129–30, 139–40.

41. "Piya Tu Ab To Aaja" ([My] Love, Do Come Now) in the thriller *Teesri Manzil* (*Third Floor*, dir. Vijay Anand, 1966) is one of the more famous examples of this type of song. For an evocative discussion of how this number constructs a "music of body," see Iyer, *Dancing Women*, 59–60. That Helen and the film characters she played were only ever known by their first names was another sign that they were disconnected from respectable family arrangements. In her analysis of Helen and other dancing women in Hindi cinema (and Indian mythology), Amita Nijhawan discusses another song from the same film, "O Haseena" (O Beautiful Woman). Nijhawan, "Excusing the Female Dancer." See also Kasbekar, "Negotiating the Myth of the Female Ideal"; Gangoli, "Sexuality, Sensuality and Belonging," esp. 148–49; Basu, "The Face That Launched a Thousand Ships."

42. Siefert, "Image/Music/Voice," 47.

43. Altman, "The Evolution of Sound Technology," 47.

44. An excellent discussion of how this process played out in South India may be found in Soneji, *Unfinished Gestures*.

45. This investment in truth and authenticity may seem paradoxical for a cinema that

has, as Sumita Chakravarty has shown, thematized doubling and mirroring throughout its history. In my estimation, Bombay cinema's play with copies and look-alikes, mirrors and veils, has mostly been elaborated in the *visual* realm (e.g., confusions regarding twins separated at birth center on how similar they look). By contrast, haunting music and voices are often what lead characters to the truth, as in *Karz* (*Debt*, dir. Subhash Ghai, 1980) and *Madhumati* (dir. Bimal Roy, 1958). Chakravarty, *National Identity in Indian Popular Cinema, 1947–1987*.

46. Weidman, "Anthropology and Voice." 39.

47. Weidman, *Singing the Classical, Voicing the Modern*.

48. The prioritization of sound in Indian cinema is evident in the notion of "picturisation," which in popular Indian parlance refers both to the process of filming a song sequence and to the audiovisual track of the song in the film. Gregory D. Booth observes that the term suggests "the priority of the song as a musical object, rather than as a visual object, since pre-existent songs are often picturised." Likewise, for Neepa Majumdar, this term is indicative of the more general tendency of Hindi cinema to privilege the aural over the visual. Booth, "Religion, Gossip, Narrative Conventions," 143n2; Majumdar, "The Embodied Voice," 167.

49. See, for example, Majumdar, "The Embodied Voice"; Srivastava, "The Voice of the Nation"; Sundar, "*Meri Awaaz Suno.*"

50. The extent to which these moral qualities attached to the actors or the singers performing the song was a more complicated matter.

51. For a rich history of how the growth of television and advertising industries in the 1990s (and MTV India, in particular) shaped film marketing, see Punathambekar, *From Bombay to Bollywood*, 79–111. I borrow the term "re-sounding" from Kate Lacey, who uses the term to chart transformations in (mediated) listening from the late nineteenth century to the present. Lacey, "Listening in the Digital Age," 11.

52. Manuel, *Cassette Culture*, 15.

53. Booth, *Behind the Curtain*. Also note Sangita Gopal's use of this term in *Conjugations*.

54. Booth, *Behind the Curtain*, 76–77.

55. Jyotika Virdi discusses the return of romance in the late 1980s and 1990s, but her focus is not the music of these films. Virdi, *The Cinematic ImagiNation*, 178–204.

56. Thank you to Aswin Punathambekar for pushing me to develop this piece of my argument.

57. As I note in my introduction, *antakshari* (lit. last letter) is a game in which players flaunt their knowledge of Hindi film songs as they take turns singing songs that begin with the letter on which the previous player's turn ended.

58. On the ties between these shows and the Bollywood film industry, see Desai-Stephens, "Tensions of Musical Re-Animation."

59. Manuel, *Cassette Culture*.

60. Kvetko, "Indipop," 126.

61. Booth, "That Bollywood Sound."

62. Chion, *The Voice in Cinema*, 172.

63. Ostensibly the first Hindi-language music video to be telecast on MTV Asia, Baba Sehgal's 1993 dance track "Dil Dhadke" ([My] Heart Beats) was meant to introduce the rest of the world to Indipop music. Speaking of the impact of that music video on his career,

Sehgal noted that with his performances, "people started watching a singer on TV." This set him apart from playback singers, who, in the main, were "back stage [and didn't] come on television." Quoted in Kvetko, "Indipop," 187. Years later, in "Female Singers' Adda," Jonita Gandhi expressed equal enthusiasm for the visibility that YouTube provides contemporary singers: "And then you feel ownership on those million [views]. Like, this is *my* video! My *face* is in this video! Like, it's such a nice feeling." "Neeti Mohan, Neha Bhasin, Aditi Singh Sharma, Jonita Gandhi | Female Singers' Adda."

64. Kvetko, "Mimesis and Authenticity," 171.

65. Kvetko, "Indipop," 124.

66. Sundar, "The Queer Sound of the Dandiya Queen, Falguni Pathak."

67. Kumar, *Gandhi Meets Primetime*. Purnima Mankekar maps the emergence of the "new Indian woman" in 1990s television narratives in *Screening Culture, Viewing Politics*.

68. *Made in India* was a collaboration between Chinai and the composer and music producer Biddu (Biddu Appaiah). Recognized globally for his work with Carl Douglas on "Kung-Fu Fighting" (1974), Biddu is famous in India for "Disco Deewane" (Crazy for Disco, 1981), which also put the singer Nazia Hassan on the map. Biddu wrote and produced albums with several Indipop artists, including Shweta Shetty, Shaan, and Sagarika. For a thorough discussion of the "Made in India" video in the context of globalization and the expansion of satellite TV in India, see Kumar and Curtin, "Made in India." Kvetko also discusses Chinai and the *Made in India* phenomenon; see Kvetko, "Indipop," 159–78. For a discussion of Nazia Hassan's work, see Jhingan, "Sonic Ruptures," esp. 221–22.

69. Kvetko, "Indipop," 168. The emphasis on *individual* desire in these videos, whether for wealth, sex, or personal fulfillment, is also in keeping with the broader ideology of pop as a form of (bourgeois) self-expression. This argument is threaded through Kvetko, "Indipop," but see in particular 237–51.

70. For an extended discussion of remixes in relation to affect and memory in India, see Duggal, "The Community of Listeners." On how *Rang De Basanti* (*Paint It Yellow*, dir. Rakeysh Omprakash Mehra, 2006) played with the notion of remixes, incorporating a "deejay aesthetic" into its soundwork and its conception of history, see Sundar, "Of Radio, Remix, and *Rang De Basanti*."

71. Beaster-Jones, "Evergreens to Remixes," 436. See, also, remix artist Shashwati Phukan's comments in Duggal, "The Hindi Film Song Remix," 9.

72. *Rahul and I* included covers as well as remixes of Hindi film songs by Leslie Lewis (of Colonial Cousins fame). See Vijayakar, "Age Hasn't Dimmed Sparkle in Asha Bhosle's Voice." R. D. Burman passed away as he was working on the music for *1942—A Love Story* (dir. Vidhu Vinod Chopra, 1994). The film catapulted him back into the limelight after years of waning stardom. Booth, "1942—A Love Story."

73. Booth, "R.D. Burman and Rhythm," 162. For an extended discussion of Burman's compositional practices and the famed percussion section of his workshop, see Booth, "Der 'Fremde' Einfluss"; Booth, *Behind the Curtain*, 154–83.

74. See Booth, "R.D. Burman and Rhythm," 157–60, for an analysis of the songs "Gulabi Ankhein" (Rose-Like Eyes) from *The Train* (dir. Ravikant Nagaich, 1970), "Gori Ke Haath Mein" (In the Fair One's Hands) from *Mela* (*Fair*, dir. Prakash Mehra, 1971), and "Shabnam" from *Kati Patang* (*Severed Kite*, dir. Shakti Samanta, 1971).

75. Booth, 159.

76. One might usefully compare Bhosle's voicing of the vamp in cabaret songs to South Indian playback stars' use of "effects," a term that distinguishes moments of "voiced emotion, such as sighing, crying, or laughing, or voiced bodily reaction, such as swooning in delight or pain, hiccupping, and so forth" from the consistently "pure" timbre and style that singers used for most film songs. Weidman, *Brought to Life by the Voice*, 113.

77. Sen, "The Sounds of Modernity," 95 (emphasis added). Sen's name for this era uses the monikers fans used for the two artists. He also acknowledges other music directors such as Laxmikant-Pyarelal, Kalyanji-Anandji, and Rajesh Roshan as prominent figures in this second revolution. But he reserves his strongest praise for Burman, Kumar, Bhosle, and Helen, hailing them as "pioneers of modern song and dance." Sen, 94, 103n28.

78. Beaster-Jones, "Evergreens to Remixes," 440–41.

79. Elsewhere I discuss the implications of Burman's bodily sound for another woman artist who often sang for him, Usha Uthup. Sundar, "Usha Uthup and Her Husky, Heavy Voice."

80. Jhingan, "Sonic Ruptures." For an eye-opening discussion of piracy, see Sundaram, *Pirate Modernity*.

81. Jhingan, "Sonic Ruptures," 230.

82. Jhingan, "Lata Mangeshkar's Voice in the Age of Cassette Reproduction," 99–103.

83. Although Arun's family does not hail from the state of Rajasthan, she identifies closely with the culture and music of this region, having grown up in Jaipur, Rajasthan.

84. This phrasing references the Rani of Jhansi, a young queen famous for her bravery and leadership during the 1856 Indian Mutiny against the British. Jhansi is a city in Uttar Pradesh, a state that borders Rajasthan. The phrase also recalls the Rann of Kutch, an extensive wetland region located in northeastern Gujarat and Sind (in Pakistan), at the lower end of Rajasthan's Thar Desert.

85. *Ghaghra-choli* refers to the long, colorful, embroidered skirt (*ghaghra* or *lehenga*) and tight blouse (*choli*) worn by women in rural Rajasthan and Gujarat. There are subtle differences in the styles of *ghaghra-cholis* from these two regions.

86. Leimbacher, "Hearing Voice(s)," 297–99. For Michel Chion, who builds on Pierre Schaeffer's notion of "reduced listening," such a focus on the sonic traits of voice can be a useful exercise in "opening up our ears and sharpening our powers of listening," even as it entails fixing sound as an object. Chion, *Audio-Vision*, 31.

87. For broader discussions of the way Rajasthan has been represented in Indian cinema, see Ayyagari, "Film Frontiers"; Bhaumik, "The Persistence of Rajasthan in Indian Cinema."

88. Periodically, the song returns to the *banjarin* woman: each new stanza begins with her verses, at which point the camera reverts to medium shots of her dancing. Toward the end of the song, the distance between the normative woman and the "other" collapses. The camera is now positioned in the folk performers' camp, so that our view is from among the *banjarins* and the star couple is in the background. Pallavi runs up to Ila Arun's character and begins dancing with her as the entranced Viren looks on. The "ethnic" voice serves as Pallavi's musical accompaniment as she dances her way to the end of the song sequence.

89. For Alka Yagnik's comments on how she imitated Mangeshkar, see Jhingan, "Lata Mangeshkar's Voice in the Age of Cassette Reproduction," 100, 104.

90. Mehta, *Censorship and Sexuality in Bombay Cinema*, 160–62.

91. Kabir, "Allegories of Alienation and Politics of Bargaining," esp., 147, 149–50.

92. See Gangoli, "Sexuality, Sensuality and Belonging"; Iyer, *Dancing Women*; Kasbekar, "Negotiating the Myth of the Female Ideal"; Kesavan, "Urdu, Awadh and the Tawaif," esp. 255.

93. Shohini Ghosh, quoted in Munshi, "A Perfect 10—'Modern and Indian,'" 170. Expectations regarding men's bodies and women's bodies have converged, to some extent, particularly in item numbers. For instance, both men and women stars are expected to be "spectacular" dancers today.

94. The term "item number" only gained traction in the late 1990s, with the last of the songs discussed in the preceding section, "Chaiyya Chaiyya." On the circulation and reanimation of item numbers in South Indian (Tamil) film culture, see Weidman, "Voices of Meenakumari." For a similar, albeit more wide-ranging and theoretical, exploration, see Brara, "The Item Number." I discuss a recent transformation of the form in chapter 2 of this book, in my discussion of item number–esque qawwalis and dancing publics.

95. For an excellent analysis of how this particular song and Madhuri Dixit's subsequent performances reconfigured women's stardom in the 1990s, see Iyer, *Dancing Women*, 179–98.

96. Iyer, 35–39.

97. Thank you to Aswin Punathambekar for emphasizing how important this was to my argument.

98. Munshi, "A Perfect 10—'Modern and Indian,'" 162. Of course, what's valorized is the display of particular *kinds* of feminine bodies—fair, taut, tall ones.

99. Munshi, 170. For a discussion of how these new ideas about the national and the international were recoded during this period in the figure of Ruby, a veejay on Channel [V], see Butcher, "Parallel Texts." To understand how contemporary conceptions of the body play out in middle-class lives, see McGuire, "How to Sit, How to Stand." I engage with this latter essay in the following section.

100. Talukdar, "Thin but Not Skinny"; Talukdar and Linders, "Gender, Class Aspirations, and Emerging Fields of Body Work in Urban India"; Anwer and Arora, *Bollywood's New Woman*.

101. Fernandes, "Nationalizing 'the Global'"; Oza, *The Making of Neoliberal India*; Chaudhuri, "Gender, Media and Popular Culture in a Global India."

102. Thapan, "Embodiment and Identity in Contemporary Society."

103. Sawhney, "The Ladies Sing the Blues."

104. My essay "Making-of Videos" discusses the central position accorded to the music director in the genre. There is, however, no denying the fact that singers, too, gain new visibility in this genre, which gives audiences a peek into studio recording sessions.

105. Sawhney, "The Ladies Sing the Blues."

106. Sawhney paraphrases how singer and music director Vishal Dadlani (of the Vishal-Shekhar team) conceives of singing voices cultivated in nonfilm contexts:

> a female voice . . . is not always expected to supplement the male voice anymore. In other words, the female vocalists of an older era had no option but to sing on a high octave because their male counterparts kept it characteristically low. . . . As

music producers became more and more flexible with the scale and texture of male vocals, and singers like Kay Kay and himself [Dadlani] arrived on the scene, *who sang at a high pitch owing to backgrounds in rock 'n' roll or Punjabi music,* female playback singers found the space to explore the rawness of a folk song, the low tenor of a Sufi song or the rock interpretation of a love song.

For the moment, I must set aside Dadlani's argument about the relationship between men's and women's voices in duets, as the study of men's playback singing falls outside the scope of this chapter. Note, though, his assumption that singers' training in nonfilm genres shaped how they approached film music, particularly the pitch in which they sang.

107. Kvetko, "Indipop"; Higgins, "Confusion in the Karnatic Capital."

108. Sawhney, "The Ladies Sing the Blues."

109. *SEL: Shankar Ehsaan Loy* (website).

110. Sawhney, "The Ladies Sing the Blues."

111. *Ehsaan Noorani* (website).

112. Film critic Bhawana Somaaya, quoted in Sawhney, "The Ladies Sing the Blues" (emphasis added). A. R. Rahman is widely credited with having changed not just the sound and quality of Hindi film music, but also the way industry insiders think about film music and musicians. Rahman's father, R. K. Shekhar, was a music director himself, which gave the young Rahman (then Dileep Kumar) a certain familiarity with the intricacies of music composition and the workings of the film industries in the South. But just as important as this film lineage is Rahman's training in Carnatic and Western classical musics, and his stint producing ad jingles.

113. Sawhney.

114. Sundar, "Making-of Videos," 224–26.

115. Majumdar, "The Embodied Voice," 172.

116. McGuire, "How to Sit, How to Stand."

117. McGuire, 118.

118. In her essay on actors Kareena Kapoor and Vidya Balan, Tupur Chatterjee explicates the simultaneous pressure on women to conform to an ultrathin bodily ideal and be authentically "Indian." Chatterjee, "Size Zero Begums and Dirty Pictures."

119. McGuire, "How to Sit, How to Stand," 124. McGuire builds on the influential work by Pinney, *Photos of the Gods.*

120. McGuire, "How to Sit, How to Stand," 128 (original emphasis).

121. A similar project unfolds in voice and accent courses for call-center workers, and in music schools for aspiring film singers. Aneesh, *Neutral Accent*; Desai-Stephens, "You Have to Feel to Sing!"

122. Rahaim, *Musicking Bodies.* Rahaim in turn borrows the term "musicking" from Small, *Musicking.*

123. Rahaim, *Musicking Bodies,* 2.

124. Rahaim, 3.

125. Rahaim, 25.

126. Weidman, "Neoliberal Logics of Voice," 185.

127. Weidman, 185.

128. Weidman, 177.

129. Whereas many singers of the past were strongly associated with particular actors—Mangeshkar was the voice of Nargis, and Mukesh that of Raj Kapoor—contemporary singers are not similarly paired with individual actors.

130. As Tamil singer Anupamaa notes, "Nowadays we should be called playfront singers, not playback singers. We are not in the back anymore." Quoted in Weidman, "Neoliberal Logics of Voice," 182. This echoes Baba Sehgal's comment about how (his) music videos changed expectations about the visibility of singers.

131. The voice/body binary of yesteryear is further disrupted when actors do their own singing. While the Bombay film industry has not reverted to the singer-actor era of the 1930s and early 1940s, when stars did their own singing, there has been an increase in the number of actors who sing a song or two. Some playback singers have also tried their hand at acting in front of the camera. All in all, the strict division of labor between acting and singing that defined the Mangeshkar era has weakened.

132. Gopal, *Conjugations*, 45.

133. Garwood, "The Songless Bollywood Film."

134. Siefert, "Image/Music/Voice," 47 (emphasis added). For a framework that emphasizes the labor of dancers and choreographers in Hindi film song-dance sequences, see Iyer, *Dancing Women*.

135. Altman, "The Evolution of Sound Technology," 47.

136. Mehta, "Authorizing Gesture," 67. Mehta adds that "visuality [has recently emerged] as a new mode for constructing and gauging vocal performances," particularly for women playback singers. Mehta, 69.

137. Weidman, "Neoliberal Logics of Voice," 188.

138. Weidman, 188.

139. In the making-of video for the Marathi film *Sau Shashi Deodhar* (*Mrs. Shashi Deodhar,* dir. Amol Shetge, 2014), for example, Mahalaxmi Iyer (who sings in Hindi and Tamil cinema as well) speaks of the challenge of singing for a montage-sequence song (i.e., a song where actors aren't lip-synching the lyrics): the implication is that it's difficult to "get into character" because the emotions are not tied to a particular figure on screen. "Song Making with Mahalaxmi Iyer & Akriti | Sau Shashi Deodhar."

140. Weidman, "Neoliberal Logics of Voice," 186.

141. RadioandMusic.com, "Major Win for ISRA, Delhi HC Rules in Favour of Singers"; RadioandMusic.com, "Singers Get Favourable Delhi High Court Order on Royalties." On the state of singers' royalties circa 2005, see Ojha, "What's Wrong with India's Music Industry?"

142. ISRA (website) (emphasis in original).

143. Hilmes, "On a Screen Near You."

## Chapter 2

1. Lacey, *Listening Publics*, 8. In theorizing "listening publics," Lacey reminds us of Walter Ong's insight that "the inescapable collectivity suggested by the word 'audience' resides in its relation to sound and listening." She also draws on Alice Rayner's work on theatrical audiences, which conceives of the audience in intersubjective terms and places listening at its core. This harks back to the first *OED* definition of audience, which emphasizes hearing: the audience is an "assembly of listeners." Lacey, 13–14.

2. Kesavan, "Urdu, Awadh and the Tawaif." Peter Manuel observes that "there are no distinctively Muslim aspects of qawwali, which freely or loosely uses melodies based on Hindustani rags, as well as tunes associated in other contexts with Hindu occasions. . . . Hindu devotees and visitors are commonly estimated to constitute around one third of those who attend Chishti shrines, especially during 'urs festivities when qawwali is featured. Further, Sufiana qawwali has traditionally accommodated Hindu performers." Manuel's observation reminds us that the "Islamicate" is a cultural category, more than a religious one. Even as the qawwali is a syncretic form and not a specifically Muslim one, it is strongly associated with the Islamicate. Manuel, "North Indian Sufi Popular Music," 380.

3. Hirschkind, *The Ethical Soundscape*, 34–35, 37–40.

4. Qureshi, "Sufi Music and the Historicity of Oral Tradition," 109.

5. Rahaim, *Ways of Voice*, 121.

6. Lacey, *Listening Publics*, 8. In both formulations, the audience is attentive and not distracted. Lacey's concepts differ from the "ubiquitous listening" that Anahid Kassabian describes as happening alongside other activities as one goes about one's daily life. Kassabian, *Ubiquitous Listening*.

7. Lacey, *Listening Publics*, 7 (original emphasis).

8. Lacey, 8.

9. Lipari, *Listening, Thinking, Being*, 186 (original emphasis).

10. Leimbacher, "Hearing Voice(s)," 293.

11. Note that both Stoever and Kheshti also offer concepts—the "embodied ear" and "playing by ear" respectively—to describe how listeners (can and do) undo the overdetermined nature of listening. Stoever, *Sonic Color Line*, 15; Kheshti, *Modernity's Ear*, xix.

12. Duggal, "The Community of Listeners"; Huacuja Alonso, *Radio for the Millions*.

13. Punathambekar and Mohan, "Sound Clouds."

14. Lacey, "Listening in the Digital Age," 11.

15. Rahaim, *Ways of Voice*, 131.

16. Hirschkind, *The Ethical Soundscape*.

17. Rice, "Listening," 101. See also footnote 20 of my introduction.

18. Rice, "Listening"; Stockfelt, "Adequate Modes of Listening."

19. Lacey, *Listening Publics*; Lipari, *Listening, Thinking, Being*.

20. I borrow the term "citizen-listeners" from Huacuja Alonso, "Radio, Citizenship, and the 'Sound Standards.'"

21. Thank you to Abhishek Amar for gently prodding me to not be so mournful about the changes of which I write.

22. Manuel, "North Indian Sufi Popular Music."

23. An embarrassingly early version of this argument appeared in a special issue of *South Asian Popular Culture* edited by Ajay Gehlawat and Rajinder Dudrah, "The Evolution of Song and Dance in Hindi Cinema."

24. Zuberi and Sarrazin, "Evolution of a Ritual Musical Genre."

25. Manuel, "North Indian Sufi Popular Music," 382.

26. Brueck, Smith, and Verma, *Indian Sound Cultures, Indian Sound Citizenship*.

27. See, for instance, Ansari, "There Are Thousands Drunk by the Passion of These Eyes"; Chadha and Kavoori, "Exoticized, Marginalized, Demonized"; Hirji, "Change of

Pace?"; Islam, "Imagining Indian Muslims"; Jain, *Muslim Culture in Indian Cinema*; Kazmi, "Muslim Socials and the Female Protagonist"; Misri, "Bollywood's 9/11"; Rai, "Patriotism and the Muslim Citizen in Hindi Films"; Ramnath, "Muslim Stereotyping in Hindi Films"; Taneja, "Muslimness in Hindi Cinema."

28. The *purdah/parda* (veil) continues to serve as the preeminent marker of Muslim otherness. Many feminist scholars offer a robust critique of this trope. See, for instance, Ahmed, *Women and Gender in Islam*; Abu-Lughod, "Do Muslim Women Need Saving?"; Mahmood, *Politics of Piety*; Moallem, *Between Warrior Brother and Veiled Sister*; Moallem, "Transnationalism, Feminism, and Fundamentalism."

29. Kesavan, "Urdu, Awadh and the Tawaif," 246.

30. One of the earliest uses of a qawwali as a song sequence comes in *Zeenat* (dir. Shaukat Hussain Rizvi, 1945), where a group of women sing "Aahein Na Bharin, Shikwein Na Kiye" ([I] Did Not Sigh nor Complain). Bhattacharjya, "Qawwali."

31. Such attire includes "skull caps and high-collared *sherwani* coats," in the case of men, and *angarakhas* and *churidars* (courtesan-style tunics and tight-fitting bottoms), *dupattas* (stoles or scarves), and veils, in the case of women. Manuel, "North Indian Sufi Popular Music," 384.

32. Zuberi and Sarrazin, "Evolution of a Ritual Musical Genre," 170.

33. Beaster-Jones, *Bollywood Sounds*, 117.

34. A good example of the merging of worldly and spiritual love in the qawwali is *Mughal-e-Azam*'s "Teri Mehfil Mein" (In Your Gathering), in which Anarkali (Madhubala) and Bahaar (Nigar Sultana) face off in a qawwali contest as they vie for the attention of Prince Salim (Dilip Kumar). The two women embody two divergent traditions of the qawwali: the witty competitive performance for love, as represented by Bahaar's performance, and the yearning for spiritual union with the beloved, embodied in Anarkali's performance. Bhaskar and Allen, *Islamicate Cultures of Bombay Cinema*, 16, 18–19.

35. Qureshi, "Sufi Music and the Historicity of Oral Tradition," 109. Qawwals' improvisations announce their spiritual and poetic sophistication, not just their musical talent: "the practice of combining *shers* (couplets) from relevant poems . . . [is] an active form of poiesis that demonstrates the prowess of the *qawwal*." Gaind-Krishnan, "Qawwali," 1776.

36. Zuberi and Sarrazin, "Evolution of a Ritual Musical Genre," 168.

37. Caldwell, "Songs from the Other Side," 256, 258 ; Rahaim, *Ways of Voice*, 5–6.

38. Asha Bhosle was the lead voice of the woman's party in several classic qawwalis. For a longer discussion of the distinctions between film and traditional qawwalis, see Morcom, *Hindi Film Songs and the Cinema*, 70–134.

39. Even with the gradual waning of Urdu from film dialogue, tropes such as *nazarein milana* (the meeting of gazes) and *nazar ke tir* (arrows of sight) permeate song lyrics. Taylor, "Penetrating Gazes," 309.

40. Emphasis added to words that refer to eyes or sight.

41. Taylor, "Penetrating Gazes," 309.

42. Taylor, 302.

43. Taylor, 307.

44. Rajadhyaksha, "The Phalke Era," 72–73.

45. Qureshi, "His Master's Voice?," 82.

46. Jhingan, "The Singer, the Star and the Chorus."

47. Jhingan.

48. For an elaboration of Christopher Faulkner's concept of "listening formation," see Devine, "Imperfect Sound Forever." In elaborating the aural cultures surrounding Hindi film music, Duggal also gestures to Ola Stockfelt's notion of "genre-normative modes of listening." Stockfelt observes that musical styles and genres are tied to particular performance contexts and relations between musicians and audience members. These culturally and historically specific "listening situations" in turn shape how one listens to a given genre. Stockfelt, "Adequate Modes of Listening," 91.

49. Radio enjoys a special place in Duggal's story, for it was the primary medium for the dissemination of film music for much of the twentieth century. Duggal, "The Community of Listeners," 48.

50. Duggal, 52.

51. While the fandom surrounding Ameen Sayani's voice and his countdown show *Binaca Geetmala* is legendary, his was not the only program that drew *pharmaishes*. Punathambekar, "Ameen Sayani and Radio Ceylon"; Huacuja Alonso, "Songs by Ballot."

52. Duggal, "Imagining Sound through the *Pharmaish*," 14.

53. Lacey, *Listening Publics*, 13–14.

54. Ong, *Orality and Literacy*, 133.

55. Lacey, *Listening Publics*, 14–15.

56. Hirschkind, *The Ethical Soundscape*, 34. See also his discussion of "listening as performance." Hirschkind, 84–88.

57. Lacey rightly points out that such a use of "merely" implies that listening does not entail any substantial or important engagement on the part of the auditor. Lacey, *Listening Publics*, 15.

58. Duggal, "The Community of Listeners."

59. See, for instance, Pauwels, "The Woman Waylaid at the Well." See also Aarti Wani's discussion of this film in Wani, *Fantasy of Modernity*, 88.

60. While the star actor's name is otherwise listed as Bharat Bhushan, the credit sequence in *Barsaat Ki Raat* spells his surname as "Bhooshan."

61. Morcom, *Hindi Film Songs and the Cinema*, 91.

62. Note that my wording in this paragraph rehearses the repetitive structure of the lyrics of "Na To Caravan."

63. Sangari, "Viraha," 268. *Kafi* is a devotional Sufi poetic genre that draws on Punjabi and Sindhi folklore.

64. Pauwels, "The Woman Waylaid at the Well," 18–19, 29n25.

65. Another qawwali in the film, "Jee Chahtha Hai" ([My] Heart Desires), includes a similar, albeit brief, turn to a traditionally Hindu idiom at the end of the song. That both Mubarak Ali's and Daulat Khan's troupes are able to incorporate lines from other poems and songs so deftly suggests that they are well-matched contestants in these high-stakes literary and musical competitions.

66. Unless otherwise noted, all translations (and emphases) are mine. The first line may also be translated as: "No wall could stop Laila from following Majnoon's voice." All sonic references are underlined.

67. Sangari, "Viraha," 280.

68. Wani, *Fantasy of Modernity*, 84.

69. Vebhuti Duggal's study of the aural cultures of Hindi film music between the 1950s and 1970s affirms Wani's argument about the entanglements of radio and film music. Duggal, "The Community of Listeners."

70. Wani, *Fantasy of Modernity*, 85.

71. Gopal, *Conjugations*, 25.

72. Sangari, "Viraha," 264, 265.

73. Gopal, 24–40..

74. Qureshi, "His Master's Voice?," 96.

75. "Haseenon ke Jalwe" (The Splendor of the Beautiful) from *Babar* (dir. Hemen Gupta, 1960) and "Tumhe Ishq Dekar Khuda ne" (Having Granted You Love) from *Jabse Tumhe Dekha Hai* (*Ever since I Saw You*, dir. Kedar Kapoor, 1963) are good examples of qawwalis staged as gendered contests.

76. The *mujra* is a seductive performance genre of *tawaifs*.

77. Akbar's other songs, "Shirdiwale Sai Baba" (Sai Baba of Shirdi) and "Tayyab Ali Pyaar Ka Dushman" (Tayyab Ali, Enemy of Love), also mobilize qawwali elements. Thank you to my student and research assistant Clara Walling for her insightful observations, for they helped me develop my analysis of this song. William Elison, Christian Lee Novetzke, and Andy Rotman read "Parda Hai Parda" and the "Muslim subplot" of *Amar Akbar Anthony* as a parody of the Muslim social. In revealing the artifice of Hindi cinema's stereotypes, the film lays bare the terms by which Muslims have been incorporated into the myth of the nation in Hindi films. See Elison, Novetzke, and Rotman, *Amar Akbar Anthony*, 74–114.

78. The tactile magic of the darshanic exchange is fully developed in another qawwali from the same film, "Shirdiwale Sai Baba." For an analysis of this song, Akbar's Nehru coat, and Maharashtra Congress's investment in Sai Baba, see Elison, Novetzke, and Rotman, 105.

79. The lyrics of "Pal Do Pal" mark the contingent nature of this gathering and the bonds formed on life's journey. The chase sequence intercut with the qawwali presents this life lesson in more literal terms, reminding us that these passengers face imminent disaster.

80. Duggal, "Imagining Sound through the *Pharmaish*," 4. In certain traditional and/or feudal contexts, such a request was a mark of patronage. For less endowed audience members, too, the *pharmaish* is a sign of investment—affective, if not economic, investment—involvement, and knowledge.

81. Duggal, "The Community of Listeners," 4.

82. Duggal, 4–5.

83. Huacuja Alonso, "Songs by Ballot," 58. .

84. For an excellent discussion of the overlaps between *bhakti*, *sant*, and Sufi traditions, and the complex resonances of love in these traditions, see Panjabi, introduction to *Poetics and Politics*.

85. Duggal, "Imagining Sound through the *Pharmaish*," 6–8.

86. Duggal, 8.

87. Orsini, *Love in South Asia*.

88. Wani, *Fantasy of Modernity*, 90.

89. Sangari, "Viraha," 256.

90. Sangari, 267.

91. See, for instance, Chakravarty, *National Identity in Indian Popular Cinema, 1947–1987*; Virdi, *The Cinematic ImagiNation*.

92. Huacuja Alonso, "Radio, Citizenship, and the 'Sound Standards,'" 133.

93. Huacuja Alonso, 130–31, 132.

94. Wani, *Fantasy of Modernity*, 30–31.

95. Sommer, *Foundational Fictions*.

96. Punathambekar, "Ameen Sayani and Radio Ceylon," 193.

97. Huacuja Alonso, "Radio, Citizenship, and the 'Sound Standards,'" 137.

98. Duggal, "The Community of Listeners," 103.

99. Duggal builds on Ravikant's scholarship about the "sonic maps" that listeners forged through their writing and participation in radio listeners' clubs. Duggal, "Imagining Sound through the *Pharmaish*," 15.

100. Wani, *Fantasy of Modernity*, 91.

101. Huacuja Alonso, "Radio, Citizenship, and the 'Sound Standards.'"

102. Lacey, "Listening in the Digital Age," 11.

103. Qureshi, "His Master's Voice?," 88, 91.

104. Qureshi, 89.

105. Gaind-Krishnan, "Qawwali Routes," 8.

106. Gaind-Krishnan, 8.

107. Jacoviello, "Nusrat Fateh Ali Khan," 324.

108. Qureshi, "His Master's Voice?," 94.

109. The album was to commemorate India's (and Pakistan's) fiftieth anniversary, but it also coincided with Nusrat Fateh Ali Khan's untimely passing in 1997. Nusrat Fateh Ali Khan composed the music for, and sang in, three Hindi films: *Aur Pyar Ho Gaya* (*And Love Happened*, dir. Rahul Rawail, 1997), *Kartoos* (*Cartridge*, dir. Mahesh Bhatt, 1999), and *Kachche Dhaage* (*Fragile Ties*, dir. Milan Luthria, 1999). Caldwell, "Songs from the Other Side," 251.

110. Gaind-Krishnan, "Qawwali Routes," 6.

111. Sonia Gaind-Krishnan notes that qawwali as a genre is linked to a certain kind of singing voice, even as other "sonic signifiers of the genre have been destabilized," and that Nusrat Fateh Ali Khan's is considered *the* qawwali voice. Gaind-Krishnan, 2.

112. Javed Akhtar used such a repetitive structure, specifically the repetition of similes, in "Ek Ladki Ko Dekha To Aisa Laga" (Seeing [The] Girl Felt Like), the R. D. Burman composition in *1942—A Love Story* (1994). While some of the same similes appear in that hit song, they are rendered in a more Sanskritized idiom than the Persianized Urdu of "Afreen Afreen."

113. Williams and Mahmood, "A Soundtrack for Reimagining Pakistan?," 112–13. *Coke Studio* (Pakistan) was conceived by musician and producer Rohail Hyatt, and he has served as producer for several seasons.

114. Williams and Mahmood, 113. The tag line was changed briefly to "One Nation—One Spirit—One Sound" in seasons 11 and 12.

115. Richard David Williams and Rafay Mahmood draw on Najia Mukhtar's unpub-

lished 2016 doctoral dissertation, entitled "Approaching Religious Difference Differently: Counter-Dominant Agents in Contemporary Pakistan." (SOAS University of London). Williams and Mahmood, 119.

116. Qureshi, "His Master's Voice?," 83.

117. "Best of Coke Studio—YouTube."

118. This and subsequent descriptors of the artist and the song are from the *Coke Studio* blurb, which is posted on the show's YouTube channel. "Coke Studio Season 9 | Afreen Afreen | Rahat Fateh Ali Khan & Momina Mustehsan."

119. Williams and Mahmood, "A Soundtrack for Reimagining Pakistan?," 121.

120. "Coke Studio Season 9 | Afreen Afreen | Rahat Fateh Ali Khan & Momina Mustehsan."

121. Rahaim, *Ways of Voice*, 3–8.

122. Beaster-Jones, "Film Song and Its Other," 101.

123. Manuel, "North Indian Sufi Popular Music," 382.

124. Shubha Mudgal, quoted in Manuel, 389.

125. I use the term "pop Sufism" when discussing this broad pop cultural domain, and reserve the term "Sufipop" for the musical genre.

126. Rahaim, *Ways of Voice*, 174. See also Caldwell, "Songs from the Other Side," 153–200; Manuel, "North Indian Sufi Popular Music," 390–91.

127. Manuel, "North Indian Sufi Popular Music," 390.

128. Manuel, 379.

129. Manuel, 382–83.

130. Abbas, "Risky Knowledge in Risky Times."

131. Rahaim, *Ways of Voice*, 216–17; Manuel, "North Indian Sufi Popular Music," 383.

132. Remarkably, Riyaaz Qawwali was also invited to perform at an event protesting that very visit; the group declined both invitations due to a prior engagement. Gaind-Krishnan, "Qawwali Routes," 2, and see 2n10.

133. Pal, "Performing Pluralism." Thank you to Matt Rahaim for pointing me to this essay.

134. Rahaim, *Ways of Voice*, 173 (original emphasis).

135. As evident in my discussion of women's playback singing in chapter 1, what Rahaim calls "filmi" vocalizing has changed dramatically over the years. Lata Mangeshkar honed her iconic sound over several decades. The hegemony of that voice was undone by the cultivation of new vocal dispositions, inside and outside cinema. That said, Rahaim's distinction between "gentle *filmi* crooning" and "high, bright, *buland* voice" does obtain. Hindi film songs do tend to be rendered in a smooth, crooning voice (by men). The difference between this vocal disposition and those used in other musical genres and styles (qawwali, Hindustani classical music, manganiyar songs, etc.) is stark.

136. Caldwell, "Songs from the Other Side," 249–50.

137. For a fuller discussion of Pakistani artists' "sonic genealogies" and careers in India, see Caldwell, "Songs from the Other Side," 201–37 (on women's voices), 238–83 (on men's voices). The "first wave" of Pakistani voices in Hindi cinema was in the 1970s, and it was composed of all women (Runa Laila, Salma Agha, and Reshma). The "second wave," which arrived in the 2000s, was composed entirely of men. Caldwell reads the 2016 ban as a cultural arm of the brinksmanship that the two nations engage in periodically. That Pakistani

singers won most of the 2011 Filmfare awards might have contributed to the animosity toward them. While the ban dealt a significant blow, some of these singers' Bollywood careers have recovered somewhat in the last few years. Caldwell, 248.

138. Caldwell characterizes Pakistani singers in Bollywood as follows:

> Within the overall space of male Pakistani vocalists, there are two articulated provinces: the qawwali and the rock province. Voices in the qawwali region, represented primarily by Rahat Fateh Ali Khan, tend to sound rooted in classical training, but with a "khulī āvāz (open voiced)" quality and hints of qawwali gāyakī. Voices in the rock region, like that of Atif Aslam, sound more rough-edged and untrained, but also more "hip." The Pakistani rock sound, as heard in Indian film song, moves between the soft, crooning end of the spectrum to the hard, straining end.

He adds that Indian singers specializing in Sufi genres tend not to be misrecognized as Pakistani, even when their Sufipop vocal style is close to that of their Pakistani peers. Caldwell illustrates the difference between the vocal timbres (and styles) cultivated by Indian and Pakistani artists through an expert analysis of the song "Noor-e Khuda" (Light of God) from *My Name Is Khan* (dir. Karan Johar, 2009), featuring the singers Shankar Mahadevan and Adnan Sami. (The latter was a Pakistani citizen at time of this song's release.) See Caldwell, 258, 240–48.

139. Caldwell, 259.

140. Kesavan, "Urdu, Awadh and the Tawaif."

141. Rahaim, *Ways of Voice*, 173–74.

142. Rahaim, 131 (original emphasis).

143. Rahaim, 178.

144. Rahaim, 133.

145. Rahaim, 177.

146. Rahaim, 101.

147. A *mahfil-e-sama* is a gathering of spiritual elites trained to listen to hear the mystical content of Sufi poetry. Qawwals sing to an assembly of Sufi aspirants, and the gathering is overseen by a *pir* (spiritual authority). The structure and hierarchy of a *mahfil-e-sama* is quite distinct from the open atmosphere of a qawwali performance at a *dargah*. Rahaim, 119–28.

148. Rahaim, 177.

149. Nusrat Fateh Ali Khan's "Afreen Afreen" was composed well before the term "Sufipop" was coined. However, as I have demonstrated, that song and others like it set the stage for the emergence of Sufipop.

150. Kvetko, "Indipop," 83.

151. Kvetko, 83–84.

152. Kvetko, "It's Rocking?," 82.

153. Kvetko, 82. As Kvetko puts it elsewhere, "Indipop evoke[d] a mode of consumption that fragments individuals away from traditional groups and located them in their own private universe (often as small as the space between their headphones)." Kvetko, "Indipop," 28.

154. Kvetko, "It's Rocking?," 82. Rahman's pre-*Roja* credits include a pop album in English

called *Set Me Free*, released by Magnasound in 1991. The album cover reads *Shubhaa Set Me Free*, after the featured singer, Malgudi Shubha.

155. Booth, *Behind the Curtain*, 7. Gregory D. Booth borrows the terms "old Bollywood" and "new Bollywood" from a journalistic piece: Virmani, "The Prodooser Is Dead! Long Live the Producer!" I have paraphrased the description of Rahman's studio practice from Beaster-Jones, *Bollywood Sounds*, 139–40.

156. Beaster-Jones, *Bollywood Sounds*, 140.

157. Sarrazin, "Global Masala," 40–41.

158. For detailed musical analyses of "Kehna Hi Kya" and "Chaiyya Chaiyya," see Beaster-Jones, *Bollywood Sounds*, 121–23, 141–43. (Note that in the Tamil version of Mani Ratnam's films, "Kehna Hi Kya" is "Kannalane" (My Love), and "Chaiyya Chaiyya" is "Thaiyya Thaiyya.") For a discussion of the Sufi references in the *Dil Se* song sequences—particularly a reading of "Chaiyya Chaiyya" as mourning the loss of the Islamicate in Hindi cinema, see Kabir, "Allegories of Alienation and Politics of Bargaining," 145–49.

159. Beaster-Jones, *Bollywood Sounds*, 139–40.

160. Rahaim, *Ways of Voice*, 178.

161. The last is a film version of the Sabri Brothers' qawwali "Bhar Do Jholi."

162. Hirschkind, *The Ethical Soundscape*.

163. Hirschkind, 35, 84–88.

164. The qawwals depicted on screen are the Nizami Bandhu (Chand Nizami and his nephews Shadab and Sohrab), the hereditary qawwals who sing regularly at Delhi's Nizamuddin Dargah. However, the voices we hear are those of Javed Ali, Mohit Chauhan, and A. R. Rahman. Soofi, "Kun Faya Kun's Love Note to Rahman 'Saab.'"

165. Bhaskar and Allen, *Islamicate Cultures of Bombay Cinema*, 161–62.

166. Bhattacharjya, "Qawwali." The CD credits Kadar Ghulam Mustafa, and the Wikipedia page for the film names Rahman, Srinivas, Kadar Ghulam Mushtafa, and Murtaza Ghulam Mushtafa as the singers.

167. Priya Kumar calls *Fiza* a "Muslim minoritarian" film; Ira Bhaskar and Richard Allen count this among "New Wave Muslim Socials." These categories indicate that despite its mainstream address, the film is doing something different in its representation of Muslim men. Moreover, "Piya Haji Ali" overlaps with "Maula Saleem Chisti" in *Garm Hava* (1973), one of the first new wave Muslim socials and a landmark film about Partition. The long shots in "Maula Saleem Chisti" similarly articulate the monumentality of its sacred location, the Ajmer Dargah. The song does not feature a hero as singer-poet; in fact, the qawwals are not visible at all, being cast in silhouette or in shadow. Finally, both qawwalis are montage sequences that have a pensive, documentary feel that fits conventions of the two social realist films. For a reading of *Fiza* that resonates with my analysis of "Piya Haji Ali," see Kumar, *Limiting Secularism*, 199–219. For a discussion of the generic categories noted above, see Kumar, 178; Bhaskar and Allen, *Islamicate Cultures of Bombay Cinema*, 91.

168. Bhaskar and Allen, *Islamicate Cultures of Bombay Cinema*, 17–18.

169. Manuel, 382–84; Mamdani, *Good Muslim, Bad Muslim*.

170. Zuberi and Sarrazin, "Evolution of a Ritual Musical Genre," 173.

171. Duggal, "The Hindi Film Song Remix," 59.

172. Duggal, 60. Whereas jhankaar beats were added to new soundtracks, remixes typically took older, "classic" Hindi film songs as their starting point, "added faster beats, inserted new lyrics (usually in English) and gave [them] a new video form." The addition of "beats" was important, for it cemented the notion that older film music was the site of melody. Duggal, 4; and see Beaster-Jones, "Evergreens to Remixes," 433.

173. Duggal, "The Hindi Film Song Remix," 7. The binary opposition of melody and rhythm crumbles when we remember that the film songs that tended to be remixed were themselves associated with dance cultures. Duggal, 4. Thus, for instance, R. D. Burman songs often appeared in cover versions and remixes, including in Asha Bhosle's *Rahul and I* (1996). The late 1990s and early 2000s is also heralded for the "return of melody," particularly in the work of A. R. Rahman. In short, melody and rhythm do not map neatly onto the past and present. Still, the binary is a powerful and persistent one.

174. Hijra is a socioreligious identity marker for certain trans women and intersex people.

175. Taneja, "From Melody to Dev D."

176. "Making of the Film | Part 2 | Bunty Aur Babli | Abhishek Bachchan | Rani Mukerji | Shaad Ali Sahgal."

177. Iyer, *Dancing Women*, 67. The virtually untranslatable terms *jhatkas* and *matkas* refer to a range of sensuous and exaggerated dance moves, usually performed by women in Hindi cinema, such as the heaving of the torso and the swaying of the hips and waist.

178. Nijhawan, "Excusing the Female Dancer," 106.

179. "Main Hoon Na | Making | Tumse Milke Dilka Hai Jo Haal / Qawwali Song | Shah Rukh Khan, Sushmita Sen."

180. Staged numbers like "Parda Hai Parda" (*Amar Akbar Anthony*) and "Hai Agar Dushman" (If There Is an Enemy [in Society]) (*Hum Kisise Kum Naheen* [*We Are as Good as the Best of Them*, dir. Nasir Hussain, 1977]) had the performers decked out in colorful clothes and deployed veils, sequins, lanterns, and roses to great effect. Some qawwalis were performed by courtesan characters, and were thus designed to be spectacular and seductive *mujras*. Examples include "Teri Mehfil Mein," the qawwali competition in *Mughal-e-Azam*, and the Rekha and Amitabh number "Pyaar Ke Rang Se" (With the Color of Love) from *Kasme Vaade* (*Sworn Promises*, dir. Ramesh Behl, 1978).

181. The song is posted on Truly Madly's YouTube channel; see "TrulyMadly Presents Creep Qawwali with All India Bakchod."

182. Thank you to Sangita Gopal for underscoring the relevance of this point for me.

183. Huacuja Alonso, "Radio, Citizenship, and the 'Sound Standards.'"

## Chapter 3

1. Shankar and Cavanaugh, "Toward a Theory of Language Materiality," 4. Thank you to Mariam Durrani for pointing me to Cavanaugh and Shankar's book.

2. Aneesh, *Neutral Accent*, 4.

3. Davé, *Indian Accents*, 3.

4. *Vikatam* is a genre in which a single mimic performs various voices and sounds. Weidman, "Sound and the City."

5. Aneesh, *Neutral Accent*, 4, 59.

6. Chow, *Not like a Native Speaker*, 58–59.

7. Chow, 11, 59. Francesca Orsini also comments on the creative energy of language mixing, especially in relation to the way the advertising industry deploys the hybrid tongue Hinglish: "The linguistic inventiveness and creativity of Hinglish is exploited . . . to create an informal, intimate connection with the viewer." Orsini, "*Dil Maange More*," 203.

8. It is worth pausing over Chow's words: "Because the native speaker is thought to occupy an uncorrupted origination point, learning a language as a nonnative speaker can only be an exercise in woeful approximation. The failure to sound completely like the native speaker is thus given a pejorative name: '(foreign) accent.' Having an accent is, in other words, the symptom precisely of discontinuity—an incomplete assimilation, a botched attempt at eliminating another tongue's competing copresence. In geopolitical terms, having an accent is tantamount to leaving on display—rather than successfully covering up—the embarrassing evidence of one's alien origins and migratory status. . . . The speech of the native speaker is deemed so natural that it is said to be without—or shall we say outside?—an accent." Chow, *Not like a Native Speaker*, 58.

9. Said, *The World, the Text, and the Critic*, 34–35.

10. See, for example, Hilmes, *Radio Voices*; Casillas, *Sounds of Belonging*.

11. Two recent special issues mark this "regional" turn in Indian cinema studies: Srinivas, "Regional Cinemas of India" (*BioScope*, 2015); and Wani, "Region" (*Studies in South Asian Film and Media*, 2016). For a theoretical and historical delineation of the concept, see Radhakrishnan, "Region/Regional Cinema." S. V. Srinivas develops the category of the "regional blockbuster" in "Rajinikanth and the 'Regional Blockbuster.'" Monika Mehta and Madhuja Mukherjee develop "network" as an alternative for studying the dynamic exchanges and "shifting geographies" of the cinemas of India in their edited volume *Industrial Networks and Cinemas of India*. Francesca Orsini writes eloquently and prolifically on the importance of multilingual frameworks for the study of literature. See her essays "How to Do Multilingual Literary History?," "The Multilingual Local in World Literature," and "Na Hindu Na Turk." Rita Kothari's essays and edited work on translation politics in India are also invaluable; see, for example, Kothari, *A Multilingual Nation*. On multilinguality and language hierarchies in Bollywood, see Ganti, "No One Thinks in Hindi Here."

12. Vasudevan, "Geographies of the Cinematic Public," 96.

13. Kothari, "Introduction," 15–16.

14. Kozloff, *Overhearing Film Dialogue*, 217.

15. For an inspiring, feminist call to resist this gendered organization of public space, see Phadke, Khan, and Ranade, *Why Loiter?* "Gully" is a Hindi word meaning "street."

16. Sundar, "Language, Region and Cinema." My argument mobilized the concept of "translation consciousness," linguist and critical theorist G. N. Devy's name for the fluid conception of language that operates on the subcontinent. Devy, "Translation Theory—An Indian Perspective."

17. For a longer discussion of how a plethora of languages mark cinematic production and distribution practices in India, particularly in South Indian film industries, see Sundar, "Language, Region and Cinema," 27–31. On the practice of dubbing Hollywood films into Hindi, and how dubbing entails much more than interlingual translation, see Ganti, "It Needs to Be More like a Hindi Film"; Ganti, "English Is So Precise, and Hindi Can Be

So Heavy!"; Ganti, "Blurring the Boundaries between Hollywood and Bollywood"; Ganti, "Creating That 'Local Connect.'"

18. Jaeckle, "Introduction," 2.

19. See, for example, Hilmes, *Radio Voices*; Smith, *Vocal Tracks*; Smith, *Spoken Word*; Verma, *Theater of the Mind*.

20. For example, John Mowitt uses the notion of "bilingual enunciation" to extend linguistic and psychoanalytic accounts of cinema, and query the foreignness of films designated as such. Hamid Naficy discerns in the work of exilic, diasporic, and postcolonial filmmakers an "accented style," emerging from histories of dislocation, both personal and collective. I, too, am interested in how the movement of peoples shapes the language(s) and aural sensorium of a place. However, my focus is on language as sound, not on style in general. Mowitt, *Re-Takes*. Naficy, *An Accented Cinema*, 22. In their edited volume *The Multilingual Screen* (2016), Tijana Mamula and Lisa Patti train our attention on how multilingualism has shaped the history and aesthetics of cinema around the world well "beyond the soundtrack." While this call for a renewed understanding of the relationship between multilingualism and cinema is an important and very welcome one, I contend there is still much more to be said about language as an audible element of cinema.

21. Kozloff, *Overhearing Film Dialogue*, 6–7.

22. Chion, *Audio-Vision*, 5–6.

23. Chion, 171–74.

24. Chion, 177–78. The term "verbal wallpaper" is from Kozloff, *Overhearing Film Dialogue*, 47.

25. "Writing voice" is Rey Chow's term for the filmic convention of rendering written correspondence in the voice of the absent letter writer. Chow, "The Writing Voice in Cinema." Dialogues and voice-overs may also be distinguished from sung lyrics (which may or may not be lip-synched) and from words that appear on screen but that are not sounded out (everything from intertitles to place names to written elements in the mise-en-scène). Chion devotes an entire monograph to writing made visible in cinema. Chion, *Words on Screen*.

26. See, especially, Eidsheim, *The Race of Sound*, 1–37.

27. My use of "deadly" here is a reference to the high stakes of linguistic nationalisms and to a (positive and superlative) turn of phrase commonly used in Indian English.

28. Kozloff argues further that underlying such critiques of cinematic speech being "too much" is the popular association of talk with femininity and terseness with masculinity. Kozloff, *Overhearing Film Dialogue*, 6–7, 11.

29. Kozloff, 18.

30. Kozloff, 91. Kozloff's first book, *Invisible Storytellers*, clarifies how voice-overs shape notions of time, space, authority, irony, and reliability in cinema, but it precludes discussion of how those voices sound. Her second monograph, *Overhearing Film Dialogues*, is keenly attuned to the performative dimensions of dialogue. Still, even this shift in topic and approach in Kozloff's corpus is instructive. Both she and Chion (as well as other scholars who conceive of voice as "disembodied") grant materiality to some kinds of speaking voices, but not others—to dialogue, but not to voice-overs. For a critique of Kozloff, see Garwood, *The Sense of Film Narration*, 102–3.

31. Garwood, *The Sense of Film Narration*, 14.

32. Kozloff makes the same argument in *Overhearing Film Dialogues*, but with less attention to timbre, texture, or technology.

33. O'Meara, *Engaging Dialogue*, 25.

34. Vazquez, *Listening in Detail*, 8.

35. Prasad, *Cine-Politics*.

36. Krishnan, "From Songs to Speech." See also Baskaran, *The Eye of the Serpent*; Hughes, "What Is Tamil about Tamil Cinema?"; Velayutham, *Tamil Cinema*.

37. Bate, *Tamil Oratory and the Dravidian Aesthetic*, xv. See also Bate, "Arumuga Navalar, Saivite Sermons, and the Delimitation of Religion, c. 1850"; Bate, "To Persuade Them into Speech and Action." Bate's important work casts Tamil oratory as a modern genre with roots in the mid-nineteenth century, when Arumuga Navalar used the form of the Protestant sermon in Saivite worship. Until this moment, such a public form of address—specifically a monologue by an individual of high status calling out to (and calling up) a large, mixed audience—had not been used in Tamil contexts, whether ritual, social, or political. He dates the extensive and systematic use of vernacular oratory for political ends to the early twentieth century, first in the Swadeshi movement (1905–8) and then, a decade later, in the Home Rule and labor movements (1917–19). By speaking in a widely understood tongue (Tamil, Telugu) and a fairly colloquial register, activists (particularly those in the labor movement) were able to speak to the concerns of ordinary people and cast themselves as one of them. Language thus broadened the reach of the intersecting political groups/movements beyond elite circles, cutting across caste and class divides. The cinematic entanglements and transformation of this speech genre into a more ornate, older-sounding form in the middle of the twentieth century is linked to the rise of Dravidianism, which effectively made oratory a fundamental feature of both cinema and mass politics in Tamilnadu. Amanda Weidman astutely notes that the institutionalization of the playback system and rise of Dravidian oratory in the 1940s and 1950s were not just contemporaneous developments; they both relied on voice amplification technologies—the microphone, in particular. Weidman, *Brought to Life by the Voice*, 4.

38. Bharatidasan was renowned as the unofficial poet of the Dravidian political revolution. His credits include the source narrative for *Ponmudi* (dir. Ellis R. Dungan, 1950) and the song lyrics for *Parasakthi* (*Goddess*, dir. Krishnan-Panju, 1952). For his part, Annadurai wrote the story and dialogues for *Velaikkari* (*Maid Servant*, dir. A.S.A. Sami, 1949) and dialogues for *Nallathambi* (dir. Krishnan-Panju, 1949), while Karunanidhi is credited with the story and dialogues of *Manthiri Kumari* (*Minister's Daughter*, dir. Ellis R. Dungan and T. R. Sundaram, 1950) and the dialogues in *Parasakthi*. Annadurai, Karunanidhi, and MGR (also Jayalalitha) would become some of the most influential of modern politicians in Tamilnadu. For an in-depth study of key Madras studios and the entrenchment of Dravidian politics in Tamil cinema of the mid-twentieth century, see Pillai, *Madras Studios*.

39. Krishnan, "From Songs to Speech."

40. Mukherjee, *Bombay Hustle*, esp. 143–84.

41. Amanda Weidman writes about the comic mimicry genre of *vikatam*, which circulated via gramophone records in early twentieth-century Madras, and Stephen Putnam Hughes finds connections between drama, gramophone, and cinema from its earliest years. Weidman, "Sound and the City"; Hughes, "Music in the Age of Mechanical Reproduction."

42. Sarkar, *The Swadeshi Movement in Bengal, 1903–1908*; Bate, "Swadeshi Oratory and

the Development of Tamil Shorthand," 71. The exquisite phrase "flood of seditious eloquence" is from a 1907 source cited by Bate and attributed to two "loyal servants of the Raj,"
G. Ramaswamy and P. Krishneyya.

43. Kumar, "Provincialising Bollywood?"

44. Gopinath, "Don't Hold Back Jack," 50.

45. Ajit was actor Hamid Ali Khan's stage name.

46. Sarah Kozloff defines a "verbal star turn" as a chance for the actors playing these
roles to flaunt their linguistic skills. Loyan, Gabbar Singh, and other characters famous for
their dialogue-*baazi* also tell us that the association of "talk" with femininity that Kozloff
identifies in Hollywood does not apply to Bombay cinema. Here, both star masculinity and
femininity (and especially the former) find articulation in dialogue. Kozloff, *Overhearing
Film Dialogue*, 11, 60–61.

47. The other protagonists of *Sholay* are also remembered for their relationship to
speech. There is the laconic Jai (Amitabh Bachchan) and his love interest, Radha (Jaya
Bhadhuri), who is traumatized into silence for much of the film. The desire for revenge also
turns the feudal landlord and ex-cop Thakur Baldev Singh (Sanjeev Kumar) into a man of
few words. The quiet of Jai, Radha, and Thakur is set against the endless chatter of Veeru
(Dharmendra) and, especially, Basanti (Hema Malini).

48. Abu Hamdan, "Aural Contract," 73.

49. For an elaboration of this argument, see the editors' introduction to Rangan et al.,
*Thinking with an Accent.*

50. Mazumdar, *Bombay Cinema*, 41–78. *Rangeela* was director Ram Gopal Varma's
debut Hindi feature.

51. Mazumdar, 41.

52. Mazumdar names *Amar Akbar Anthony* (dir. Manmohan Desai, 1977) as the first
film to include a *tapori* as a hero, in the form of Bachchan's Anthony. Mazumdar, 44, 77.

53. Mazumdar, 220n6.

54. Mazumdar, 45.

55. Lahiri, "An Idiom for India," 62.

56. The limits of this utopianism—the potential of Hindustani to unite a "nation"—are
of course evident in that it was not the language of everyday life in huge swaths of southern
India (not to mention other parts the subcontinent).

57. Mazumdar, *Bombay Cinema*, 43. In making this claim, Mazumdar builds on Alok
Rai's recounting of the tensions between the Nagari and Persian streams of the Hindi language debates. Rai, "Making a Difference."

58. Rai, "Making a Difference," 255.

59. Francesca Orsini defines Hinglish as "a moniker used to cover a wide range of code-
switching and mixed language phenomena that combine English and Hindi," and adds that
such mixing is common in other languages as well. Orsini, "*Dil Maange More*," 199.

60. LaDousa, *Hindi Is Our Ground, English Is Our Sky.* Akshya Saxena also establishes
how English has been used by Dalit and ethnic minority groups to protest the hegemony of
the Indian state and elite groups. Saxena, *Vernacular English.*

61. Orsini, "*Dil Maange More*," 200 (original emphasis). Commenting on the widespread
use of Hinglish in political discourse in North India, Orsini adds that "if we pay attention

to *accent, fluency,* and *rhetorical skills,* very different types of Hinglish and bilingualism emerge, not just due to a politician's background and education, but also aimed at sending out particular signals to voters." Orsini, 206 (original emphasis).

62. Orsini, 200–201.

63. For more on the use of English and Hinglish in Bombay cinema, see Sundar, "Language, Region and Cinema," 34–35; Garwood, "The Songless Bollywood Film," 173–76; Saxena, *Vernacular English,* 148–77.

64. Gopalan, "Bombay Noir." See also Mazumdar, *Bombay Cinema,* 149–96.

65. *Satya* garnered Filmfare nominations for Best Film, Best Director, Best Actress (Urmila Matondkar), Best Supporting Actor (Bajpayee), Best Supporting Actress (Chhaya), and Best Villain (Govind Namdeo). Bajpayee, Chhaya, and lead actor J. D. Chakravarthy also came away with Star Screen Awards for their acting.

66. Other Telugu films of the 1990s would draw out the distinction between the "old city" and the "new city" in more blatant ways. In these mainstream films, the old city is populated by Muslims and lower-caste Hindus who speak in the Telangana dialect. It is a space of criminality and backwardness that must be brought to heel by the hero, representative of the "new city." The latter is imagined as a modern, "dialect-less" space (read: where everyone speaks the coastal Andhra dialect). Srinivas, "Cardboard Monuments," 92.

67. Film critic Uday Bhatia treats the film as a "subtle ideological victory" for a different reason. Shiv Sena leadership loved *Satya* and granted it "tax-free" status, despite the fact that it was made by a team of people who were "outsiders" to Bombay. Bhatia, *Bullets over Bombay,* 198.

68. Mazumdar, *Bombay Cinema,* 44.

69. Srinivas, "Cardboard Monuments." See also Srinivas's broader scholarly corpus.

70. Srinivas, 91.

71. Perhaps the most famous aural (and visual) stereotype of a South Indian in Hindi cinema is the Tamilian music teacher Master Pillai, played by comedian Mehmood in *Padosan* (*Neighbor,* dir. Jyoti Swaroop, 1968). His Hindi accent is immortalized in the duet "Ek Chathur Naar" (A Smart Woman), where the spoken parts are in Mehmood's voice and the sung lyrics in Manna Dey's. The song exemplifies the use of comedy to cast non-Hindi speakers as other, with not one but two voices simultaneously lampooning South Indian speakers and Carnatic music.

72. Biswas, "Mourning and Blood Ties," 7.

73. While the name Mumbai is used by one and all now, it was a contentious choice in the late 1990s. People were very deliberate in staking their position in the name-change debate.

74. Lippi-Green, "The Myth of Non-Accent," 46. On Chander's Bambaiyya argot, see Bhatia, *Bullets over Bombay,* 127–28.

75. The first Hollywood blockbuster to be released in Indian theaters in its dubbed versions (in Hindi, Telugu, and Tamil), *Jurassic Park* is famous for having rendered "dinosaur" as *badi chipkali* (big lizard) for Hindi-speaking audiences. Ramnath, "Jurassic Park"; Ganti, "It Needs to Be More like a Hindi Film," 55–56.

76. The narrator's words are: "Isi mahaul mein, kahin se ek aadmi aaya" (In[to] this atmosphere, there came a man, from somewhere). The reference here is to the riots

that followed the demolition of the sixteenth-century Babri Masjid by Hindutva zealots in December 1992, and the series of retaliatory bomb blasts that ravaged Bombay Stock Exchange and other important commercial venues in the city in March 1993.

77. Film critic Uday Bhatia concurs that Satya is likely "from one of [the] southern states" and that it was important to Varma that his protagonist be a migrant to the city. Bhatia, *Bullets over Bombay*, 198.

78. Bhatia, 204.

79. Bhatia, 204.

80. Kozloff, *Overhearing Film Dialogue*, 212. Kozloff also notes the liberal use of "accents" in the gangster genre, stressing the characters' "separateness from official American culture, privilege, and power." Kozloff, 206–7.

81. Kumar, "Writing My Own Satya," 99; Bhatia, *Bullets over Bombay*, 204–8.

82. Mazumdar, *Bombay Cinema*, 41.

83. A Hindi remake, *Dayavan* (*Compassionate One*, dir. Feroz Khan, 1988), starring Vinod Khanna, was released the following year, but it did not enjoy the critical and popular acclaim that the Tamil film did. The tepid response to *Dayavan* belies the enormous impact that *Nayakan* had on both Hindi and Tamil cinema, particularly on the gangster genre. *Nayakan*'s reach was considerable as it was broadcast (with English subtitles) in Doordarshan's regional cinema slot on Sunday afternoons.

84. Hansen, *Wages of Violence*.

85. Creekmur, "Bombay Bhai."

86. VT station or Victoria Terminus was renamed Chhatrapati Shivaji Terminus as part of Shiv Sena's campaign to proclaim Maratha glory. This location also ties *Satya* to *Nayakan*. Bhatia, *Bullets over Bombay*, 25.

87. Gopalan, *Cinema of Interruptions*.

88. Shankar, *Flesh and Fish Blood*, 113–24.

89. This role is essayed by Janakaraj, who also plays Velu *nayakar*'s wingman and translator in *Nayakan* (1987).

90. Amar's last name, Varma, perhaps suggests that his is a Malayali family. However, this ambiguity does little to unsettle his hegemonic position. It is the three women in his life—the unnamed *banjarin* with whom he dances atop a train (see chapter 1), his love interest Meghna, and his fiancée Preeti—who, in different ways, articulate a critique of nationalist desire. Note that Malayalam lyrics form the chorus in "Jiya Jale" (My Heart Burns), the engagement ceremony song that we might read as Preeti's fantasy. With the *moorsing* and *mridangam* also playing prominent roles in framing Preeti's Hindi lyrics, this song has a distinct, if vague, South Indian feel to it. Kabir, "Allegories of Alienation and Politics of Bargaining."

91. Some cast and crew members, such as Anurag Kashyap, thought the "in-your-face" score and sound design were strengths of the film. Others, such as Saurabh Shukla and Gerard Hooper, found the sound too loud and distracting; some colleagues advised Varma to turn down the sound, if only so that the actors' lines would be more audible. Bhatia, *Bullets Over Bombay*, 252–54.

92. Bhatia, 216–18. Bhatia describes the distorted sound effects in this scene—what I hear as "Boom. Boom. Aaaa!"—as "Morricone-like 'hoh!'"

93. Garwood, *The Sense of Film Narration*, 10.

94. *Alaap* is the improvised, unmetered elaboration of a *raga* (melodic mode) at the beginning of a song in Indian classical music.

95. The song is sometimes referred to as "Kallu mama." See, for instance, Mazumdar, *Bombay Cinema*, 180. The lyrics for this song were penned by the poet and lyricist Gulzar.

· 96. Here is how Amitava Kumar weaves *dhishoom dhishoom* into his prose: "There are more direct evocations too [of the history of Hindi cinema]. Not only in the way in which Bhiku Mhatre asks Satya during their first, violent encounter if he imagines he is Amitabh Bachchan, but also the way in which violence, with revenge as its engine, reminds us of all the *dhishoom-dhishoom* fights we have witnessed in 1970s movies like *Deewar.*" Kumar, "Writing My Own Satya," 100–101.

97. Thank you to Ani Maitra and Nina Sun Eidsheim: our conversation following my presentation at the Thinking with an Accent conference helped me clarify this point about the cinephilic musicality of *dhichkiaoon.*

98. Pettman, "Pavlov's Podcast," 154–60. In this essay, and in his book *Sonic Intimacy*, Dominic Pettman extends Roland Barthes's notion of the punctum in photography to apply to another one of Barthes's concepts, the grain of the voice. Here, I take "aural punctum" to apply to an evocative and layered word/sound, *dhichkiaoon*, more than a voice. The effect is as piercing as ever.

99. Chion, *Audio-Vision*, 178.

## Coda

1. Gopal, *Conjugations*, 58. New Bollywood, she explains, "no longer needs the song-and-dance sequence to deliver the sensations of coupling, and the narrative allows the couple access to sovereignty." Gopal, 57.

2. Shahani, "Queer Intimacy during Seditious Times," 15.

3. I have written elsewhere about how we might depart from our "listening habitus." See my essay "Listening with an Accent" in Rangan et al., *Thinking with an Accent.*

4. "We see it as a love scene, a crime scene, an ambush, as spectacle. It's as if the film is showing us the many lenses Indian society uses to view homosexuality." Bhatia, review of *Aligarh.*

5. In 2018, the Supreme Court ruled Section 377 unconstitutional in *Navtej Singh Johar v. Union of India.*

6. Dyer, *In the Space of a Song.*

7. In their original form, both songs are picturized on a couple and have the woman singing to her lover. They are solo numbers, voiced by Lata Mangeshkar alone. In *Aligarh*, we hear both Siras's voice (actor Bajpayee's voice) and Lata Mangeshkar's in the first whiskey and music scene; it is thus, arguably, a romantic duet. And yet, it works differently than such romantic numbers usually do.

8. Shahani, "Queer Intimacy during Seditious Times," 11.

9. Shahani, 11, 13–14.

10. Shahani, 10. Shahani also reads Irfan's trace in the wound on Deepu's face, which Siras inquires about and which comes from being beaten up when he (Deepu) goes looking for Irfan in his neighborhood. Shahani, 15–16; Puar, *Terrorist Assemblages.*

11. Shahani's use of "touch" is indebted to Judith Butler's theorization of how we are undone by one another. Butler, *Undoing Gender*.

12. Weidman, "Voices of Meenakumari."

13. Duggal, "The Hindi Film Song Remix," 146.

14. Jhingan, "Re-Embodying the 'Classical,'" 173.

15. Gopal, "The Audible Past," 809 (original emphasis).

16. Siras won the annual literary prize of the Maharashtra Sahitya Parishad in 2002 for this collection.

17. This is a moment that supports Ruth Vanita's argument that Hindi cinema uses the very same tropes to represent intense homosocial and homoerotic bonds, as it does straight romance. Vanita, "Dosti to Tamanna."

18. Chow, "The Writing Voice in Cinema." By naming this particular use of the voice-over the "writing voice," Chow historicizes the convention and links its cinematic usage to long-standing debates in literary studies, philosophy, and sound theory. She notes that Chion's theorization of the voice in cinema—and the aurality of the medium itself—adds a material, tangible dimension to the interventions of theorists like Mikhail Bakhtin, Jacques Derrida, and Mladen Dolar, who have elaborated on "the internal rupture, disembodiment and nonoriginariness" of voice in more abstract and nonvisual terms. In framing Chion's acousmêtre as coextensive of the way voice emerges in other cultural texts, Chow underscores a point often lost in film-centric discussions: "The voice is, on the one hand, always a sound effect, the materiality of which is inevitably entangled with the technicalities of film as a medium; on the other hand, the voice is inherently imaginary, always carrying a surplus of significance that defies its confinement to the cinematic apparatus." Apprehending the complexity of voice in both its material and imaginary dimensions requires that we push beyond disciplinary borders. Chow, 21, 18.

19. For Chion, it is precisely the fact that the speaker is unseen—that the voice seems to come from nobody and nowhere—that gives the acousmatic voice its power. The writing voice is an aural form that is at least partly visualized on screen (in the form of a letter); it is, by definition, both visual and aural. Chion, *Audio-Vision*, 71–73, 128–31.

20. Chatterjee, "Language That Binds, Language That Frees."

21. Siras expresses his frustration with the translation first to Deepu and then to a group of men he meets at the gay party. When one of them quotes the first two lines of "O Beloved Moon" and asks what he thinks of the translation, Siras quips, "Angrezi achchi nahi thi" (The English wasn't good).

22. Deepu's Hindi accent marks him as a South Indian, just as the lawyer Prathamesh Tripathy's English accent suggests that he comes from the Hindi-speaking belt in the north. (Tripathy quotes "O Beloved Moon" while welcoming Siras to the gay party.)

23. Chow, *Not like a Native Speaker*, 59.

24. Jaaware, *Practicing Caste*.

25. On how Dalit writing dismantles casteist injunctions against touch through the embrace of English, see Saxena, *Vernacular English*, 60–123.

26. Campt, *Listening to Images*, 99–100.

27. Campt, 6–7, 71–72.

28. Sedgwick, "Paranoid Reading and Reparative Reading."

# Bibliography

Abbas, Shemeem Burney. "Risky Knowledge in Risky Times: Political Discourses of Qaw-wālī and Sūfīana-Kalam in Pakistan-Indian Sufism." *Muslim World* 97, no. 4 (October 2007): 626–39.

Abu Hamdan, Lawrence. "Aural Contract: Forensic Listening and the Reorganization of the Speaking Subject." In *Forensis: The Architecture of Public Truth*, 65–82. Berlin: Sternberg and Forensic Architecture, 2014.

Abu-Lughod, Lila. "Do Muslim Women Need Saving? Reflections on Cultural Relativism and Its Others." *American Anthropologist* 104, no. 3 (2002): 783–90.

Ahmed, Leila. *Women and Gender in Islam: Historical Roots of a Modern Debate*. New Haven, CT: Yale University Press, 1992.

Ahmed, Sara. *Complaint!* Durham, NC: Duke University Press, 2021.

Ahmed, Sara. *Living a Feminist Life*. Durham, NC: Duke University Press, 2017.

Altman, Rick. "The Evolution of Sound Technology." In *Film Sound: Theory and Practice*, edited by Elisabeth Weiss and John Belton, 44–53. New York: Columbia University Press, 1985.

André, Naomi Adele. *Voicing Gender: Castrati, Travesti, and the Second Woman in Early-Nineteenth-Century Italian Opera*. Bloomington: Indiana University Press, 2006.

Aneesh, A. *Neutral Accent: How Language, Labor, and Life become Global*. Durham, NC: Duke University Press, 2015.

Ansari, Usamah. "'There Are Thousands Drunk by the Passion of These Eyes': Bollywood's Tawa'if: Narrating the Nation and 'The Muslim.'" *South Asia: Journal of South Asian Studies* 31, no. 2 (August 2008): 290–316.

Anwer, Megha, and Anupama Arora, eds. *Bollywood's New Woman: Liberalization, Liberation, and Contested Bodies*. New Brunswick, NJ: Rutgers University Press, 2021.

Appadurai, Arjun, and Carol Appadurai Breckenridge. "Museums Are Good to Think: Heritage on View in India." In *Museums and Communities*, edited by Ivan Karp, Christine Mullen Kreamer, and Steven D. Lavine, 34–55. Washington, DC: Smithsonian Institution Press, 1992.

Arnold, Alison E. "Hindi Filmī Gīt: On the History of Commercial Indian Popular Music." PhD diss., University of Illinois at Urbana-Champaign, 1991.

Ashcroft, Bill, Gareth Griffiths, and Helen Tiffin, eds. *The Empire Writes Back: Theory and Practice in Post-Colonial Literatures*. London: Routledge, 1989.

Ayyagari, Shalini. "Film Frontiers: Imagining Rajasthan in Contemporary Bollywood Film."

In *Music in Contemporary Indian Film: Memory, Voice, Identity*, edited by Jayson Beaster-Jones and Natalie Sarrazin, 147–61. New York: Routledge, 2017.

Barkin, Elaine, and Lydia Hamessley, eds. *Audible Traces: Gender, Identity, and Music*. Zurich: Carciofoli Verlagshaus, 1999.

Barthes, Roland. "The Grain of the Voice." In *Image-Music-Text*, by Roland Barthes, 179–89. New York: Hill and Wang, 1977.

Barthes, Roland. "Listening." In *The Responsibility of Forms*, by Roland Barthes, translated by Richard Howard, 245–60. Los Angeles: University of California Press, 1985.

Baskaran, S. Theodore. *The Eye of the Serpent: An Introduction to Tamil Cinema*. Chennai: Tranquebar Press, 2013.

Basu, Anustup. "'The Face That Launched a Thousand Ships': Helen and Public Femininity in Hindi Film." In *Figurations in Indian Film*, edited by Meheli Sen and Anustup Basu, 139–57. New Delhi: Orient Blackswan, 2013.

Bate, Bernard. "Arumuga Navalar, Saivite Sermons, and the Delimitation of Religion, c. 1850." *Indian Economic and Social History Review* 42, no. 4 (2005).

Bate, Bernard. "Swadeshi Oratory and the Development of Tamil Shorthand." *Economic and Political Weekly* 47, no. 42 (2012): 70–75.

Bate, Bernard. *Tamil Oratory and the Dravidian Aesthetic: Democratic Practice in South India*. New York: Columbia University Press, 2009.

Bate, Bernard. "'To Persuade Them into Speech and Action': Oratory and the Tamil Political, Madras, 1905–1919." *Comparative Studies in Society and History* 55, no. 1 (2013): 142–66.

Beaster-Jones, Jayson. "A.R. Rahman and the Aesthetic Transformation of Indian Film Scores." *South Asian Popular Culture* 15, no. 2–3 (2017): 155–71.

Beaster-Jones, Jayson. *Bollywood Sounds: The Cosmopolitan Mediations of Hindi Film Song*. Oxford: Oxford University Press, 2015.

Beaster-Jones, Jayson. "Evergreens to Remixes: Hindi Film Songs and India's Popular Music Heritage." *Ethnomusicology* 53, no. 3 (Fall 2009): 425–48.

Beaster-Jones, Jayson. "Film Song and Its Other: Stylistic Mediation and the Hindi Film Song Genre." In *More Than Bollywood: Studies in Indian Popular Music*, edited by Gregory Booth and Bradley Shope, 97–113. Oxford: Oxford University Press, 2014.

Becker, Judith. *Deep Listeners: Music, Emotion, and Trancing*. Bloomington: Indiana University Press, 2004.

"Best of Coke Studio—YouTube." YouTube playlist, uploaded by Coke Studio. Accessed August 22, 2021. https://www.youtube.com/playlist?list=PLlYsrzDvIU9Rl3KTGvX2tPr6yBwPPjaH0

Bhaskar, Ira, and Richard Allen. *Islamicate Cultures of Bombay Cinema*. New Delhi: Tulika Books, 2009.

Bhatia, Uday. *Bullets over Bombay: Satya and the Hindi Film Gangster*. Noida, India: HarperCollins, 2021.

Bhatia, Uday. Review of *Aligarh*, directed by Hansal Mehta. *Mint*, March 28, 2016. https://lifestyle.livemint.com/smart-living/innovation/film-review-aligarh-111651818076712.html

Bhattacharjya, Nilanjana. "Qawwali." March 27, 2017. Personal communication.

Bhaumik, Kaushik. "The Persistence of Rajasthan in Indian Cinema: One Region, So Many Views." *Journal of the Moving Image* 10 (2011): 13–39.

Biswas, Moinak. "Mourning and Blood Ties." *Journal of the Moving Image* 5 (2006): 1–9.

Bonenfant, Yves. "Queer Listening to Queer Vocal Timbres." *Performance Research: A Journal of the Performing Arts* 15, no. 3 (2010): 74–80.

Booth, Gregory D. *Behind the Curtain: Making Music in Mumbai's Film Studios*. New York: Oxford University Press, 2008.

Booth, Gregory D. "Der 'Fremde' Einfluss in R. D. Burmans Diskurs und musikalischer Praxis" (The "Foreign" Influence in Discourse and Practice in the Music of R. D. Burman). In *Fokus Bollywood: Das indische Kino in wissenschatlichen Diskursen*, edited by Claus Tieber, 67–83. Vienna: Lit Verlag, 2009.

Booth, Gregory D. "1942—A Love Story: R. D. Burman's Posthumous Comeback at the End of Old Bollywood." In *Music in Contemporary Indian Films: Memory, Voice, Identity*, edited by Jayson Beaster-Jones and Natalie Sarrazin, 21–34. New York: Routledge, 2017.

Booth, Gregory D. "R.D. Burman and Rhythm: 'Making the Youth of This Nation to Dance.'" *BioScope: South Asian Screen Studies* 3, no. 2 (2012): 147–64.

Booth, Gregory D. "Religion, Gossip, Narrative Conventions and the Construction of Meaning in Hindi Film Songs." *Popular Music* 19, no. 2 (2000): 125–45.

Booth, Gregory D. "That Bollywood Sound." In *Global Soundtracks: Worlds of Film Music*, edited by Mark Slobin, 85–113. Middletown, CT: Wesleyan University Press, 2008.

Brara, Rita. "The Item Number: Cinesexuality in Bollywood and Social Life." *Economic and Political Weekly* 45, no. 23 (2010): 67–74.

Brett, Philip, Elizabeth Wood, and Gary C. Thomas, eds. *Queering the Pitch: The New Gay and Lesbian Musicology*. London: Routledge, 1994.

Brueck, Laura, Jacob Smith, and Neil Verma, eds. *Indian Sound Cultures, Indian Sound Citizenship*. Ann Arbor: University of Michigan Press, 2020.

Butcher, Melissa. "Parallel Texts: The Body and Television in India." In *Image Journeys: Audio-Visual Media and Cultural Change in India*, edited by Christiane Brosius and Melissa Butcher, 165–96. New Delhi: Sage, 1999.

Butler, Judith. *Undoing Gender*. New York: Routledge, 2004.

Caldwell, John. "Songs from the Other Side: Listening to Pakistani Voices in India." PhD diss., University of North Carolina, 2021.

Campt, Tina M. *Listening to Images*. Durham, NC: Duke University Press, 2017.

Casillas, Dolores Inés. *Sounds of Belonging: U.S. Spanish-Language Radio and Public Advocacy*. New York: New York University Press, 2014.

Chadha, Kalyani, and Anandam P. Kavoori. "Exoticized, Marginalized, Demonized: The Muslim 'Other' in Indian Cinema." In *Global Bollywood*, edited by Anandam P. Kavoori and Aswin Punathambekar, 131–45. New York: New York University Press, 2008.

Chakravarty, Sumita S. *National Identity in Indian Popular Cinema, 1947–1987*. Austin: University of Texas Press, 1993.

Chatterjee, Niladri. "Language That Binds, Language That Frees." *Wire*, March 5, 2016. https://thewire.in/film/language-that-binds-language-that-frees

Chatterjee, Partha. "The Nationalist Resolution of the Women's Question." In *Recasting*

*Women: Essays in Indian Colonial History*, edited by Kumkum Sangari and Sudesh Vaid, 233–53. New Delhi: Kali for Women, 1989.

Chatterjee, Tupur. "Size Zero Begums and Dirty Pictures: The Contemporary Female Star in Bollywood." *Synoptique: Journal of Film and Moving Image Studies* 3, no. 1 (Winter 2014). https://www.synoptique.ca/issue-3-1

Chattopadhyay, Budhaditya. "The Auditory Spectacle: Designing Sound for the 'Dubbing Era' of Indian Cinema." *New Soundtrack* 5, no. 1 (2015): 55–68.

Chattopadhyay, Budhaditya. "The Cinematic Soundscape: Conceptualising the Use of Sound in Indian Films." *SoundEffects: An Interdisciplinary Journal of Sound and Sound Experience* 2, no. 2 (2012): 65–78.

Chattopadhyay, Budhaditya. "Sound Memories: In Search of Lost Sounds in Indian Cinema." *Journal of the Moving Image* 6 (2007): 1–12.

Chaudhuri, Maitrayee. "Gender, Media and Popular Culture in a Global India." In *Routledge Handbook of Gender in South Asia*, edited by Leela Fernandes, 145–59. London: Routledge, 2014.

Chion, Michel. *Audio-Vision: Sound on Screen*. Translated by Claudia Gorbman. New York: Columbia University Press, 1994.

Chion, Michel. *The Voice in Cinema*. Translated by Claudia Gorbman. New York: Columbia University Press, 1999.

Chion, Michel. *Words on Screen*. Translated by Claudia Gorbman. New York: Columbia University Press, 2017.

Chow, Rey. *Not like a Native Speaker: On Languaging as a Postcolonial Experience*. New York: Columbia University Press, 2014.

Chow, Rey. "The Writing Voice in Cinema: A Preliminary Discussion." In *Locating the Voice in Film: Critical Approaches and Global Practices*, edited by Tom Whittaker and Sarah Wright, 17–30. Oxford: Oxford University Press, 2016.

"Coke Studio Season 9 | Afreen Afreen | Rahat Fateh Ali Khan & Momina Mustehsan." Uploaded by Coke Studio, August 19, 2016. YouTube video, 6:44. https://www.youtube.com/watch?v=kw4tT7SCmaY

Creekmur, Corey K. "Bombay Bhai: The Gangster in and behind Popular Hindi Cinema." In *Images of Justice: Cinema, Law, and the State in Asia*, edited by Corey K. Creekmur and Mark Sidel, 29–43. New York: Palgrave Macmillan, 2007.

Cusick, Suzanne. "On Musical Performances of Gender and Sex." In *Audible Traces: Gender, Identity, and Music*, edited by Elaine Barkin and Lydia Hamessley, 25–49. Zurich: Carciofoli Verlagshaus, 1999.

Davé, Shilpa. *Indian Accents: Brown Voice and Racial Performance in American Television and Film*. Urbana: University of Illinois Press, 2013.

Dechamma C. C., Sowmya, and Elavarthi Sathya Prakash, eds. *Cinemas of South India: Culture, Resistance, Ideology*. Oxford: Oxford University Press, 2010.

Denning, Michael. "Decolonizing the Ear: The Transcolonial Reverberations of Vernacular Phonograph Music." In *Audible Empire: Music, Global Politics, Critique*, edited by Ronald Radano and Tejumola Olaniyan, 25–44. Durham, NC: Duke University Press, 2016.

Deo, Aditi, and Vebhuti Duggal. "Radios, Ringtones, and Memory Cards, or How the Mobile Phone Became Our Favourite Music Playback Device." *South Asian Popular Culture* 15, no. 1 (2017): 41–56.

Desai-Stephens, Anaar. "Tensions of Musical Re-Animation from Bollywood to Indian Idol." In *Music in Contemporary Indian Films: Memory, Voice, Identity*, edited by Jayson Beaster-Jones and Natalie Sarrazin, 76–90. New York: Routledge, 2017.

Desai-Stephens, Anaar. "'You Have to Feel to Sing!': Popular Music Classes and the Transmission of 'Feel' in Contemporary India." *Culture, Theory, and Critique* 61, no. 2–3 (2020): 187–207.

Devine, Kyle. "Imperfect Sound Forever: Loudness, Listening Formations, and the Historiography of Sound Reproduction." PhD diss., Carleton University, 2012.

Devy, G. N. "Translation Theory—An Indian Perspective." In *In Another Tongue: Essays on Indian English Literature*, by G. N. Devy, 134–52. Frankfurt: Peter Lang, 1993.

Douglas, Susan. *Listening In: Radio and the American Imagination*. Minneapolis: University of Minnesota Press, 2004.

Duggal, Vebhuti. "The Community of Listeners: Writing a History of Hindi Film Music Aural Cultures." PhD diss., Jawaharlal Nehru University, 2015.

Duggal, Vebhuti. "The Hindi Film Song Remix: Memory, History, Affect." MPhil thesis, Jawaharlal Nehru University, 2010.

Duggal, Vebhuti. "Imagining Sound through the *Pharmaish*: Radios and Request-Postcards in North India, c. 1955–1975." *BioScope: South Asian Screen Studies* 9, no. 1 (2018): 1–23.

Dyer, Richard. *In the Space of a Song: The Uses of Song in Film*. London: Routledge, 2012.

Ehrick, Christine. *Radio and the Gendered Soundscape: Women and Broadcasting in Argentina and Uruguay, 1930–1950*. New York: Cambridge University Press, 2015.

*Ehsaan Noorani* (website). Accessed July 13, 2018. http://www.ehsaannoorani.com/about.html

Eidsheim, Nina Sun. *The Race of Sound: Listening, Timbre, and Vocality in African American Music*. Durham, NC: Duke University Press, 2019.

Elison, William, Christian Lee Novetzke, and Andy Rotman. *Amar Akbar Anthony: Bollywood, Brotherhood, and the Nation*. Cambridge, MA: Harvard University Press, 2016.

Fernandes, Leela. "Nationalizing 'the Global': Media Images, Cultural Politics and the Middle Class in India." *Media, Culture & Society* 22, no. 5 (2000): 611–28.

Fleeger, Jennifer. *Mismatched Women: The Siren's Song through the Machine*. New York: Oxford University Press, 2014.

Furlonge, Nicole Brittingham. *Race Sounds: The Art of Listening in African American Literature*. Iowa City: University of Iowa Press, 2018.

Gaind-Krishnan, Sonia. "Qawwali." In *The Sage International Encyclopedia of Music and Culture*, edited by Janet Sturman, vol. 1, 1776–77. Thousand Oaks, CA: Sage, 2019.

Gaind-Krishnan, Sonia. "Qawwali Routes: Notes on a Sufi Music's Transformation in Diaspora." *Religions* 11, no. 12 (2020).

Gangoli, Geetanjali. "Sexuality, Sensuality and Belonging: Representations of the 'Anglo-Indian' and the 'Western' Woman in Hindi Cinema." In *Bollyworld: Popular Indian Cinema through a Transnational Lens*, edited by Raminder Kaur and Ajay J. Sinha, 143–62. New Delhi: Sage, 2005.

Ganti, Tejaswini. "Blurring the Boundaries between Hollywood and Bollywood: The Production of Dubbed Films in Mumbai." In *Industrial Networks and Cinemas of India: Shooting Stars, Shifting Geographies and Multiplying Media*, edited by Monika Mehta and Madhuja Mukherjee, 208–21. New York: Routledge, 2021.

Ganti, Tejaswini. "Creating That 'Local Connect': The Dubbing of Hollywood into Hindi." In *The Routledge Companion to Media Industries*, edited by Paul McDonald, 329–39. London: Routledge, 2022.

Ganti, Tejaswini. "'English Is So Precise, and Hindi Can Be So Heavy!': Language Ideologies and Audience Imaginaries in a Dubbing Studio in Mumbai." In *Anthropology, Film Industries, Modularity*, edited by Ramyar D. Rossoukh and Steven C. Canton, 41–61. Durham, NC: Duke University Press, 2021.

Ganti, Tejaswini. "'It Needs to Be More like a Hindi Film': Dubbing Hollywood in India." *IIC (India International Centre) Quarterly* 47, no. 3–4 (Winter 2020–Spring 2021): 53–73.

Ganti, Tejaswini. "'No One Thinks in Hindi Here': Language Hierarchies in Bollywood." In *Precarious Creativity: Global Media, Local Labor*, edited by Michael Curtin and Kevin Sanson, 118–31. Oakland: University of California Press, 2016.

Garwood, Ian. *The Sense of Film Narration*. Edinburgh: Edinburgh University Press, 2013.

Garwood, Ian. "The Songless Bollywood Film." *South Asian Popular Culture* 4, no. 2 (2006): 169–83.

Gehlawat, Ajay, and Rajinder Dudrah, eds. "The Evolution of Song and Dance in Hindi Cinema." Special issue, *South Asian Popular Culture* 15, no. 2 (2017).

Genette, Gerard. *Paratexts: Thresholds of Interpretation*. Translated by Jane E. Lewin. Cambridge: Cambridge University Press, 1997.

Gopal, Sangita. "The Audible Past, or What Remains of the Song-Sequence in New Bollywood Cinema." *New Literary History* 46, no. 4 (Autumn 2015): 805–22.

Gopal, Sangita. *Conjugations: Marriage and Form in New Bollywood Cinema*. Chicago: University of Chicago Press, 2011.

Gopal, Sangita, and Sujata Moorti, eds. *Global Bollywood: Travels of Hindi Song and Dance*. Minneapolis: University of Minnesota Press, 2008.

Gopalan, Lalitha. "Bombay Noir." In *A Companion to Film Noir*, edited by Andrew Spicer and Helen Hanson, 496–511. Malden, MA: Blackwell, 2013.

Gopalan, Lalitha. *Cinema of Interruptions: Action Genres in Contemporary Indian Cinema*. London: British Film Institute, 2002.

Gopinath, Praseeda. "'Don't Hold Back Jack': Ranveer Singh, Masculinity, and New Media Ecology." In *Stardom in Contemporary Hindi Cinema: Celebrity and Fame in Globalized Times*, edited by Aysha Iqbal Viswamohan and Clare Wilkinson, 45–58. Singapore: Springer, 2020.

Gorbman, Claudia. "The Master's Voice." *Film Quarterly* 68, no. 2 (Winter 2014): 8–21.

Gorbman, Claudia. *Unheard Melodies: Narrative Film Music*. Bloomington: Indiana University Press, 1987.

Gray, Jonathan. *Show Sold Separately: Promos, Spoilers, and Other Media Paratexts*. New York: New York University Press, 2010.

Hansen, Thomas Blom. *Wages of Violence: Naming and Identity in Postcolonial Bombay*. Princeton, NJ: Princeton University Press, 2001.

Higgins, Niko. "Confusion in the Karnatic Capital: Fusion in Chennai, India." PhD diss., Columbia University, 2013.

Hilmes, Michele. "The New Materiality of Radio: Sound on Screens." In *Radio's New Wave: Global Sound in the Digital Era*, edited by Jason Loviglio and Michele Hilmes, 43–61. New York: Routledge, 2013.

Hilmes, Michele. "On a Screen Near You: The New Soundwork Industry." *Cinema Journal* 52, no. 3 (Spring 2013): 177–82.

Hilmes, Michele. *Radio Voices: American Broadcasting, 1922–1952*. Minneapolis: University of Minnesota Press, 1997.

Hirji, Faiza. "Change of Pace? Islam and Tradition in Popular Indian Cinema." *South Asian Popular Culture* 6, no. 1 (April 2008): 57–69.

Hirschkind, Charles. *The Ethical Soundscape: Cassette Sermons and Islamic Counterpublics*. New York: Columbia University Press, 2006.

Hodgson, Marshall G. S. *The Venture of Islam: Conscience and History in a World Civilization*. Vol. 1, *The Classical Age of Islam*. Chicago: University of Chicago Press, 1974.

Hu, Brian. "The KTV Aesthetic: Popular Music Culture and Contemporary Hong Kong Cinema." *Screen* 47, no. 4 (Winter 2006): 407–24.

Huacuja Alonso, Isabel. "Radio, Citizenship, and the 'Sound Standards' of a Newly Independent India." *Public Culture* 31, no. 1 (2019): 117–44.

Huacuja Alonso, Isabel. *Radio for the Millions: Hindi-Urdu Broadcasting across Borders*. New York: Columbia University Press, 2023.

Huacuja Alonso, Isabel. "Songs by Ballot: *Binaca Geetmala* and the Making of a Hindi Film-Song Radio Audience, 1952–1994." *BioScope: South Asian Screen Studies* 13, no. 1 (June 2022): 38–73.

Hughes, Stephen Putnam. "Music in the Age of Mechanical Reproduction: Drama, Gramophone, and the Beginnings of Tamil Cinema." *Journal of Asian Studies* 66, no. 1 (2007): 3–34.

Hughes, Stephen Putnam. "What Is Tamil about Tamil Cinema?" *South Asian Popular Culture* 8, no. 3 (October 2010): 213–29.

Indraganti, Kiranmayi. "Of 'Ghosts' and Singers: Debates around Singing Practices of 1940s Indian Cinema." *South Asian Popular Culture* 10, no. 3 (October 2012): 295–306.

Islam, Maidul. "Imagining Indian Muslims: Looking through the Lens of Bollywood Cinema." *Indian Journal of Human Development* 1, no. 2 (2007): 403–22.

ISRA (Indian Singers' Rights Association) (website). "About ISRA." Accessed January 8, 2019. http://isracopyright.com/about_isra.php

Iyer, Usha. *Dancing Women: Choreographing Corporeal Histories of Hindi Cinema*. Oxford: Oxford University Press, 2020.

Jaaware, Aniket. *Practicing Caste: On Touching and Not Touching*. New York: Fordham University Press, 2018.

Jacoviello, Stefano. "Nusrat Fateh Ali Khan: The Strange Destiny of a Singing Mystic. When Music Travels . . ." *Semiotica* 183, no. 1/4 (2011): 319–41.

Jaeckle, Jeff. "Introduction: A Brief Primer for Film Dialogue Study." In *Film Dialogue*, edited by Jeff Jaeckle, 1–16. London: Wallflower Press, 2013.

Jain, Jasbir, ed. *Muslim Culture in Indian Cinema*. Jaipur: Rawat, 2011.

Jarman-Ivens, Freya. *Queer Voices: Technologies, Vocalities, and the Musical Flaw*. New York: Palgrave Macmillan, 2011.

Jay, Martin, and Sumathi Ramaswamy, eds. *Empires of Vision: A Reader*. Durham, NC: Duke University Press, 2014.

Jenkins, Henry. *Convergence Culture: Where Old and New Media Collide*. New York: New York University Press, 2006.

Jhingan, Shikha. "Lata Mangeshkar's Voice in the Age of Cassette Reproduction." *BioScope: South Asian Screen Studies* 4, no. 2 (2013): 97–114.

Jhingan, Shikha. "Re-Embodying the 'Classical': The Bombay Film Song in the 1950s." *BioScope: South Asian Screen Studies* 2, no. 2 (2011): 157–79.

Jhingan, Shikha. "The Singer, the Star and the Chorus." *Seminar* 598 (June 2009). https://www.india-seminar.com/2009/598/598_shikha_jhingan.htm

Jhingan, Shikha. "Sonic Ruptures: Music, Mobility and the Media." In *Media and Utopia: History, Imagination and Technology*, edited by Arvind Rajagopal and Anupama Rao, 209–34. New York: Routledge, 2016.

Kabir, Ananya Jahanara. "Allegories of Alienation and Politics of Bargaining: Minority Subjectivities in Mani Ratnam's *Dil Se*." *South Asian Popular Culture* 1, no. 2 (2003): 141–59.

Kasbekar, Asha. "Negotiating the Myth of the Female Ideal in Popular Hindi Cinema." In *Pleasure and the Nation: The History, Politics, and Consumption of Public Culture in India*, edited by Rachel Dwyer and Christopher Pinney, 298–300. New Delhi: Oxford University Press, 2001.

Kassabian, Anahid. *Ubiquitous Listening: Affect, Attention, and Distributed Subjectivity*. Berkeley: University of California Press, 2013.

Kazmi, Fareed. "Muslim Socials and the Female Protagonist." In *Forging Identities: Gender, Communities and the State in India*, edited by Zoya Hasan, 226–43. New Delhi: Kali for Women, 1994.

Kesavan, Mukul. "Urdu, Awadh and the Tawaif: The Islamicate Roots of Hindi Cinema." In *Forging Identities: Gender, Communities and the State in India*, edited by Zoya Hasan, 244–57. New Delhi: Kali for Women, 1994.

Kheshti, Roshanak. *Modernity's Ear: Listening to Race and Gender in World Music*. New York: New York University Press, 2015.

Kothari, Rita. "Introduction: When We Are 'Multilingual,' Do We Translate?" In *A Multilingual Nation: Translation and Language Dynamic in India*, edited by Rita Kothari, 1–22. New Delhi: Oxford University Press, 2018.

Kothari, Rita, ed. *A Multilingual Nation: Translation and Language Dynamic in India*. New Delhi: Oxford University Press, 2018.

Kozloff, Sarah. *Invisible Storytellers: Voice-Over Narration in American Fiction Film*. Berkeley: University of California Press, 1988.

Kozloff, Sarah. *Overhearing Film Dialogue*. Berkeley: University of California Press, 2000.

Krishnan, Rajan. "From Songs to Speech." *Seminar* 598 (June 2009). http://www.india-seminar.com/2009/598/598_rajan_krishnan.htm

Kumar, Akshaya. "Provincialising Bollywood? Cultural Economy of North-Indian Small-Town Nostalgia in the Indian Multiplex." *South Asian Popular Culture* 11, no. 1 (2013): 61–74.

Kumar, Amitava. "Writing My Own Satya." In *Lunch with a Bigot: The Writer in the World*, by Amitava Kumar, 97–105. Durham, NC: Duke University Press, 2015.

Kumar, Priya. *Limiting Secularism: The Ethics of Coexistence in Indian Literature and Film*. Minneapolis: University of Minnesota Press, 2008.

Kumar, Shanti. *Gandhi Meets Primetime: Globalization and Nationalism in Indian Television*. Urbana: University of Illinois Press, 2006.

Kumar, Shanti, and Michael Curtin. "'Made in India': In between Music Television and Patriarchy." *Television & New Media* 3, no. 4 (November 2002): 345–66.

Kun, Josh. *Audiotopia: Music, Race, and America*. Berkeley: University of California Press, 2005.

Kunreuther, Laura. *Voicing Subjects: Public Intimacy and Mediation in Kathmandu*. Berkeley: University of California Press, 2014.

Kvetko, Peter. "Indipop: Producing Global Sounds and Local Meanings in Bombay." PhD diss., University of Texas at Austin, 2005.

Kvetko, Peter. "It's Rocking? Exploring Sound and Intimacy through Mumbai's Faltering Indipop Music Industry." In *Indian Sound Cultures, Indian Sound Citizenship*, edited by Laura Brueck, Jacob Smith, and Neil Verma, 72–87. Ann Arbor: University of Michigan Press, 2020.

Kvetko, Peter. "Mimesis and Authenticity: The Case of 'Thanda Thanda Pani' and Questions of Versioning in North Indian Popular Music." In *More Than Bollywood: Studies in Indian Popular Music*, edited by Gregory Booth and Bradley Shope, 160–78. New York: Oxford University Press, 2014.

Lacey, Kate. *Feminine Frequencies: Gender, German Radio, and the Public Sphere, 1923–1945*. Ann Arbor: University of Michigan Press, 1997.

Lacey, Kate. "Listening in the Digital Age." In *Radio's New Wave: Global Sound in the Digital Era*, edited by Jason Loviglio and Michele Hilmes, 9–23. New York: Routledge, 2013.

Lacey, Kate. *Listening Publics: The Politics and Experience of Listening in the Media Age*. Sussex: Polity, 2013.

LaDousa, Chaise. *Hindi Is Our Ground, English Is Our Sky: Education, Language, and Social Class in Contemporary India*. New York: Berghahn Books, 2014.

Lahiri, Madhumita. "An Idiom for India." *Interventions* 18, no. 1 (2016): 60–85.

Leimbacher, Irina. "Hearing Voice(s): Experiments with Documentary Listening." *Discourse* 39, no. 3 (2017): 292–318.

Lipari, Lisbeth. *Listening, Thinking, Being: Toward an Ethics of Attunement*. University Park: Pennsylvania State University Press, 2014.

Lippi-Green, Rosina. "The Myth of Non-Accent." In *English with an Accent: Language, Ideology, and Discrimination in the United States*, 2nd ed., 44–54. London: Routledge, 2012.

Mahmood, Saba. *Politics of Piety: Islamic Revival and the Feminist Subject*. Princeton, NJ: Princeton University Press, 2004.

"Main Hoon Na | Making | Tumse Milke Dilka Hai Jo Haal / Qawwali Song | Shah Rukh Khan, Sushmita Sen." Uploaded by Red Chillies Entertainment, March 28, 2016. YouTube video, 1:09. https://www.youtube.com/watch?v=y4gtawLmZ7c

Majumdar, Neepa. "Beyond the Song Sequence: Theorizing Sound in Indian Cinema." In *Sound and Music in Film and Visual Media: A Critical Overview*, edited by Graeme Harper, 303–24. New York: Continuum International, 2009.

Majumdar, Neepa. "The Embodied Voice: Song Sequences and Stardom in Popular Hindi

Cinema." In *Soundtrack Available: Essays on Film and Popular Music*, edited by Pamela Robertson Wojcik and Arthur Knight, 161–81. Durham, NC: Duke University Press, 2001.

Majumdar, Neepa. *Wanted Cultured Ladies Only! Female Stardom and Cinema in India, 1930s–1950s*. Urbana: University of Illinois Press, 2009.

"Making of the Film | Part 2 | Bunty Aur Babli | Abhishek Bachchan | Rani Mukerji | Shaad Ali Sahgal." Uploaded by YRF, January 31, 2009. YouTube video, 5:25. https://www.you tube.com/watch?v=eybtH0RosG0

Mamdani, Mahmood. *Good Muslim, Bad Muslim: America, the Cold War, and the Roots of Terror*. New York: Pantheon Books, 2004.

Mamula, Tijana, and Lisa Patti, eds. *The Multilingual Screen: New Reflections on Cinema and Linguistic Difference*. New York: Bloomsbury Academic, 2016.

Mankekar, Purnima. *Screening Culture, Viewing Politics: An Ethnography of Television, Womanhood, and Nation in Postcolonial India*. Durham, NC: Duke University Press, 1999.

Manuel, Peter. *Cassette Culture: Popular Music and Technology in North India*. Chicago: University of Chicago Press, 1993.

Manuel, Peter. "North Indian Sufi Popular Music in the Age of Hindu and Muslim Fundamentalism." *Ethnomusicology* 52, no. 3 (2008): 378–400.

Mazumdar, Ranjani. *Bombay Cinema: An Archive of the City*. Minneapolis: University of Minnesota Press, 2007.

McClary, Susan. *Feminine Endings: Music, Gender, and Sexuality*. Minneapolis: University of Minnesota Press, 1991.

McGuire, Meredith Lindsay. "'How to Sit, How to Stand': Bodily Practice and the New Middle Class." In *A Companion to the Anthropology of India*, edited by Isabelle Clark-Decès, 117–36. Oxford: Wiley Blackwell, 2011.

Mehta, Monika. "Analyzing Credit Sequences." In *Writing about Screen Media*, edited by Lisa Patti, 163–68. New York: Routledge, 2019.

Mehta, Monika. "Authorizing Gesture: Mirchi Music Awards and the Re-Calibration of Songs and Stardom." In *Music in Contemporary Indian Film: Memory, Voice, Identity*, edited by Jayson Beaster-Jones and Natalie Sarrazin, 61–75. New York: Routledge, 2017.

Mehta, Monika. *Censorship and Sexuality in Bombay Cinema*. Austin: University of Texas Press, 2011.

Mehta, Monika. "DVD Compilations of Hindi Film Songs: (Re)Shuffling Sound, Stardom, and Cinephilia." *South Asian Popular Culture* 10, no. 3 (October 2012): 237–48.

Mehta, Monika. "*Fan* and Its Paratexts." *Framework* 58, no. 1–2 (Spring–Fall 2017): 128–43.

Mehta, Monika, and Madhuja Mukherjee, eds. *Industrial Networks and Cinemas of India: Shooting Stars, Shifting Geographies and Multiplying Media*. London: Routledge, 2021.

Mishra, Vijay. *Bollywood Cinema: Temples of Desire*. New York: Routledge, 2002.

Misri, Deepti. "Bollywood's 9/11: Terrorism and Muslim Masculinities in Popular Hindi Cinema." In *Global Asian American Popular Cultures*, edited by Shilpa Davé, Nishime LeiLani, and Tasha Oren, 276–89. New York: New York University Press, 2016.

Moallem, Minoo. *Between Warrior Brother and Veiled Sister: Islamic Fundamentalism and the Politics of Patriarchy in Iran*. Berkeley: University of California Press, 2005.

Moallem, Minoo. "Transnationalism, Feminism, and Fundamentalism." In *Women, Gender, and Religion: A Reader*, edited by Elizabeth A. Castelli, 119–45. New York: Palgrave, 2001.

Morcom, Anna. *Hindi Film Songs and the Cinema*. London: Routledge, 2016.

Mowitt, John. *Re-Takes: Postcoloniality and Foreign Film Languages*. Minneapolis: University of Minnesota Press, 2005.

Mukherjee, Debashree. *Bombay Hustle: Making Movies in a Colonial City*. New York: Columbia University Press, 2020.

Munshi, Shoma. "A Perfect 10—'Modern and Indian': Representations of the Body in Beauty Pageants and the Visual Media in Contemporary India." In *Confronting the Body: The Politics of Physicality in Colonial and Post-Colonial India*, edited by James H. Mills and Satadru Sen, 162–82. London: Anthem Press, 2004.

Murch, Walter. Foreword to *Audio-Vision: Sound on Screen*, by Michel Chion, translated by Claudia Gorbman, vii–xxiv. New York: Columbia University Press, 1994.

Murphy, Kate. *Behind the Wireless: A History of Early Women at the BBC*. London: Palgrave Macmillan, 2016.

Naficy, Hamid. *An Accented Cinema: Exilic and Diasporic Filmmaking*. Princeton, NJ: Princeton University Press, 2001.

Nakassis, Constantine. "A Tamil-Speaking Heroine." *BioScope: South Asian Screen Studies* 6, no. 2 (July 2015): 165–86.

"Neeti Mohan, Neha Bhasin, Aditi Singh Sharma, Jonita Gandhi | Female Singers' Adda." Uploaded by Film Companion, June 12, 2017. YouTube video, 37:20. https://www.youtube.com/watch?v=9LgEHWktl3I

Nijhawan, Amita. "Excusing the Female Dancer: Tradition and Transgression in Bollywood Dancing." *South Asian Popular Culture* 7, no. 2 (2009): 99–112.

Ochoa Gautier, Ana María. *Aurality: Listening and Knowledge in Nineteenth-Century Colombia*. Durham, NC: Duke University Press, 2014.

Ojha, Abhilasha. "What's Wrong with India's Music Industry?" Rediff.com, September 5, 2005. http://www.rediff.com/money/2005/sep/05spec.htm

O'Meara, Jennifer. *Engaging Dialogue: Cinematic Verbalism in American Independent Cinema*. Edinburgh: Edinburgh University Press, 2018.

Ong, Walter. *Orality and Literacy: The Technologizing of the Word*. New York: Routledge, 1982.

Orsini, Francesca. "*Dil Maange More*: Cultural Contexts of Hinglish in Contemporary India." *African Studies* 74, no. 2 (August 2015): 199–220.

Orsini, Francesca. "How to Do Multilingual Literary History? Lessons from Fifteenth- and Sixteenth-Century North India." *Indian Economic Social History Review* 49, no. 2 (June 2012): 225–46.

Orsini, Francesca, ed. *Love in South Asia: A Cultural History*. Cambridge: Cambridge University Press, 2006.

Orsini, Francesca. "The Multilingual Local in World Literature." *Comparative Literature* 67, no. 4 (2015): 345–74.

Orsini, Francesca. "Na Hindu Na Turk: Shared Languages, Accents, and Located Meanings." In *A Multilingual Nation: Translation and Language Dynamic in India*, edited by Rita Kothari, 50–69. New Delhi: Oxford University Press, 2018.

Oza, Rupal. *The Making of Neoliberal India: Nationalism, Gender, and the Paradoxes of Globalization*. New York: Routledge, 2006.

Pal, Felix. "Performing Pluralism: Why the BJP Wants Muslim Friends." *New Mandala* (blog), February 20, 2019. https://www.newmandala.org/performing-pluralism-why -the-bjp-wants-muslim-friends/

Panjabi, Kavita. Introduction to *Poetics and Politics of Sufism and Bhakti in South Asia: Love, Loss and Liberation*, edited by Kavita Panjabi, 1–52. New Delhi: Orient Blackswan, 2011.

Pauwels, Heidi. "'The Woman Waylaid at the Well' or Paṇaghaṭa-Līlā: An Indian Folk Theme Appropriated in Myth and Movies." *Asian Ethnology* 69, no. 1 (2010): 1–33.

Pettman, Dominic. "Pavlov's Podcast: The Acousmatic Voice in the Age of Mp3s." *Differences* 22, no. 2–3 (2011): 140–67.

Pettman, Dominic. *Sonic Intimacy: Voice, Species, Technics (or, How To Listen to the World)*. Stanford, CA: Stanford University Press, 2017.

Phadke, Shilpa, Sameera Khan, and Shilpa Ranade. *Why Loiter? Women and Risk on Mumbai Streets*. New Delhi: Penguin Books India, 2011.

Pillai, Swarnavel Eswaran. *Madras Studios: Narrative, Genre, and Ideology in Tamil Cinema*. New Delhi: Sage, 2015.

Pinney, Christopher. *"Photos of the Gods": The Printed Image and Political Struggle in India*. London: Reaktion Books, 2004.

Prasad, M. Madhava. *Cine-Politics: Film Stars and Political Existence in South India*. New Delhi: Orient Blackswan, 2014.

Puar, Jasbir K. *Terrorist Assemblages: Homonationalism in Queer Times*. Durham, NC: Duke University Press, 2007.

Punathambekar, Aswin. "Ameen Sayani and Radio Ceylon: Notes towards a History of Broadcasting and Bombay Cinema." *BioScope: South Asian Screen Studies* 1, no. 2 (2010): 189–97.

Punathambekar, Aswin. *From Bombay to Bollywood: The Making of a Global Media Industry*. New York: New York University Press, 2013.

Punathambekar, Aswin, and Sriram Mohan. "Sound Clouds: Listening and Citizenship in Indian Public Culture." In *Indian Sound Cultures, Indian Sound Citizenship*, edited by Laura Brueck, Jacob Smith, and Neil Verma, 19–43. Ann Arbor: University of Michigan Press, 2020.

Qureshi, Regula Burckhardt. "His Master's Voice? Exploring Qawwali and 'Gramophone Culture' in South Asia." *Popular Music* 18, no. 1 (1999): 63–98.

Qureshi, Regula Burckhardt. "Sufi Music and the Historicity of Oral Tradition." In *Ethnomusicology and Modern Music History*, edited by Stephen Blum, Phillip V. Bohlman, and Daniel M. Neuman, 103–20. Urbana: University of Illinois Press, 1993.

Radano, Ronald M., and Philip V. Bohlman, eds. *Music and the Racial Imagination*. Chicago: University of Chicago Press, 2000.

Radhakrishnan, Ratheesh. "Region/Regional Cinema." *BioScope: South Asian Screen Studies* 12, no. 1–2 (2021): 162–65.

RadioandMusic.com. "Major Win for ISRA, Delhi HC Rules in Favour of Singers." August 18, 2016. http://www.radioandmusic.com/biz/regulators/high-court/160818-major -win-isra-delhi-hc-rules-favour-singers

RadioandMusic.com. "Singers Get Favourable Delhi High Court Order on Royalties." January 5, 2015. http://www.radioandmusic.com/biz/regulators/high-court/151030-singe rs-get-favourable-delhi-high-court-order

Rahaim, Matthew. *Musicking Bodies: Gesture and Voice in Hindustani Music.* Middletown, CT: Wesleyan University Press, 2012.

Rahaim, Matthew. *Ways of Voice: Vocal Striving and Moral Contestation in North India and Beyond.* Middletown, CT: Wesleyan University Press, 2021.

Rai, Alok. "Making a Difference: Hindi, 1880–1930." In *Multiculturalism, Liberalism, Democracy,* edited by Rajeev Bhargava, Amiya Kumar Bagchi, and R. Sudarshan, 248–64. New Delhi: Oxford University Press, 1999.

Rai, Amit. "Patriotism and the Muslim Citizen in Hindi Films." *Harvard Asia Quarterly* 7, no. 3 (Summer 2003): 4–15.

Rajadhyaksha, Ashish. "The 'Bollywoodization' of the Indian Cinema: Cultural Nationalism in a Global Arena." *Inter-Asia Cultural Studies* 4, no. 1 (2003): 25–39.

Rajadhyaksha, Ashish. "The Phalke Era: Conflict of Traditional Form and Modern Technology." *Journal of Arts & Ideas,* no. 14–15 (December 1987): 47–78.

Ramnath, Nandini. "Jurassic Park: When Dinosaurs Ruled the Indian Box Office." *Mint,* March 25, 2013. https://www.livemint.com/Consumer/fQpy8CgHElhfHyrKsqTHEK /Jurassic-Park-When-dinosaurs-ruled-the-Indian-box-office.html

Ramnath, Nandini. "Muslim Stereotyping in Hindi Films: 'We Cannot Allow Ourselves to Forget What Constitutes Us.'" *Scroll.In,* September 20, 2021. https://scroll.in/reel/100 5662/

Ranade, Ashok Damodar. *Hindi Film Song: Music beyond Boundaries.* New Delhi: Promila, 2006.

Rangan, Pooja, Akshya Saxena, Ragini Tharoor Srinivasan, and Pavitra Sundar, eds. *Thinking with an Accent: Toward a New Object, Method, and Practice.* Berkeley: University of California Press, 2023.

Rice, Tom. "Listening." In *Keywords in Sound,* edited by David Novak and Matt Sakakeeny, 99–111. Durham, NC: Duke University Press, 2015.

Said, Edward W. *The World, the Text, and the Critic.* Cambridge, MA: Harvard University Press, 1983.

Samuels, David W., Louise Meintjes, Ana María Ochoa, and Thomas Porcello. "Soundscapes: Toward a Sounded Anthropology." *Annual Review of Anthropology* 39 (2010): 329–45.

Sangari, Kumkum. "Viraha: A Trajectory in the Nehruvian Era." In *Poetics and Politics of Sufism and Bhakti in South Asia: Love, Loss and Liberation,* edited by Kavita Panjabi, 256–87. New Delhi: Orient Blackswan, 2011.

Sarkar, Sumit. *The Swadeshi Movement in Bengal, 1903–1908.* 2nd ed. New Delhi: Permanent Black, 2010.

Sarrazin, Natalie. "Global Masala: Digital Identities and Aesthetic Trajectories in Post-Liberalized Indian Film Music." In *More Than Bollywood: Studies in Indian Popular Music,* edited by Gregory Booth and Bradley Shope, 38–59. Oxford: Oxford University Press, 2014.

Sawhney, Isha Singh. "The Ladies Sing the Blues." *Caravan: A Journal of Politics and Culture*, January 31, 2013. http://www.caravanmagazine.in/reviews-and-essays/ladies-sing-blues

Saxena, Akshya. *Vernacular English: Reading the Anglophone in Postcolonial India*. Princeton, NJ: Princeton University Press, 2022.

Sedgwick, Eve Kosofsky. "Paranoid Reading and Reparative Reading, or You're So Paranoid, You Probably Think This Introduction Is about You." In *Novel Gazing: Queer Readings in Fiction*, edited by Eve Kosofsky Sedgwick, 1–37. Durham, NC: Duke University Press, 1997.

*SEL: Shankar Ehsaan Loy* (website). Accessed July 14, 2018. http://www.shankarehsaanloy.com/

Sen, Biswarup. "The Sounds of Modernity: The Evolution of Bollywood Film Song." In *Global Bollywood: Travels of Hindi Song and Dance*, edited by Sangita Gopal and Sujata Moorti, 85–104. Minneapolis: University of Minnesota Press, 2008.

Shahani, Nishant. "Queer Intimacy during Seditious Times: Revisiting the Case of Ramchandra Siras." *South Asia Multidisciplinary Academic Journal* 20 (2019). https://doi.org/10.4000/samaj.5230

Shankar, S. *Flesh and Fish Blood: Postcolonialism, Translation, and the Vernacular*. Berkeley: University of California Press, 2012.

Shankar, Shalini, and Jillian R. Cavanaugh. "Toward a Theory of Language Materiality: An Introduction." In *Language and Materiality: Ethnographic and Theoretical Explorations*, edited by Jillian R. Cavanaugh and Shalini Shankar, 1–28. Cambridge: Cambridge University Press, 2017.

Siefert, Marsha. "Image/Music/Voice: Song Dubbing in Hollywood Musicals." *Journal of Communication* 45, no. 2 (1995): 44–64.

Sjogren, Britta. *Into the Vortex: Female Voice and Paradox in Film*. Urbana: University of Illinois Press, 2006.

Small, Christopher. *Musicking: The Meanings of Performing and Listening*. Middletown, CT: Wesleyan University Press, 1998.

Smith, Jacob. *Spoken Word: Postwar American Phonograph Cultures*. Berkeley: University of California Press, 2011.

Smith, Jacob. *Vocal Tracks: Performance and Sound Media*. Berkeley: University of California Press, 2008.

Smith, Jeff. "Black Faces, White Voices: The Politics of Dubbing in Carmen Jones." *Velvet Light Trap*, no. 51 (Spring 2003): 29–42.

Smith, Mark M. "Futures of Hearing Pasts." In *Sounds of Modern History: Auditory Cultures in 19th- and 20th-Century Europe*, edited by Daniel Morat, 13–22. New York: Berghahn Books, 2014.

Sommer, Doris. *Foundational Fictions: The National Romances of Latin America*. Berkeley: University of California Press, 1991.

Soneji, Davesh. *Unfinished Gestures: Devadāsīs, Memory, and Modernity in South India*. Chicago: University of Chicago Press, 2012.

"Song Making with Mahalaxmi Iyer & Akriti | Sau Shashi Deodhar." Uploaded by Sau. Shashi Deodhar, February 10, 2014. YouTube video. https://www.youtube.com/watch?v=DGHXmRn5BnM (removed from site).

Soofi, Mayank Austen. "Kun Faya Kun's Love Note to Rahman 'Saab.'" *Mint*, March 3, 2017. https://www.livemint.com/Leisure/PtZ8OCPUN9tZVabC8ldGeK/Kun-Faya-Kuns-lo ve-note-to-Rahman-saab.html

Spivak, Gayatri Chakravorty. "Can the Subaltern Speak?" In *Marxism and the Interpretation of Culture*, edited by Cary Nelson and Lawrence Grossberg, 271–313. Urbana: University of Illinois Press, 1988.

Srinivas, S. V. "Cardboard Monuments: City, Language and 'Nation' in Contemporary Telugu Cinema." *Singapore Journal of Tropical Geography* 29, no. 1 (2008): 87–100.

Srinivas, S. V. "Rajinikanth and the 'Regional Blockbuster.'" *Working Papers of the Chicago Tamil Forum* 3 (2016). http://chicagotamilforum.uchicago.edu/working-papers/table -of-contents/ctf-toc.html

Srinivas, S. V., ed. "Regional Cinemas of India." Special issue, *BioScope: South Asian Screen Studies* 6, no. 2 (July 2015).

Srivastava, Sanjay. "The Voice of the Nation and the Five-Year Plan Hero: Speculations on Gender, Space, and Popular Culture." In *Fingerprinting Popular Culture: The Mythic and the Iconic in Indian Cinema*, edited by Vinay Lal and Ashis Nandy, 122–55. New Delhi: Oxford University Press, 2006.

Sterne, Jonathan. *The Audible Past: Cultural Origins of Sound Reproduction*. Durham, NC: Duke University Press, 2006.

Sterne, Jonathan. "Sonic Imaginations." In *The Sound Studies Reader*, edited by Jonathan Sterne, 1–17. New York: Routledge, 2014.

Stockfelt, Ola. "Adequate Modes of Listening." In *Audio Culture: Readings in Modern Music*, edited by Christoph Cox and Daniel Warner, 88–93. New York: Continuum, 2005.

Stoever, Jennifer Lynn. *Sonic Color Line: Race and the Cultural Politics of Listening*. New York: New York University Press, 2016.

Sundar, Pavitra. "Language, Region and Cinema: Translation as Politics in *Ek Duuje Ke Liye*." *Studies in South Asian Film & Media* 7, no. 1 (2016): 25–43.

Sundar, Pavitra. "Making-of Videos: Of Placeless Studios and Pioneering Music Directors." In *Industrial Networks and Cinemas of India: Shooting Stars, Shifting Geographies and Multiplying Media*, edited by Monika Mehta and Madhuja Mukherjee, 222–37. New York: Routledge, 2021.

Sundar, Pavitra. "*Meri Awaaz Suno*: Women, Vocality, and Nation in Hindi Cinema." *Meridians* 8, no. 1 (2008): 144–79.

Sundar, Pavitra. "Of Radio, Remix, and *Rang De Basanti*: Rethinking History through Film Sound." *Jump Cut: A Review of Contemporary Media* 56 (Fall 2014). https://www.ejum pcut.org/archive/jc56.2014-2015/index.html

Sundar, Pavitra. "The Queer Sound of the Dandiya Queen, Falguni Pathak." *Sounding Out!* (blog), October 23, 2017. https://soundstudiesblog.com/2017/10/23/

Sundar, Pavitra. "Usha Uthup and Her Husky, Heavy Voice." In *Indian Sound Cultures, Indian Sound Citizenship*, edited by Laura Brueck, Jacob Smith, and Neil Verma, 115–51. Ann Arbor: University of Michigan Press, 2020.

Sundaram, Ravi. *Pirate Modernity: Delhi's Media Urbanism*. London: Routledge, 2010.

Talukdar, Jaita. "Thin but Not Skinny: Women Negotiating the 'Never Too Thin' Body Ideal in Urban India." *Women's Studies International Forum* 35, no. 2 (2012): 109–18.

Talukdar, Jaita, and Annulla Linders. "Gender, Class Aspirations, and Emerging Fields of Body Work in Urban India." *Qualitative Sociology* 36, no. 1 (2013): 101–23.

Taneja, Anand Vivek. "Muslimness in Hindi Cinema." *Seminar* 598 (June 2009). https://www.india-seminar.com/2009/598/598_anand_vivek_taneja.htm

Taneja, Nikhil. "From Melody to Dev D." *Hindustan Times*, December 31, 2009.

Taylor, Jessica. "'Speaking Shadows': A History of the Voice in the Transition from Silent to Sound Film in the United States." *Journal of Linguistic Anthropology* 19, no. 1 (2009): 1–20.

Taylor, Woodman. "Penetrating Gazes: The Poetics of Sight and Visual Display in Popular Indian Cinema." In *Beyond Appearances? Visual Practices and Ideologies in Modern India*, edited by Sumathi Ramaswamy, 297–322. New Delhi: Sage, 2003.

Thapan, Meenakshi. "Embodiment and Identity in Contemporary Society: Femina and the 'New' Indian Woman." *Contributions to Indian Sociology* 38, no. 3 (2004): 411–44.

Thomas, Rosie. "Sanctity and Scandal: The Mythologization of Mother India." *Quarterly Review of Film and Video* 11, no. 3 (1989): 11–30.

Thompson, Emily. *The Soundscape of Modernity: Architectural Acoustics and the Culture of Listening in America, 1900–1933*. Cambridge: MIT Press, 2002.

Thoraval, Yves. *The Cinemas of India*. Delhi: Macmillan India, 2000.

"TrulyMadly Presents Creep Qawwali with All India Bakchod." Uploaded by TrulyMadly, October 8, 2015. YouTube video, 4:55. https://www.youtube.com/watch?v=gEC0pK HJKNM

Vanita, Ruth. "*Dosti* to *Tamanna*: Male-Male Love, Difference, and Normativity in Hindi Cinema." In *Everyday Life in South Asia*, edited by Diane Mines and Sarah Lamb, 146–58. Bloomington: Indiana University Press, 2002.

Vasudevan, Ravi. "Geographies of the Cinematic Public: Notes on Regional, National and Global Histories of Indian Cinema." *Journal of the Moving Image*, 2010, 94–117.

Vazquez, Alexandra T. *Listening in Detail: Performances of Cuban Music*. Durham, NC: Duke University Press, 2013.

Velayutham, Selvaraj, ed. *Tamil Cinema: The Cultural Politics of India's Other Film Industry*. London: Routledge, 2008.

Verma, Neil. *Theater of the Mind: Imagination, Aesthetics, and American Radio Drama*. Chicago: University of Chicago Press, 2012.

Vijayakar, R. M. "Age Hasn't Dimmed Sparkle in Asha Bhosle's Voice." *India-West*, May 24, 1996.

Virdi, Jyotika. *The Cinematic ImagiNation: Indian Popular Films as Social History*. New Brunswick, NJ: Rutgers University Press, 2003.

Virdi, Jyotika. "A National Cinema's Transnational Aspirations? Considerations on 'Bollywood.'" *South Asian Popular Culture* 15, no. 1 (2017): 1–22.

Virmani, Ashish. "The Prodooser Is Dead! Long Live the Producer!" *Man's World*, February 2004, 77–79.

Wani, Aarti. *Fantasy of Modernity: Romantic Love in Bombay Cinema of the 1950s*. Delhi: Cambridge University Press, 2016.

Wani, Aarti, ed. "Region." Special issue, *Studies in South Asian Film and Media* 7, no. 1–2 (April 2016).

Weheliye, Alexander G. *Phonographies: Grooves in Sonic Afro-Modernity*. Durham, NC: Duke University Press, 2005.

Weidman, Amanda. "Anthropology and Voice." *Annual Review of Anthropology* 43 (2014): 37–51.

Weidman, Amanda. *Brought to Life by the Voice: Playback Singing and Cultural Politics in South India*. Berkeley: University of California Press, 2021.

Weidman, Amanda. "Neoliberal Logics of Voice: Playback Singing and Public Femaleness in South India." *Culture, Theory, and Critique* 55, no. 2 (April 2014): 175–93.

Weidman, Amanda. *Singing the Classical, Voicing the Modern: The Postcolonial Politics of Music in South India*. Durham, NC: Duke University Press, 2006.

Weidman, Amanda. "Sound and the City: Mimicry and Media in South India." *Journal of Linguistic Anthropology* 20, no. 2 (2010): 294–313.

Weidman, Amanda. "Voices of Meenakumari: Sound, Meaning, and Self-Fashioning in Performances of an Item Number." *South Asian Popular Culture* 10, no. 3 (October 2012): 307–18.

Williams, Richard David, and Rafay Mahmood. "A Soundtrack for Reimagining Pakistan? Coke Studio, Memory and the Music Video." *BioScope: South Asian Screen Studies* 10, no. 2 (2019): 111–28.

Zuberi, Irfan, and Natalie Sarrazin. "Evolution of a Ritual Musical Genre: The Adaptation of Qawwali in Contemporary Hindi Film." In *Music in Contemporary Indian Film: Memory, Voice, Identity*, edited by Jayson Beaster-Jones and Natalie Sarrazin, 162–75. New York: Routledge, 2017.

Zuberi, Nabeel. "Listening while Muslim." *Popular Music* 36, no. 1 (2017): 33–42.

# INDEX

*Note:* Page numbers in italics refer to the illustrations.